GW01090547

MURDER MOST LOCAL

Historic Murders of

EAST CORK

PETER O'SHEA

Murder Most Local
Historic Murders of East Cork by Peter O'Shea
ISBN: Soft Cover 978-1-9163796-0-2
ISBN: Hard Cover
Copyright©2019 Peter O'Shea
ALL RIGHTS RESERVED. International copyright secured.

Published by Most Local Press

Printed in Poland by Totem

No part of this publication, including illustrations
or photographs, may be reproduced or transmitted
in any form or by any means, electronic or mechanical,
including photocopy, recording or any
information storage and retrieval system, without
permission in writing from the author.

Acknowledgements

It's difficult to write acknowledgements when you are writing about murders. Many people don't want to be mentioned at all and who could blame them.

One day I called someone I didn't know to try to find out the motive behind one of the cases. She had not heard of it at all but was intrigued as she lived so near to the murder location. She ended our conversation with "leave it with me". Two weeks later the phone rang, the woman had done her research and gave me a clue about why this murder took place and pointed me in the right direction. I mentioned when I finally put it in a book what name should I put on the acknowledgements page. She said don't mention a thing about where the information came from but when the book comes out let her know as they would read a few of them up her way.

It was after this conversation and others like it that I realised the acknowledgements page would be short. I decided not going to mention anybody who gave information about any of the cases. Another example was the man I met at the Annual Field Day in Ballinrostig. He was able to tell me in that same field over 200 years ago there was a murder.

To all the people who said you can't write about murders, a special thanks to you as it only made me more motivated to complete this book.

I am very grateful to all the people who have offered continuous support and helped me through it, especially those who kept asking was I finished yet. Special thanks to Jerry and Mary Rose Lynch for all the support the last time around and the fantastic book launch. (Sorry I should have written this at least a year ago). Thanks to John O'Shea for digging in the briars and showing me the stone in Ballingarrane on that cold wet Sunday so long ago now. I honestly cannot thank the proof readers and editors enough - Karen Casey, Kathleen Forrest, Janett Murray and Nessa O'Shea. A near impossible task but I am very appreciative.

Finally to all the people who bought my last book- **Well, Here I am in Ballycotton**, I really enjoyed receiving your feedback, thank you for your support.

Table of Contents

Murder Map

Introduction

Where do you start with an introduction for a book like this! First let me explain what it's all about and how it began. While writing my last book *Well, here I am in Ballycotton* in 2015, I included one story about a murder near Ballycotton. Many were intrigued with this story having heard bits about it over the years. The most feedback I received was about this one murder story and this set the seed. Like everything it was put on the shelf as an idea for many reasons.

The concept kept coming back up though and I decided to research one local story and see what people thought of it. I started writing and within months I had found many more interesting stories and it grew from there.

Each story is unique; there are times when you think you know who did it and others where we will never know for sure. In some cases it is obvious from the very start who done it, but will they get away with it or not? Comparing the different cases there are times when the chief suspect can't be proven guilty. While in other cases a suspect ends up paying with their life when less evidence is produced.

All the cases are actual real events that have taken place in the last 200 years with the most recent being 60 years ago.

For many years in Ireland being found guilty ended with the murderer paying for the crime with their life. In the early 1800's executions were held in public and served as a grim warning to others not to do likewise. Any lesser crime such as manslaughter would see the person transported to a far flung colony but petty crimes were punished similarly back then. Those found guilty of murder but insane generally meant life imprisonment. Despite the severe punishment people were still driven to killing for many reasons as you shall see. It should be stressed that murder was still uncommon and one report over 10 years to shows 51 murders in Cork County from nearly 5000 crimes committed.

With the foundation of the Irish Free State murder seems to have become more uncommon in the 1920's and 30's. For this reason the rare cases in this period generated a huge amount of public interest. Some are still talked about to this day while others are long forgotten.

In Ireland now we sometimes think crime is a modern problem. Although it's more prevalent these days after reading these pages you can't but be convinced there was always crime. There are various reasons why someone would be driven to committing murder - land, jealousy, sex, money and of course drink. Most of these motives are still similar to those in today's society.

She tried her best to avoid him
Lissanisky, Cobh 1880

The Cotter family lived in a quiet part of Great Island about a mile north of the town of Cobh is the townland of Lissanisky. Like any other rural place in Ireland it comprised mostly of farmers and those that worked for farmers. Mary Prudence Cotter was the daughter of a local farmer. She was only twenty two years old and still living at home with her father James and mother Catherine and her younger brother James aged 20.

On Sunday the 29th of February 1880 she went out with two sisters, Hannah and Mary Cashman to visit some neighbours. The group were visiting a nearby farm belonging to John Higgins in the townland to the south called Ballyleary. They walked down the road and took a shortcut across some fields to get to the farm. When crossing the fields they met a neighbour called Patrick Allen who asked to speak to Mary. He said to her "surely Miss Cotter it is not from me you are running away. I want to say something to you". Mary replied sternly to him "what is it" and he said "tis not much" as he was really only trying to get her attention. Hannah and Mary Cashman walked ahead, leaving the two talking. The sisters waited in the next field for Mary Cotter to catch up.

Mary had known Patrick since childhood and he seemed to have an attachment towards her. In their younger days they were courting each other for a while. However Allen had been in the lunatic asylum for a period, since then she no longer encouraged him and even tried her best to avoid him. Over the years she had come to dislike him more and more, and had recently become afraid of him. For some reason he wasn't taking the hints and kept trying to approach her becoming annoyed with her lack of interest in him.

That day whatever transpired between them, ten minutes later she ran crying after the two Cashman girls. She told the sisters that Patrick Allen had hit her "a clout on the cheek with his closed fist". Mary was quite upset over what happened and no longer wanted to go to Higgins house. She feared meeting Allen again and the Cashman sisters offered to walk home with her. Mary told her two companions that she would be fine if she went home by the road where he wouldn't do anything to her. It was now after four in the afternoon and what the sisters didn't know yet was they would never see their friend alive again.

At twenty minutes to five two other women were out for a walk. Near a small cottage they found the body of a young woman lying on the road. There was blood all over the road and her head was beaten in. The women ran on and told an old man who they thought would do something, but he didn't and went on his way. The nearest farmer to the cottage was said to be occupied by an elderly deaf man, this was probably him. Coincidentally they met Dr Corbett walking up the road, he subsequently took charge of the situation and sent someone for the police.

Later a large posse of police arrived from the town. They inspected the body and the scene of the crime on the road. After hearing what had occurred earlier, they arrested Patrick Allen at his Uncle David Burke's house. For the last year after being released from the asylum he had been helping out at his uncle's farm. When the police arrived there around seven, they found Allen in bed. He made no statement nor did they find any traces of blood on his clothes. None the less Patrick Allen was arrested and placed in custody in the nearest barracks in the town.

An inquest was held on the 2nd of March by Coroner Rice. A jury of thirteen men from the locality were sworn in. As the accused Patrick Allen was not brought before the jury, the evidence called would only show the cause of death.

Denis McCarthy another farmer in the townland of Lissanisky, was called to give evidence as he lived near the murder scene. Dr Corbett had just left his house that afternoon but returned minutes later saying there was a body of a young girl on the road. McCarthy quickly returned to the scene with Corbett and saw the huge pool of blood on the road. There was nobody else seen around at that time. Between them they moved the body to Donoghue's cottage nearby and raised the alarm.

Dr Creagh Downing told the jury that on Sunday the 29th of February he was called to attend the scene. That evening he carried out a superficial examination of the body finding severe head injuries. There were five lacerated wounds on the head all penetrating the skull. The doctor said the injuries seemed to have been inflicted by a large sharp triangular shaped stone.

The Coroner after hearing the evidence returned an open verdict. He said Mary Cotter met her death from injuries caused by some persons unknown. Later that day a huge crowd attended Mary Cotter's funeral which proceeded to Carrigtwohill graveyard.

On Thursday the 4th of March a special sitting of the petty sessions was held at Queenstown courthouse to investigate if there was a case to answer. Several Magistrates sat on the bench including Mr Beamish and Mr Starkie while Mr Rice from Fermoy prosecuted for the crown. The accused was brought to court and placed among four other men so the witnesses could identify him. He had no solicitor to represent him but despite this he appeared quite cool in court. He displayed also no signs of insanity whatsoever. A huge crowd gathered at the courthouse in the town to catch a glimpse of the man accused of this brutal murder.

Mary Cashman bravely gave her side of the story, telling how she was with Mary Cotter just before she was murdered. The Cashman sisters were more than likely the last to have seen her alive. She recalled how Mary's cheek was red after being struck by Allen in the field. Afterwards she said Patrick Allen headed in the direction of the road leading to Cotter's house. The girls waited a few minutes in the field, deciding what they were going to do, hoping Allen had gone. Mary Cotter headed through the fields towards the road. Meanwhile Hannah and Mary Cashman went in the opposite direction towards Higgins's farm. It was over an hour later when Mary Cashman heard the news that her friend Mary Cotter had been killed. Her sister gave the same evidence of what had happened that day.

The next witness Hannah Grogan told how she was walking on the road from Carrigaloe to Lissanisky on the afternoon in question. Near a little cottage in Lissanisky they met a man on the road. She identified that man as the prisoner in court Patrick Allen. It was twenty minutes past four when she saw him but there was no body on the road at this time. The hearing was adjourned until the 11th of March, when the remainder of the witnesses would be heard.

The following Thursday the court sat again and the accused displayed the same calm expression in the courthouse.

Denis McCarthy was called again and he told how he had helped Dr Corbett move the body off the road and into Donoghue's cottage. After giving the same evidence of events as he did previously, he now added more information. He said he knew Mary Cotter and the accused quite well. In the past he often saw them together but not since Patrick had come out of the asylum. However about three months before he saw them talking on the road. Patrick said to her "how are you Mary?" but she replied "don't speak to me", Patrick referred to their past relationship saying "you would speak to me one time". Mary Cotter took up a stone threw it at him but missed. Denis recalled a more recent conversation he had with the accused. Patrick told him "if I thought this girl above put me in the asylum I'd have her life". He knew that Allen was referring to Mary Cotter and pointed out that he would suffer for it if he did anything to her. Allen told McCarthy that he would do it when nobody was looking. He also said he had a hatchet and intended to cut out her heart and feed it to the dogs.

**Modern picture of the road at Lissanisky
probably near the murder scene**

Dr W. Downing was called next and told how he was called to Donoghue's cottage the evening of the murder to inspect the body. He gave testimony similar to the inquest, stating how Mary had suffered five blows to the head. The doctor also told how there were also wounds on her hands, from trying to protect herself. The first blow was struck on the pole of the head and the doctor concluded that would have been enough to kill her.

A farm servant called Hannah Savage was next called to the stand and told the court that she worked at Denis McCarthy's farm. The evening before the murder, Mary Cotter who she knew well came into McCarthy's farmhouse. Not long after Patrick Allen arrived as if he was following Mary because he was not in the habit of going there normally. He spoke to Mary but she didn't reply to him at all. Not getting any satisfaction from her he spoke to Hannah saying Mary didn't care for much as she was to be married soon. He sat down alongside Mary on the bench she occupied. Mary got up and avoided him by going to the well for water with Hannah; she didn't want to be left alone with Patrick. Hannah said that Mary left ten minutes later but Patrick Allen followed her and wouldn't leave her alone. Mary ran back to McCarthy's farm house ran inside and locked the door. Finding herself trapped, she climbed out of the kitchen window on the other side of the house and made her escape. Hearing this evidence the accused spoke for the first time saying "did I run after Mary Cotter? No, don't you think I could have caught her if I wished".

David Burke uncle of the accused told of his nephew's movements that Sunday afternoon. They had their dinner at three and Patrick Allen left the house an hour after. He didn't return home until half past six, at which time he went to bed. The police arrived ten minutes later and arrested him. Burke told how the clothes Allen wore all day were those he was arrested in.

Catherine Cotter mother of the deceased was called next. Before the magistrates she said how she was unaware that her daughter was at one time courting Patrick Allen. She added though that they were very young then. Allen she said was often at their house back then. Since being released from the asylum, Mary no longer encouraged him but he kept coming back. Several times Catherine Cotter told him that he wasn't wanted there as her daughter was annoyed and upset when he called.

As the evidence was all so circumstantial there were many witnesses needed to build a case against Patrick Allen. Even so nobody actually saw him murder Mary but all the witness statements placed him near the scene. They also showed that he was in the habit of confronting Mary Cotter and how she tried to avoid him. It took two more days in court, where many more witnesses told what they saw that day and the goings on of Patrick Allen.

The most interesting witness was one farmer of the locality J. Connell. His testimony shows Patrick Allen's frame of mind after the murder took place. Connell told how Allen arrived at his house between five and six that evening. Patrick was in a most excited state, saying he needed to avoid the police. He told Connell how he had hit a girl earlier and seemed to be very worried.

After several days of hearing evidence the magistrates quickly came to a decision on the 17th of March. Despite nobody seeing the murder and the accused making no statement, the magistrates obviously felt that they had heard enough. They returned the case to trial before a jury at the next assizes and all the witnesses were bound over to attend again. As Patrick Allen still had no legal representation he was asked if he had anything to say before the court but he refused.

The case was called at the Cork summer Assizes in June, before Justice Barry. A solicitor named Mr Green for the crown applied for a postponement of the case as the accused was currently being held in the lunatic asylum. He said there was no point in taking him out of it. The judge agreed and postponed the case until the next Assizes in December.

On the 14th of December, the case was finally called at the Cork Winter Assizes before Justice Fitzgerald. Solicitor Mr Roche defended the case while four queens counsel solicitors prosecuted. The judge said before the court that he had already adjourned several cases until January. When asked about another case he quipped that he hadn't the time to adjourn it today and needed to press on with the current one. Evidence for the prosecution was next called.

First to the stand was Denis Mulcahy who gave circumstantial evidence which the accused had told him. Sometime before the murder, Allen told him how Mary Cotter was the reason he had gone to the lunatic asylum. He also told Mulcahy he was going to murder Mary Cotter.

Roche spoke for the prisoner and addressed the jury. He said if Patrick had committed the crime he was not responsible on account of being insane. This was the whole of the case for the defence.

Medical Superintendent of the Cork Lunatic Asylum Dr Eames, was next examined in court. He told how he had known Patrick Allen who had been an inmate from July 1876 until released in February 1879. He told how occasionally Allen became extremely violent and uncontrollable. Several times he assaulted the attendants there. It normally happened when he was interfered with and he went out of his mind with fury. Allen had been quiet for the last year before being released, but the doctor said these types of patients could have sudden relapses. Allen had been readmitted to the asylum on June 3rd, over 3 months after the murder. When the doctor was questioned by the judge he replied that jealousy would indeed be a cause to excite the accused to a state of fury. Dr Townsend, another doctor in the asylum, gave similar evidence having experienced Patrick Allen state of mind also.

As the defence's case was only trying to prove the prisoners insanity. Mr Roche told the court that there were several more doctors present. They were also willing to give testimony having been in charge of Patrick Allen at some point of his custody. The judge however had heard enough and said there was no need to hear anymore medical evidence.

Mr Roche for the defence summed up the case and asked the jury to find his client insane and not responsible for the crime he had committed.

The jury only needed a short time to deliberate and retuned to the courtroom with the verdict. They found that Patrick Allen was not guilty on grounds of insanity.

The judge ordered the prisoner to be detained *at the Lord Lieutenant's pleasure* which in effect was indefinitely.

A feud between Neighbours
Rochemount, Near Trabolgan 1902

The families of the Smiddy's and Duhig's were neighbours and friends. Thomas Smiddy, 36, was a labourer, married with two young children Richard 7 and Mary 3. Maurice Duhig was also a married labourer aged 36. However he had a much larger family to support, six children aged between five and fourteen years old. Both men and women were employed by James Smyth on the Rochemount farm estate only a few hundred yards west of the gates to Trabolgan. Thomas Smiddy's family lived in the lodge house just inside the entrance gate to Rochemount estate in the townland of Ballyhook. James Smyth had purchased the estate of over 400 acres in the early 1880's and employed many farm workers in the area.

In July of 1902 the two men fell out for some reason. Maurice told his wife that Thomas Smiddy had thrown two stones at him in a field. However when Duhig accused Smiddy of it he refused to talk to him.

On August 24th 1902 the trouble between the two families intensified. Maurice was returning home from Lower Aghada when he turned into the entrance of Rochemount. Inside the gate he had to pass Thomas Smiddy's lodge to get home. He was only about 130 yards from his own house when he stopped on the road and called out as something blocked his way. Maybe Smiddy's children were playing out on the road. Mrs Smiddy came out of the house first and then her husband. Duhig turned away from them in his cart and was struck from behind. This blow knocked him out of the cart and he didn't recall another blow. Thomas had some drink taken but was later able to recall hitting Duhig.

The next day Maurice Duhig went to Midleton Hospital where it was found he had a fracture in his skull. Within a few days he had developed further complications due to the fracture. On the right side of his neck a large abscess formed and he also developed an inflammation around his heart. He had to remain in hospital due to his serious condition. Almost three months later on 13th November Maurice Duhig died in Midleton

Aghada where Maurice Duhig passed through before going home that evening. Image courtesy of the National Library of Ireland

Workhouse Hospital. The cause was said to have been a fractured skull as a result of the blow he received back in August.

The following Saturday the 15th November an inquest was held at Midleton Hospital to determine the cause of Maurice Duhig's death. First to give evidence before the jury was wife of the deceased Johanna Duhig. She stated her husband had been a labourer employed by Mr James Smyth of Rochemount. She recalled that day in August when her husband was struck. He had left and gone to Lower Aghada with a donkey and cart. When the donkey arrived home at eight thirty that evening without her husband she suspected something was amiss. She untackled the donkey and went down the road to look for him. At this time she thought he was probably lying drunk somewhere. She found him lying on the green opposite Thomas Smiddy's house near the entrance gate to Rochemount. Maurice was lying face down with his hand on his forehead. His wife assumed he had a lot of drink taken but when she reached him he was able to tell her he had not. She noticed that he was bleeding badly from an injury to his head. She asked him who had done this to him and he replied Thomas Smiddy. Mrs Smiddy came out of her house and said to her "Hyse him out of that with ye" to which she replied "God forgive ye are after settling him". Several of the Duhig children arrived on the scene and assisted their mother in taking Maurice home. Dr Higgins of Aghada arrived the same night to Duhig's house and bandaged up his head injury but could not do a lot for his condition. The next day Maurice was taken to Midleton Hospital where he was to remain until his death.

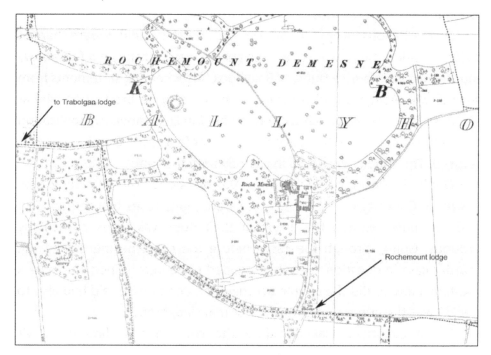

Map from the period showing the Rochemount Estate

Next before the jury was Sergeant Morgan of the RIC who was stationed at Whitegate. He said on the day in question he saw Maurice Duhig driving his donkey and cart at 4:30 in Lower Aghada. Later he saw him at Longpoint about 6:15 and he appeared to be going in the direction of home. Later in the night when he received information of what had happened to Duhig, he went to his house. Maurice was lying in bed with his head bandaged up. Morgan enquired as to what had happened to him. Maurice told how Thomas Smiddy had assaulted him outside Smiddy's gate not 130 yards from his own house. Morgan proceeded to take a statement from Duhig as to what had happened.

Several more witnesses gave evidence of seeing Maurice Duhig going home that evening going up Trabolgan hill and stopping outside the gate. Those that saw him on the way home noticed there was nothing amiss and that he had drink taken but was not drunk at all.

The jury of the inquest without too much deliberation returned the verdict, "we find that death resulted from the effects of wounds as described by the medical evidence, but otherwise we have no evidence of who inflicted such wounds"

On the 18th on November both Thomas and Mary Smiddy were charged before Resident Magistrate Gray. The charge was that they did *feloniously murder and kill* Maurice Duhig at Ballyhook. After hearing statements from several witnesses the judge returned the case to be brought to trial at the next Cork Assizes which were to be held in December. An application for bail was made by the solicitor for the defence, Mr Dunlea, but was refused. The couple were held in custody until the trial.

On the 3rd December 1902 Justice Barton opened the Munster winter assizes in Cork city courthouse. There were many cases before the court and the judge warned the jury that their duty was to be particularly arduous. Going through the cases before the court he mentioned the murder case in question. He said it needed to be determined who struck the fatal blow or did the couple act together. The jury he said had also to decide was the crime that of murder or manslaughter.

When eventually called before the court a few days later, Mr O'Mahony appeared for the Smiddy's. He said his clients had been of good character before and never involved with trouble of any kind. Thomas and Mary Smiddy pleaded guilty to the events which led to the death of Maurice Duhig. Before the court they regretted that Duhig had died as a result of their actions. By pleading guilty it made the case much more straightforward and several character witnesses were called for the accused. The judge then said in court "only one stone had been thrown and only one blow given, which prisoner had it been?" If he knew which it was he said he "could take a merciful view in the case of the other". The court was adjourned for the day and would reconvene for sentencing on the 12th of December.

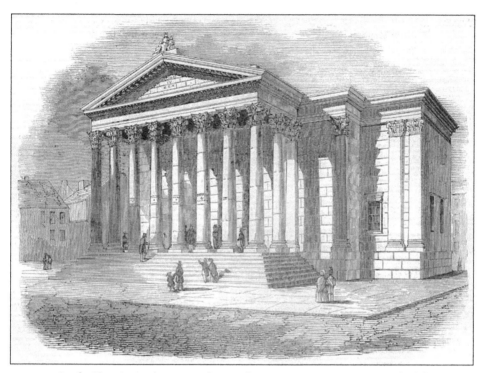
Cork City Courthouse where the Winter Assizes were held

When the court did sit again for sentencing of the case, Justice Barton stated that death was caused by a stone being thrown. He said Thomas Smiddy had not intended to kill Duhig. The court was not in a position where it could overlook the fact that a death had taken place due to Thomas Smiddy's deliberate action. The judge imposed a sentence of eighteen months hard labour on Thomas. Mrs Smiddy had also pleaded guilty but the court found she had no serious responsibility for the actions of her husband and had not thrown the stone. She had already been held in custody for twenty five days and was sentenced to the same period to run from the time of arrest. The judge ordered that Mary Smiddy be discharged by the end of the day and free to return home to her family.

A stone's throw from home
Conna 1849

On Saturday the 9th June 1849, at seven in the morning Johanna Doody was sent on an errand by her brother. She was to go to the nearby village of Conna, to get some tobacco. Johanna was twenty years of age and lived in the townland of Currabeha about two miles north of Conna.

She reached the village, bought her brothers tobacco and started on her journey home. Returning home she met a local young man on the road in the townland of Clashaganniv. She probably knew him as he had recently been in trouble for attacking people in the area. He set upon her and beat her on the head with a heavy stone, before making his escape. When Johanna didn't arrive home, her family became worried. They went out looking for her and found her on the side of the road. When the body was found she was barely recognisable as her face had been beaten so badly.

The police arrived and the local Sergeant Cuthbert made a search of the area where he found traces of blood. The trail of blood led to the house of a seventeen year old young man James Dooly. He lived with his father who was a labourer. The Sergeant found that Dooly had recently washed himself, which would have been unusual back then. He also found traces of blood in the house and duly arrested the suspect. James at first admitted to meeting the girl on the road and also said that he had hit her. Following advice he later remained silent as to what had happened.

There was no obvious motive for why Dooly had killed the young girl. At one stage he even told the police that God had sent him to commit it.

An inquest was held on the Wednesday after and it returned the verdict that James Dooly had committed the murder while in a state of insanity.

Modern image of the village of Conna where Johanna came on the errand

A Grave day
Cloyne 1914

Around about 1911 a disagreement developed about an unmarked grave plot in Cloyne. A brother of Michael Manning from Ballylanders had died that year and was buried at the edge of the graveyard in Cloyne adjoining the Cathedral. James O'Brien from Cloyne was also claiming the plot and the men fell out over it. James a labourer lived in Spittal Street in Cloyne with his wife and young children. Manning an elderly farmer lived in his farm at Ballylanders with his sister.

The disagreement remained unresolved until of course when the plot was to be used again. This time Michael Manning's sister Bridget O Keeffe who had been living in Ballycrenane passed away in 1914. On the day of his sister's wake, Manning and O'Brien had an argument on the street in Cloyne over the plot. Several people heard them rowing and name calling in the middle of town. It got so bad that Sergeant Grace had to come between the men to put a stop to it. In the finish O'Brien said aloud "don't open the grave".

At about ten the next morning James O'Brien went to the plot in question and met Thomas Walton the Sexton (in charge of the plots in the graveyard) there. O'Brien said "they are a long time coming to open this grave". Walton replied "they may not open it at all as I have given them one by the side of it". Later that Tuesday morning after the wake Manning went to Cloyne to make arrangements and for the grave plot to be opened. He travelled to Cloyne by donkey and cart accompanied by two men Michael Scannell and Matthew Condon. As he arrived in Cloyne going up Church lane at about 11:30 James O'Brien was standing around Daly's corner. He got word that Manning was heading towards the graveyard. O'Brien immediately set off towards the graveyard to catch up with him. Michael Manning entered the graveyard alone; the other two men went about other errands. The man in charge of the graveyard was in his house just inside the gate, as he read the newspaper he saw Manning go past alone. Shortly after O'Brien appeared beside Manning in the graveyard. The two men walked towards the grave but said nothing to each other. When Manning got to the grave where he intended to bury his sister O'Brien seized his opportunity, with no one else present in the graveyard. Again without saying a word O'Brien attacked and threw the older man back against a gravestone. He lashed out and kicked him in the stomach several times.

**The cathedral a few years before with sexton's house
to the right in the corner of graveyard.
Image courtesy of the National Library of Ireland**

After the assault Manning managed to get up and leave the graveyard. Thomas Walton who was going to meet Manning encountered him leaving and saw that he was holding his abdomen. Manning went directly to the police barrack and informed Constable George McDermott about what had occurred. Both men returned to the scene of the crime and found that James O'Brien was still there. O'Brien in front of the constable denied the accusations, he said he only gave the old man a shove and he fell over. Afterwards when Thomas Walton arrived, he made arrangements to have

Mrs O'Keeffe buried in another plot. An application to open the grave had already been made to Walton the previous Sunday by two young nephews of Manning's but Walton had refused to let the grave be opened. The reason he said was the law stated that nine years had not passed since the last internment in that plot. This length of time was necessary from a sanitary point of view.

However that Sunday the two young men, who were from Ballycotton, told Walton that the grave would have to be opened as it was needed. When Manning had arrived at the grave earlier he had not known that the sexton would not allow the plot to be opened but O'Brien had and still fought over it. To make matters worse another plot was arranged to bury Mrs O'Keeffe and James O'Brien who was still in the graveyard even helped open that grave.

Dr Murphy from Cloyne attended to Manning after the assault and stated he was suffering from acute pain. The doctor advised him to go home where his sister could look after him. Things didn't get better for Michael Manning and the next day a telegram was sent to the doctor asking him to come to Ballycotton. The doctor found that Manning was unable to retain either food or drink. Again the next day the doctor travelled to Ballycotton as he was concerned for his patient. He found that Manning had begun to show symptoms of peritonitis a bacterial infection caused by the rupturing of his intestines and knew his condition was serious. There were no antibiotics at the time and the infection could only be monitored. The doctor would have known that little could be done and nearly 90% of people died from such infections at that time. The following day the doctor found his patient to be in an even worse condition than the day before. Knowing what the likely outcome was Jeremiah Healy was summoned to where Manning was dying to take a deposition from him of what had occurred in the graveyard. Manning was able to tell Healy that he was assaulted by James O'Brien and kicked in the stomach at least five or six times.

On the 8th of March Michael Manning died from the injuries he sustained a week before. An inquest was held at Ballycotton on March 11th to determine what had caused his death. The inquest was presided over by Coroner Richard Rice who was a solicitor from Fermoy. The jury was sworn in of which John Mahony local postmaster was foreman. Giving evidence was Matthew Condon and Michael Scannell who had accompanied Manning to the graveyard on the day but had not entered. Mrs Sloane a sister of the deceased gave evidence of identification. Constable McDermott of Cloyne stated he went back to the graveyard after the assault took place. Dispensary doctors Dr D. J Murphy from Cloyne and Dr P J O'Brien who had carried out the post-mortem both gave medical evidence.

The inquest jury returned a verdict that Manning died from inflammation of the intestines. The death was caused by violent injuries inflicted on him by a person not present at the inquest.

On the 19th of March at Midleton court sessions an application was made to further remand James O'Brien in custody. Sergeant Grace of Cloyne said he had further inquiries to make in the case before O'Brien could be charged.

Later in the month on the 27th of March, there was a special sitting of the court in Midleton before John French resident magistrate. James O'Brien was charged with having caused the death of Michael Manning by assault.

Dr Murphy of Cloyne gave medical evidence having attended to the deceased man's injuries for several days before he died. He also gave evidence of the post mortem examination, he found the intestines to be inflamed and in his opinion violence had at some point been inflicted on Manning. He went on to say that death was certainly a result of the violence and could have been caused by being kicked or by a blunt instrument. After hearing several more witness statements the district inspector asked to have the accused committed to trial at the next Cork Assizes. Mr Barry solicitor for the defence claimed there was no direct evidence linking the death to his client. Barry said "the whole thing was an accident or a common assault". As there was to be no assizes held in Cork for three months Barry applied to have his client released on bail. Judge French decided that the case should indeed be returned for trial at the next assizes and refused the application of bail for O'Brien.

The Cork Assizes were opened in the Cork courthouse by Justice Moloney on the 16th of July. The were fifteen cases to be heard that week including two of murder, two of manslaughter, two of indecent assault, larceny and one of concealment of birth. The judge addressed the court and summed up each case briefly for the jury. When it came to the Cloyne case he said "it was straight forward enough and presented no features of any difficulty to gentlemen of the experience of the jury".

When the case was called after hearing several other cases, James O'Brien pleaded not guilty. Sergeant McSweeney opened the case for the prosecution and gave the facts of the case. He mentioned the longstanding feud over the plot and that evidence would be given before the court of how James O'Brien brutally kicked the old farmer whilst in the graveyard. The Sergeant stated that the crown prosecution was taking a very lenient view of the case in only charging the accused with manslaughter. In other places where the law was rigorously enforced, O'Brien could be tried for murder and sentenced to life imprisonment with hard labour. The Sergeant stated the most regrettable thing about the case was that the sexton of the graveyard found a resolution to the feud. He had found another adjoining plot was free and Manning's sister had since been buried there.

Jeremiah Healy justice of the peace of Verdun Terrace Ballycotton read to the court the deposition he had taken from Michael Manning just before his death.

Matthew Condon who went to Cloyne with the deceased man on the day in question next gave evidence. He stated that he did not see the assault nor did he hear the elderly farmer screaming. He entered the graveyard after the assault had taken place. When he did get there O'Brien was being accused by Manning and heard him denying that it had taken place. Thomas Walton was next to the stand. He said he supervised the burials in the graveyard and was responsible for the grave plots. He had seen Manning pass into the graveyard that morning before the assault had taken place. However he did not hear the screams as he was inside his house reading the newspaper.

Thomas Canavan was next questioned by the Sergeant; he had been standing at Daly's Corner when Manning went to the graveyard. He heard others say to O'Brien that Manning had come to get the grave opened. He said O'Brien immediately quickly took off after Manning and entered the graveyard.

Dr P.J O'Brien gave medical evidence before the court, having carried out the post mortem examination. He had found inflammation of the intestines and peritonitis. He said that this was the cause of death and was consistent with injuries inflicted five days before. The injuries were a result of violence which could have occurred when the victim was kicked but could not have been caused by falling against a gravestone. Dr Murphy again gave evidence of having treated the victim for several days after the assault. He concurred with the medical evidence already given.

Mr Ronayne for the accused still argued that the ground was slippery that day and the injuries could have been caused by a fall. He also argued that the prosecution had not removed all doubt of how the injuries could have happened. He said that the jury should conclude that doubt exists and give the accused the benefit of that doubt.

The judge summed up the case and went into the evidence given in detail. The jury retired to decide on the case and returned after half an hour with the verdict of guilty of assault. Both the prosecution and the judge agreed that the verdict could not be upheld. The judge addressed the jury and said he knew what they were thinking but this was not expressed in a legal manner. He said when an assault causes a man's death it is undeniably manslaughter. The jury again retired to consider the case and returned after twenty minutes. The foreman of the jury said that they all couldn't agree. The judge asked them once more to try again and said they had agreed on the fact that the man was indeed assaulted and on the medical evidence of the cause of death.

Finally after another half an hour of deliberation the jury returned to court with a verdict that the judge could accept. James O'Brien was found guilty of manslaughter but with a strong recommendation for mercy. The judge replied that he understood the jury's decision and intended to impose a light sentence under the circumstances. Mr Ronayne stated that his client had already been under arrest for over four months and was the father of seven children. The judge sentenced O'Brien to eight months hard labour to run from the time of his arrest.

The Blacksmith's wife.
Dromadda Beg, Ladysbridge 1895

On the morning of the 27th of June 1895 the normally peaceful village of Ladysbridge was thrown into horror and disbelief. Michael Lawton, the local blacksmith had been married to his wife for about seventeen years, he was fifty six years old and she was seven years younger than him. They had no children and were sometimes said to have been living together on bad terms and that they only lived peacefully as long as he was sober. Trouble broke out at times when Michael had drink taken.

Lawton had been off the drink for one year exactly and on the night of the 26th of June was seen in the village of Ladysbridge drinking in the pubs. His wife Mary was seen looking for him in the village earlier in the evening. The blacksmith went home from the pub at about ten pm and screams were heard to come from the house around midnight. Shortly afterwards Michael was seen leaving the house but the neighbours thought it was just another quarrel.

Early in the morning at about half seven, Michael ran to the local priest Fr O'Connor's house and roused him from his bed. In the priest's kitchen, Lawton tried to explain to him what had happened. The priest must have got the impression from Lawton's demeanour that something bad had happened and refused to listen to his statement. Instead he followed the blacksmith back to his house and went inside to find Mary Lawton lying dead in her bed, in a pool of blood. Lawton was now in a very agitated state and wanted to flee the scene but the priest advised him to remain.

A young boy was sent to Castlemartyr to alert the police there of the terrible happenings. It was around half eight that Constable Dillon arrived from Castlemartyr and found Michael Lawton at the cross in Ladysbridge. He immediately arrested him on the suspicion that he had killed his wife. At that time Lawton made no statement. Straighaway the constable went to see the crime scene with Fr O'Connor and Dr O'Connell who had also arrived from Castlemartyr. The woman was found in bed in her clothes and her face was covered in blood. There was a round puncture wound on her right cheek and a similar wound on her forehead. There was blood on the sheets and also on the wall. Dr O'Connell thought the woman had been dead eight or ten hours as the body was getting cold and rigid.

On the 28th of June 1895 coroner Richard Rice held an inquest at Ladysbridge to ascertain the facts of what had occurred. The jury was made up of people from the locality including Maurice Pomphrett farmer from Ballymacoda, John Flavin shopkeeper and newsagent Ladysbridge, Daniel Ahern farmer Bridgefield, blacksmiths David Murnane from Bohillane and James Cahill Ladysbridge.

District Inspector Ewart from Youghal represented the police while the husband of the deceased had the solicitor James Dunlea. The coroner addressed the jury and said that he knew virtually nothing about the case before them. He also made it clear that their role was to "ascertain the cause of death and bring their local knowledge to bear on the evidence". He said it was not to incriminate any person even though someone had been arrested there was nobody on trial before them.

First to give evidence at the inquest was Fr Michael O'Connor and he told how he knew the couple. He described the events the previous morning when he was brought to the house by Michael Lawton. He told the jury that he had refused to listen to the blacksmith talk about what had happened until he saw for himself, but he had his suspicions. The priest found her to be dead and said to the blacksmith "your wife is dead, what do you want me for now?" the blacksmith replied that he would run away. The priest however insisted that he should wait for the authorities to arrive. When questioned by the coroner about Lawton's state that morning Fr O'Connor said the man was terrified. He said "I do not believe that Lawton was in his right mind for years and he became a perfect madman when he took a drop of drink". As the inquest was not going to convict anyone for murder the priest should have saved this until the trial. But he didn't and continued on saying he knew Lawton well and that when the blacksmith became excited "he was then perfectly out of himself". He also told the jury Lawton didn't know what he was doing and was cruel to his wife even in the last twelve months when he was a teetotaller. When again questioned by the coroner about the cruelty, he said "he hunted that poor woman, who is dead like a hare, in my own presence".

Next before the jury of the inquest was Dr O'Connell who said he arrived at the house at nine forty the morning before. Later in the day he carried out an examination aided by another doctor, Dr Curran. They had found in addition to the head injuries she had a ruptured liver and lung as a result of broken ribs. He concluded that cause of death was a result of the rupture of the liver. The doctor informed the jury that the head injuries were caused by both the poker and the hammer found nearby. The chest injuries and broken ribs were a result of being kicked. There were also some marks on the woman's wrists that were evidence of a struggle with the murderer.

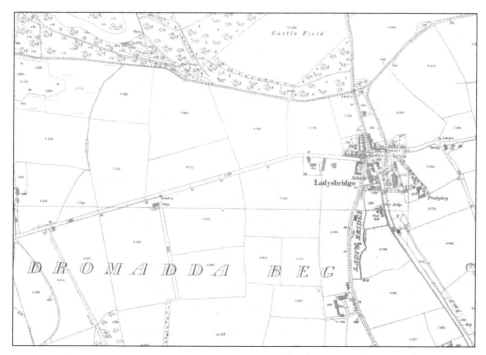

Map showing village of Ladysbridge and townland of Dromadda Beg

The coroner addressed the jury and spoke about the case. Unusually for an inquest he spoke about Mr Lawton who had been arrested on suspicion of killing his wife. Normally an inquest would not comment on any individual. Inquests were only to give a verdict on how the deceased died but not by whom. The coroner said to the jury that this man was totally devoid of rational control and that his mental weakness should exonerate him from the highest degree of guilt. He said that it would not affect a magisterial investigation but the coroner had already pre-empted the verdict of a court. Solicitor Dunlea representing Lawton asked to have the verdict left open as to by whom it had been committed.

The jury retired to deliberate on an outcome that seemed to be obvious. Not fifteen minutes later they returned to court and the foreman of the jury returned the following verdict. "We do find that the said Mary Lawton died at Dromadda Beg on the night of the 26th or the morning of the 27th of June 1895, of rupture of the liver and shock caused by violence inflicted by Michael Lawton whilst labouring under temporary insanity".

On the 8th of July the case was heard at the Castlemartyr petty sessions before Resident Magistrate Cronin. The accused was brought into court and charged that on the night of the 26th or the morning of the 27th at Dromadda Beg, feloniously, wilfully and with malice aforethought, killed and murdered his wife Mary Lawton.

The court in Castlemartyr sat again on the 11th of July to hear the remainder of the evidence. Several witnesses from the village were called and some gave evidence of how the couple had been getting on before the murder. One Michael Duggan said he was in Lawton's forge the Friday before the murder took place. He was there when Mary entered the forge and her husband asked her to leave. The witness told the court that she was a saucy woman and told her husband she wouldn't leave. After again asking his wife a few times the blacksmith told Duggan that his "wife's temper was up and no good would be got out of her". He eventually shoved his wife out of the forge before he continued his work.

After hearing the case Resident Magistrate Cronin said it was clear before the court and he asked the accused Michael Lawton if he had anything to say. He spoke before the court and said "I am not guilty your worship". The case was returned for trial at the next sitting of the Cork Assizes.

It was only five days later that the Summer Assizes sat in Cork and on the 17th the case was called before Justice Andrews. Michael Lawton was present in court and again charged with murdering his wife in Ladysbridge on the 27th June. He pleaded not guilty on the charges. Solicitors for the prosecution spoke and made an application to have the case postponed to the next assizes later in the year. They produced an affidavit from District

Inspector Ewart that said the investigation had not yet been completed. Only in the last twenty four hours had more evidence been found which had a serious bearing on the case. Mr Dunlea for the prisoner opposed the application to have the case postponed and wished to proceed with the case. The judge agreed with the application and postponed the case leaving the police more time to investigate.

The Cork winter Assizes sat on the 10th of December before Justice O'Brien at the Cork city courthouse. When the case was called in court Michael Lawton pleaded not guilty to murdering his wife. Solicitor Ronan for the crown prosecution addressed the jury. He said it was a case of whether there was doubt Lawton killed his wife or by the wildest speculation did someone else do it. He spoke about the witnesses the prosecution would call in court and what would be proved. On the evening in question he said it would be shown how Lawton was in two public houses in the village. His wife watched from outside one public house checking up on her husband. He went home and later screams were heard yet nobody else was in the house.

Mary Hegarty managed a public house in Ladysbridge for her mother. On the night of the 26th between nine and ten Lawton was there and drank three and a half glasses of sherry. When he left before ten that night his wife was waiting outside for him to leave. Another publican from Ladysbridge was Miss Fitzgerald. She said on the night in question Lawton entered her place at quarter to ten. He stayed there only a few minutes but drank three glasses of wine in a short time. While there he told her how his twelve months were up and now he was drinking again. When he left she thought he was sober.

John Dunlea was next called to give evidence and said how he met Lawton going home that night. Living nearby Dunlea heard a woman's screams later that night and afterwards saw Lawton leave his house and walk towards the village.

Resident Magistrate Cronin who had presided over the trial at Castlemartyr was called to the stand. He read a deposition he had taken from Kate Dunlea who had since died. Kate had seen the wife sober heading towards the village that night looking for her husband. Kate also said how Mary Lawton in the past had on occasions sheltered in her house from her husband and sometimes had marks on her face.

District Inspector Frederick Ewart was questioned by Mr Ronan and said at 1pm on the 27th he arrived at the crime scene in Ladysbridge. He warned Michael Lawton about not having to say anything but anything he did say would be written down and used against him. Lawton immediately began to make a statement which the inspector read before the court. "I don't want to make any statement except that I am not guilty. I was at work until after eight yesterday. I was after shoeing the priest's horse and I came home after eight and found the wife drunk. I found her dead in the bed and went and told the priest. I heard a rap at the door and got up and answered the call. I did not know then the wife was dead, but when I came in from the door I found her dead. I was talking to John Cronin at the door. I did not tell him she was dead. I did not know it at the time. I gave myself up to the police, at least I sent for them and gave myself up to them and as soon as they came for me I went with them. I mean that I found my wife dead this morning. I sent for Father O'Connor and gave him up the keys. That's all I wish to say, sorry I have so much to say can't be helped".

The inspector was asked in court how was the accused when he made the statement he replied that he was "cool and collected" but had the appearance of a man who had been drinking. His statement doesn't read like that of a calm man but one who was in a confused state.

Thomas McDonald a Constable in Castlemartyr told the court how he held the prisoner in the barracks on the 27th. He went to Lawton's cell and when he knocked on the door the prisoner made a statement to him. "I want a glass of brandy the sergeant promised to get me a drink. I'm a fool, I acted very foolishly. Constable Dillon did not arrest me I gave myself up to him. The deed was there and nobody in the house but myself. I slept very little last night. I never was so sick before. I want to send a telegram to my brother's son Tom near Midleton, about the pigs. Some one must have them now. I will be kept here or some other place".

Called to give medical evidence was Dr O Connell from Castlemartyr, who was there the morning Mary Lawton was found dead and also saw her in the bed. The next day he carried out a post mortem with Dr Curran from Killeagh. From the position of the body he concluded that she had gotten into bed and someone had killed her afterwards. He stated that the head injury and injury on the jaw bone were somewhat circular and most likely inflicted by a hammer. A hammer was produced in court and the doctor said he had compared the injuries to it and was satisfied it was the murder weapon.

After the case for the prosecution concluded, Mr Barry addressed the jury for the defence. He told the jury if the death was a result of a row between the couple the jury should reduce the charge to manslaughter. He said the only person who could tell that was Lawton himself but the law prevented him from saying anything. Barry himself believed a row took place but that Mrs Lawton died as result of a fall and hit against the furniture. Barry then concluded that the jury should find a verdict of manslaughter.

The crown prosecution solicitor Mahony disagreed and told the court there was no case to reduce the charge to manslaughter. Mahony said "if a man gave way to drink, if a fit of passion came upon him, if his wife tried to save him from himself, if he then and there brutally murdered her it was not manslaughter and the prisoner should suffer the consequences of it".

The judge proceeded to sum up the case before the jury and said there was no real question at all in the case. It was now for the jury to decide on the evidence and come to a verdict that they found right. He said reducing the charge to that of manslaughter would not mean a sacrifice of the prisoner's life. He warned that not all provocation would reduce the charge to manslaughter, words and gestures no matter how offensive would not change murder to manslaughter. One of the jury asked would the accused being drunk make it manslaughter and the judge replied it would not if he knew what he was doing was wrong. The jury retired to consider the case and returned to court over an hour later. They were still in doubt about the verdict and asked the judge to define the difference between manslaughter and murder. He answered the question with a very technical legal explanation and afterwards the jury retired again. The jury deliberated for a further thirty minutes and were recalled to court by the judge. He advised if reasonable doubt existed they should find a verdict of manslaughter. After a short spell out of the court the foreman of the jury returned and said they acquitted Lawton for murder but found him guilty of manslaughter.

Finally the judge addressed Lawton and told him the jury had taken a very lenient view of the case. The judge remarked that he could very well have been found guilty of murder and nobody could have said it wasn't a right verdict. The sentence was then passed that Michael Lawton shall be kept in penal servitude for the remainder of his natural life.

Murder in the middle of nowhere
Barrafohona, North of Midleton 1905

The townland of Barrafohona is located about seven miles north of Midleton on the road between Dungourney and Castlelyons. Back at the turn of the century it was a sparsely populated area with only sixteen houses in the townland, despite it being a large townland of over 900 acres. It was a rural area with all families except one being farmers or farm labourers. Like most places in the country they were all related to each other, the most common surname in the area was Mulcahy. Of the ninety five people living there, twenty three were Mulcahy's

One such family living there was farmer Michael Mulcahy. He had married his wife Margaret Dineen in early 1893 and started a family not long afterwards. Margaret was twenty three years younger than her husband; she was only twenty four getting married while he was forty seven. She was from a labouring family while Mulcahy was a farmer with land. However despite this and the age difference the couple were said to have got on well together and been very affectionate. After getting married Margaret's sister Kate and brother Patrick moved in with them. Despite the fact their parents were still living in the nearby townland of Peafield. Her parent's Maurice Dineen and Mary Curtin had several other children and all were farm labourers. Sending two off to work on the farm with the Mulcahy's who needed them was convenient for all parties. There is but one anomaly that maybe shows the couple were still sensitive about the age difference. The 1901 census shows both their ages as being forty seven, while he was in fact fifty five and she was only thirty two. By 1905 they had five children Michael aged eleven, Maggie nine, Mary eight, Hannah five and Ellie only just two years old.

On the 10th of July, Michael and his wife went to the fair in Midleton and conducted some business there as normal. To the outside world there wasn't the least sign that anything was amiss. The morning after the fair, the family all had breakfast together. They noticed Michael was very quiet withdrawn and generally down in himself. His wife tried to cheer him up but didn't succeed at all. After he went about his normal duties around the farmyard but Margaret kept an eye on him as she thought he was not right. At one pm the family had dinner together and again Michael was extremely quiet. After dinner he got up and walked about the house without saying a word to any of them. Then suddenly he made for the door and his wife went out after him because she thought he was not well. Michael told her to go back to the house, as he wanted to be alone. She knew something was wrong and would not return as he requested. Margaret's sister stood at the door of the farmhouse and watched the pair for some time. She never thought for a second that anything bad was going to happen as Michael had never ill treated his wife. When the pair went over the hill and out of sight she ceased watching them. For a while she went about her normal duties and forgot all about them. When they didn't return to the house later she wasn't worried at first. It was then it dawned on her something her sister had said earlier about her husband not being right. She must have panicked for she sent the eldest child Michael out to look for his parents. When he returned crying she was very worried that something was really wrong.

Kate worried went to the nearest house and got a neighbour Johanna Mulcahy to go and look with her. They set out in the direction that the couple had earlier gone, towards Portavarrig. Both women walked up the hill that Katie had watched her sister walk not long before. They found nothing and went back in the direction they had come from. They spotted Michael alone just standing there and not looking at all himself. Kate immediately blurted out "where is Margaret?" He replied "Margaret is fine" but the women weren't at all convinced by him and began to feel very uneasy. Johanna Mulcahy for some reason said "maybe you have killed her". This terrified Michael and he said to them "if I didn't somebody else did" and with that he fled. He ran towards a nearby wood and disappeared from view.

It was only then the women realised what had transpired when they saw Margaret Mulcahy lying on the ground with her head against a ditch. They knew straight away she was dead and realised their worst fears had come true. It was now about four in the afternoon and there was nobody at all about in this remote and desolate place. Somehow they raised the alarm and eventually word was got to the police in Midleton. District

Inspector Webster from the Midleton barracks gathered a large posse to begin a manhunt. He got police from Ballinacurra and Castlemartyr and proceeded to the scene as fast as he could.

The area near where the murder took place

The body was removed to the Mulcahy's farmhouse, a further search of the area for the husband and the culprit of the crime ensued. The police must have watched the farmhouse all night worried he would return. By dawn on the Wednesday morning the plantation of trees that Mulcahy was last seen entering was surrounded by twenty constables. With the light of the morning they searched every part of the wood but didn't find him there. It took a few more hours of searching when at about seven thirty am Sergeant Beddy spotted someone emerge from hiding. It was indeed Mulcahy he had been lying under some bushes and looked to be in a terrible state. He didn't resist arrest at all but gave himself up, trembling with fear. The police thought he had the appearance of someone who had only just come to realise what he had done. He seemed sorry for what he had done and told the police "oh why did we do it we were such friends". Michael Mulcahy was taken to Midleton Barracks where he was questioned. He seemed to realise what had happened and knew what punishment he was going to face before the law. The police asked him as to his state of health and he told them "wisha I'm fair trying to hould up me courage, sure I know the journey ahead of me".

Wasting no time, on the evening of Wednesday the 12th merely hours after the culprit had been apprehended the inquest was held at Mulcahy's farmhouse. The well known Coroner Rice from Fermoy presided before a last minute jury from the locality, while District inspector Webster represented the police. Key to the case was the testimony of both Kate Dineen and neighbour Johanna Mulcahy who found the body. They both told their story to the jury of the events leading up to the terrible discovery. It transpired that Michael Mulcahy had spent some time in a lunatic asylum back in 1889 a few years before being married.

Dr Walter Long from Midleton told the jury how he had earlier in the day carried out a post mortem with Dr Michael Lawton. He said the deceased appeared to be in perfect health before the recent occurrence. Marks were found on the neck and cheek of Mrs Mulcahy that appeared to be caused by fingernails. Her lungs and brain were congested which was further indication the woman died from strangulation. The coroner remarked on the very sad features of the case and commended District Inspector Webster for his handling of it.

After hearing the evidence the jury found a verdict that Margaret Mulcahy was found dead in a field near to her house. The cause of death was due to suffocation by strangulation by her husband Michael Mulcahy who is of insane mind.

Also held on the evening of the 12th Mulcahy appeared at Midleton Court house. He was charged before Justice of the Peace Mr Walsh with having murdered his wife. The District Inspector applied to remand the accused for a further eight days to further investigate the circumstances. Mulcahy sat listening to the charges against him but couldn't bear to look at Walsh who he knew well. When asked by the magistrate to "stand up Michael" he replied "wisha tis sad news sir god help me". It was no surprise that Michael Mulcahy looked to be very bothered in court and moved about as if his mind was in agony. The magistrate coming to the end of the proceeding asked the prisoner if he had anything to say. He replied "yerrah, I have no questions to ask him for I know my end and he needn't be asking me any questions either".

On the 2nd of August at a special sitting of the Petty sessions in Rathcormac, Michael Mulcahy was charged that he murdered his wife at Portavarrig Bog. The case was heard before Resident Magistrate W.A Hardy and Peace Commissioner William Barry. There was a huge amount of interest in the case in the locality and a crowd gathered at the courthouse. The District Inspector Webster who led the investigation prosecuted on behalf of the crown while solicitor Dunlea from Midleton represented the accused.

Again the evidence of Kate Dineen was the most important to the case. Kate told the court how she had lived with her sister for the past eleven years. She recalled the events which unfolded on the 11th of July clearly in the court house. Kate disclosed that she had in fact gone out looking for the couple herself before meeting Johanna Mulcahy that day. She had seen Michael alone in one of his own fields in the direction of Portavarrig bog. Returning for home it was then she met Johanna and the pair went off searching together. After encountering Michael he fled the scene. The pair went in the direction of a gap where they had seen Michael standing and found the body. Kate screamed aloud when she saw her sister there, Michael was still in view and ran even faster hearing the screams. She was lying on her back with her hair drawn over her face completely covering it. They instantly knew she was dead and saw three marks on her neck.

Dr Long from Midleton told the court how he first examined the body at her house at four in the morning of the 12th. Later in the afternoon he carried out a post-mortem exam assisted by Dr Lawton. He told how the scratches on her face and neck indicated that a struggle had taken place. The marks on the neck he said were from pressure of fingers against her throat causing death by strangulation.

Witness being sworn in

Eleven year old Michael Mulcahy junior was called to give evidence but seemed tormented with giving evidence against his own father. He refused several times to kiss the bible and be sworn in, despite being encouraged to do so. A brother-in-law of the accused was then called to give some unusual evidence. Michael Dineen was from the nearby townland of Peafield, which is the next one west of Portavarrig. He told how he had received a letter from Michael Mulcahy on the 23rd of July. He produced the letter in court. As a result of getting the letter he went to visit Mulcahy in Cork jail. The prisoner was very worried about everything he had done saying god help us "I didn't know what I had done until I went back". Mulcahy especially wanted to know how the children were doing as they were now in the care of his sister-in-law Kate. He asked Dineen to make sure the children went to school and learned their prayers. He added "I learned my prayers and didn't mind them god help me". The topic then turned to his wife's funeral and he asked about the arrangements, where she was buried? What day? Which priest was there? The man seemed to be racked with guilt for what he had done. He told his brother-in-law that he would give anything to bring her back to life again.

Young Michael Mulcahy was again brought to the stand after earlier failing to be sworn in. He was still very distressed and crying. He told how when he went out searching for his father that day that he did come across him. He asked where his mother was but his father said he didn't know. The boy then asked his father to come down to the house with him; initially he did and went across two fields in the direction of home. His father stopped and asked who was there in the house and when he told him who was at home he headed in the opposite direction.

Sergeant Beddy who was stationed at Castlemartyr was called to give testimony having arrested the prisoner. He told how he was outside the wood before dawn on the morning of the 12th waiting for daylight to search for the fugitive. Some time after not far away the sergeant came on a man coming out from his hiding spot. He spoke to him and said "perhaps you are the man I'm looking for". It was indeed Michael Mulcahy and he gave his name without any trouble. The sergeant then arrested him on suspicion of having murdered his wife and Michael was keen to talk. Mulcahy said "I have nothing to say, but a little dispute arose between us. She is a sore loss to me. She is the mother of my children. I was coming up the mountain about cattle and she was following me and wanted me to go back. I wanted her to go back. I then caught her and strangled her. I remained in a bush of furze all night below there". Walking back to the road the prisoner kept talking and even mentioned he would never have been found if he remained in his hiding spot. To the sergeant he revealed something else that was playing on his mind. He told the sergeant. "I have another farm down there and herself and her brother wanted to do me out of it, and that would not do me, and my temper rose". Sergeant Beddy told the court how he returned to the scene days after the arrest. Retracing he found the place where the body was found and where Mulcahy hid were only 320 yards apart.

Acting sergeant John Corbett told the court how he was at the Midleton barracks when the prisoner was brought in. Mulcahy asked

Corbett if he knew his brother-in-law Michael Dineen. He wanted him to call to places in Cork and settle some debts for him. This didn't really sound like someone who was unwell. He also asked the Acting Sergeant to pass another message "tell him too that I said it would be better for them all to live together than to be trying to manage as they were".

When District Inspector John Webster gave evidence detailing the investigation it concluded the case for the crown. The defence solicitor didn't cross examine the witness. When asked did he have something to say the prisoner replied "I have no questions to ask, I know my end". When called the defence solicitor James Dunlea reserved his defence. The District Inspector applied to have the case returned for trial by jury before the next Cork Assizes. The magistrates agreed with the application and concluded that there was indeed a case to answer. The accused would be held in custody until the next sitting of the assizes.

The case was called before the Cork Winter Assizes on December 15th. The jury found Michael Mulcahy to be insane and sentenced him to be imprisoned at his majesty's pleasure. This was a legal term which meant an indefinite sentence which usually turned out to be a life sentence. The children all stayed at home and were cared for by their relations the Dineen's. Their uncle Patrick and aunt Kate continued living with them as before.

Fix your bayonets and charge.
Midleton 1888

On the evening of Thursday 1st November 1888 a battle broke out between the police and several locals in Midleton. The police tried to arrest a man called Mansfield for being drunk but he resisted arrest as he wasn't drunk and this attracted people to the scene. His father said he would take him home and they could charge him later. However this was refused by the police and both Mansfield and his father then resisted arrest. The police fearing the crowd that had gathered dragged both the Mansfield's off the street and into the hall of Cashman's drapery shop. Head Constable Higgins arrived with two other policemen and ordered that the two held captive be released as he realised that Mansfield wasn't drunk at all. The police put their backs against the front door to prevent the crowd outside pushing their way in. Outside on the street they became agitated and began throwing stones, some of which smashed the fanlight over the door.

In the hallway, the five constables held their ground for nearly an hour before backup arrived. District inspector Creagh accompanied by five more constables came armed with fixed bayonets on their rifles. On the street outside the newly arrived constables trained their guns on some of the crowd gathered across the street. The police seemed to be intent on firing at the men but parish priest Fr O'Donoghue rushed up and intervened. The priest begged Creagh to withdraw his men and he would endeavour to keep the peace. However Creagh didn't withdraw and did quite the opposite, he ordered his men to fix their bayonets and charge to disperse the crowd.

In the course of the charge one young man Patrick Ahern, emerged from a pub unaware of what had transpired and was stabbed in the groin. He managed to get up from the street and stagger towards home but fell a few steps later. He was helped to his house which was nearby and a doctor was called.

The day after the outrage in the town Patrick Ahern was in his house in Dickinson's lane. He gave an account of what had occurred to justice of the peace Hallinan. Despite his injuries Patrick told how he emerged from

Hennessy's public house on the previous night hearing the commotion. Up until then he did not know what was going on out on the street. He had drunk four or five pints of porter in Hennessy's but was in no way drunk. He was on the street for a very short time when he was stabbed in the groin by a bayonet from a police constable but he couldn't identify who it was. Later that day Patrick Ahern died at home from the massive blood loss he has suffered the night before. He was only twenty three years of age and had been employed as a labourer by Mr P.J Tattan.

A young woman called Anne French was only a few yards from Ahern when it occurred. She saw Patrick leaning on a railing when a police constable rushed over and thrust his bayonet at him.

On the day following the trouble in the town the matter was brought to the attention of resident magistrate Mr Redmond. He didn't instigate an inquiry into what had happened but took an altogether different view. He instructed the police to watch the offices of Patrick Ahern's solicitor and arrest those that entered so that they could be charged for riotous behaviour. The police then served summonses on at least eight young men for being part of an alleged riot. Local solicitor Leahy who represented Patrick Ahern approached District Inspector Creagh and asked could the police bayonets be inspected. He wanted to ascertain by whom Ahern had been stabbed but after consulting with Head Constable Higgins, Creagh refused.

Coincidently in court that day 2nd of November Head Constable Higgins brought seven local young men to court on charges of public disorder on the 29th of October. Before the court Higgins refused to give evidence and said "I have no desire for these men to be punished but I think it is my duty to bring them before the court". While Higgins took a level headed view on the disturbances in the town Inspector Creagh took the opposite view. Creagh told the court he believed "it might be the beginning of a worse state of things". Consequently thirty extra police had to be drafted into the town of Midleton.

The Coroner opened the inquest at the Midleton courthouse the day following Ahern's death. Hundreds were said to have been present when the coroner arrived at the courthouse. The courthouse was packed and the crown took a keen interest in the proceedings. Solicitors Mr Leahy and Mr Barry represented the Ahern family while Solicitor Julian was for the police and District Inspector Seymour was brought from Mitchelstown to represent the crown. Twenty four people from the area had been summoned to attend the inquest as the jury by the police. Such was the feeling of distrust of the police in the town that only twelve attended. The coroner remarked it was extraordinary in a town like Midleton that a jury could not be found. It was stated at the inquest that people had left the town that morning to avoid the inquest. The coroner thought there was more sympathy for the deceased but obviously people were afraid that the police would have it in for the jury depending on the finding.

There was much speculation in the town about the jury, as it was the police who was selected them. It was said the police selected the jurors who they thought would be unable to attend and passed over people from the town that had sympathy with the deceased. It was also alleged that the police had gone out of their way to find jurors in Ballinacurra. Finally in the afternoon a jury of fourteen was sworn in and the inquest adjourned until the next day.

The town of Midleton and all the businesses were shut for most of the day of the 5th and a feeling of mourning was felt throughout the town. Despite this the police brought an extra twenty constables into the town. Large crowds attended the funeral of young Patrick Ahern in the evening despite terrible weather. People from all over the area attended and followed the procession two miles out of the town to the graveyard in Churchtown.

The feeling of unease in the town didn't die down nor was it going to, after what had happened. To make matters far worse on Wednesday the 7th Constable Swindle was seen out on the town dressed in full uniform carrying out his normal duties. This was despite most of the townspeople knowing he was the one who stabbed poor Ahern. The people were surprised and dismayed by this as they believed Swindle had left the town.

John Leahy wrote to Creagh warning him that he was not to prevent any of the constables from attending the inquest or any subsequent inquiry. If he did he would make Creagh legally responsible for his actions.

On the 10th of November William Lane Member of Parliament for East Cork asked Arthur Balfour the Chief Secretary of Ireland in the House of Commons about the case. The MP inquired whether Creagh and his constables would be suspended until the inquiry was complete. The Chief Secretary refused to comment on the case pending the outcome of the inquest.

Meanwhile the police in Midleton were taking their own steps in order to justify their actions on the night of the 1st November. They issued summonses to several of the young men who were there on the night hoping to have them prosecuted before the inquest was completed. Patrick Twomey of Charles Street Midleton (now called Connolly Street) was summonsed for resisting, obstructing and assaulting acting sergeant McLean. Maurice Murphy and Patrick Mansfield both of *Freeschool Lane* were also summonsed for the same offences on Mclean. The defendants claimed their innocence of such offences but were called to appear before the court on the 15th of November.

Before charges were brought against the defendants the inquest sat again in Midleton courthouse on the 13th of the November. First called to the stand was acting sergeant McLean, who described at great length the events on the 1st. He stated that he and Constable Swindle arrested Mansfield for being drunk and obstructing the footpath. He recalled how they had released Mansfield but stayed in the hallway hiding from the crowd. The crowd on the street called on "Balfour's bloodhounds" to come out but they remained until Creagh arrived. Under Creagh's orders they fixed their bayonets and charged the crowd until nobody was left on the streets. However McLean said he was surprised when he heard someone had been stabbed on the streets that night.

On the third day of the Inquest Dr Lawton who had attended Ahern before he died gave evidence. On the night of the 1st he was called to Dickinson's lane to the home of Patrick Ahern at ten minutes past nine. He found the patient unconscious and he saw he had lost a lot of blood. When examined he found a puncture wound an inch deep inflicted by a sharp instrument. The doctor suspected the femoral vein had been severed due to the blood loss. A police bayonet was shown in court and the doctor stated that it would inflict such a wound with only moderate force being necessary. The doctor said the cause of death was large haemorrhage of blood and he knew early on that the injury would prove fatal. The only

Charles Street Midleton, now Connolly Street
Image courtesy of National Library of Ireland

other wound found on Ahern was a laceration on chin, as if he had fallen and landed on his chin. The solicitor for the police Julian argued that a very slight prod or even if someone walked into a stationery bayonet would cause a similar injury. The doctor resumed his evidence saying he was there the next day when Patrick Ahern gained consciousness. He also witnessed the statement that Patrick gave to the justice of the peace Hallinan.

Head Constable Higgins recalled being in the hall of Cashman and Co on the 1st of November. He had been told it was safe to go back out onto the street after Mansfield had been released but said he had waited as he didn't want to use violence, if it could be avoided. He also recalled saying on the night that it would be better if Creagh had not arrived as "there was strong feeling of hostility against him".

After a break for lunch Phillip Creagh District Inspector was called and questioned by Mr Seymour. He was at dinner that night when word arrived that there was a row on the street. He blamed the trouble on a speech given in the town four days before by Dr Tanner M.P for Cork. Tanner a member of the National League had spoken to a large group in the town and allegedly told people to resist the police.

When he arrived on the scene there was a crowd across the road booing but once Creagh was recognised they threw stones at him. When he arrived outside Cashman's he ordered the men inside to come out and fix their bayonets. They then charged, cleared the crowd from the streets and some of the pubs in the town. It was only afterwards that he heard a man had been stabbed but he didn't believe it could have been one of his men. Barry asked the witness why the constables were not armed with batons that night instead of swords and rifles but Creagh refused to produce the Constabulary regulations. Under intense cross examination by Barry, Creagh refused to answer several questions but eventually was heard to say "if a man was stabbed that night it was his own fault". Barry asked had he found blood on any of his constable's swords and he replied he had not. Again Barry kept up the pressure and asked did the police in Midleton stab Ahern but Creagh replied he hadn't seen it happen. Barry asked if a man was indeed stabbed in the town what steps had the police taken to find out by whom. Creagh replied that they had done nothing to find out. He denied he was neglecting his duties in not trying to find out who had done it.

When asked was he hated by the people of the town, Creagh denied it. He said he was on good terms with the respectable people of Midleton but for the lower orders he did not care a bit. Even this statement by Creagh wasn't true as only a few months before in April he had trouble with a newsagent in the town. Timothy Murray had displayed a political poster in his shop window calling for land reform and better rights for tenant farms. Creagh upon seeing the poster burst into the shop and a struggle ensued. The poster was taken down and Murray said he would just get another. Creagh later summonsed Murray to court for displaying the *Plan of Campaign* poster.

On the same day the normal petty sessions sat in Midleton. Creagh asked for an adjournment of some of the cases as the accused were to be called as witnesses for the inquest. Patrick Mansfield was charged with drunkenness and assaulting Mc Lean.

Also summoned was Walter Mansfield, John Twomey, Patrick Knowles and Maurice Murphy on resisting and obstructing McLean. Summoned on the lesser charge of riot and unlawful assembly were Timothy Holland,

Patrick Condon, John Walsh and Maurice Hennessy. The hearing of the case was adjourned for two weeks.

The inquest had by now reached its fifth day in the courthouse. Most inquests lasted merely a couple of hours even in a murder case. The interest in the case amongst the town people had not waned and if anything the crowd in the courthouse increased.

Solicitor Julian questioned Patrick Mansfield about when he left Cashman's hall on the night in question. Mansfield said there were two or three dozen people on the street when he was released and causing no trouble at all. He also said while being held in the hall constable Swindell choked him until he became exhausted. McLean deliberately bit Mansfield's finger until he drew blood, in response the prisoner punched McLean in the face.

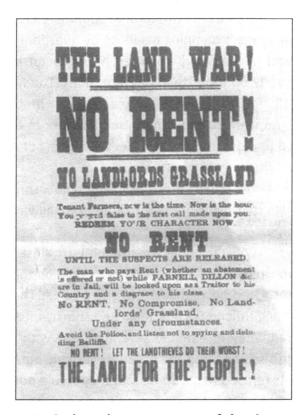

Typical Land League poster of the time

Anne French a fish seller from *Charles Street* was called next to give evidence. She was out on the street that night looking for her husband, when the police passed her by. She recalled seeing their bayonets fixed to the rifles glittering under the gas streetlamps. A little later she saw Ahern leaning against the railing when several police including Creagh came up the street towards him. Then she said one of the Constables made a drive towards Ahern and stabbed him with something without warning. She said the two constables shoved him along until he fell and heard Creagh say "have at him". This caused a sensation in the courthouse but she continued her statement. She shouted "Oh don't ye kill the man altogether" and as a result the head constable shoved her knocking her young child out of her arms. However she said no more to the police in fear she would also be attacked. When asked who stabbed Ahern she identified Constable Swindell by pointing him out in the courthouse. This caused an outburst of shouting from the crowd until the coroner suppressed it. Julian tried to undermine Anne French's damning evidence by questioning her motives against the police. Anne freely admitted having been fined for being drunk and disorderly on more than one occasion. The May before she was also fined 15s for being drunk but pleading her innocence refused to pay the fine and went to gaol. She raised laughter in the courthouse when she replied to cross examination "oh the highest of quality goes to gaol these days".

Another young man called Patrick from *Freeschool Lane* told what he saw on the streets that night. He had hidden in a hallway when Creagh ordered the charge.

After he saw two Constables had a man jammed against Tattan's railings one had a weapon in his hand. He also saw a woman on the street nearby while the police shoved his namesake to the ground. Then the witness went into the Young Ireland Society's hall and shortly afterwards several constables arrived. They threatened several people with their bayonets and rifles. Creagh also appeared and ordered everyone out onto the street but the occupants refused to go. Some said they would not be put out on the street only to be stabbed by a bayonet or maybe the police would do it in the hall. Creagh became extremely annoyed and threatened to arrest any one he could on the streets.

Patrick Desmond friend of Patrick Mansfield recalled how the two stood on the street earlier on the 1st when McLean came up and ordered them home. Mansfield was arrested and Desmond went home. Desmond recalled how later he had heard his friend was released and he went to his house and found him in bed. Daniel Cotter told the jury that he saw from the corner of Charles Street two constables rush at Patrick Ahern while he was standing by Tattan's railings. He saw Ahern being pushed along the footpath by the constables. The young man didn't get a chance to defend himself and had his hands at his hips and his head was hanging down. Suddenley Ahern fell onto the street in a helpless state.

Next called to the stand was licensed publican Catherine Hennessy from Charles Street. On the night in question she saw on the street opposite her premises a man down on the street. There were three or four police around him one of which she said was the District Inspector. She ran into the street shouting at the police for "god's sake don't murder him" but one of the Constables faced her and she fled in fright. Afterwards when everyone had left she saw a pool of blood on the footpath where the man had been lying. Creagh, Higgins and Mclean were recalled to the stand and swore that the evidence just heard as to what had happened on Charles Street was completely false.

The next witness called to the inquest was Edward Barry town commissioner. He told how he saw Mansfield being dragged away by two constables as they entered the hall. He lived near Cashman's and saw Creagh come down the street towards the crowd. When more police arrived he saw the crowd of mostly juveniles disperse as a result of Fr O'Donoghue's intervention. This had all happened before the police came out of the hall. Barry heard Creagh's order "draw your swords, steady now boys, keep together". After strenuous objecting from Mr Julian, solicitor Barry was eventually allowed by the coroner to ask the witness his question. "Will you say that the police charge was necessary for the safety of their lives that night?" To the question the witness answered "certainly not."

The witness then said he thought there were about one hundred people on the street when Mansfield was released. However he said they were a good humoured crowd who enjoyed the fact that the police were trapped in a hall. The witness said nobody except the Father interfered with Mansfield being arrested. He also said there was no reason the police went into the hall, except maybe they were tired from dragging young Mansfield. The inquest adjourned until the following week when it would be concluded.

When the inquest sat again it was to be its last day. They were to hear from a few more witnesses and then a verdict would be reached. First Creagh approached the Coroner and wished to change a comment he had previously made. He said a man could not possibly have been stabbed at Tattan's railing that night without him seeing it.

A Miss Margaret Russell was questioned by solicitor Barry. She had heard Creagh shout orders that night and then saw a man stagger near Tattan's railings. This same man was shoved back by the police against the railings. She saw others run down the street with the police pursuing them. When cross examined by Julian, Margaret admitted shouting at the police that night, when had Creagh passed by she said "Creagh you murderer, you are all Balfour's murderers."

The last witness at the inquest was John Walsh a shop assistant in the town. He had seen a man near Tattan's that night and saw the police run at him. He didn't see any more of what had happened to the man.

When the evidence was finished Julian spoke at length in defence of the police especially the actions of Creagh. At this stage, after the long inquest the exchanges between solicitors Barry and Julian had grown bitter. However in their speeches the only thing they agreed on was the professional manner of the coroner Mr Rice throughout the inquest. When it came to their opinions of the case they were completely opposed.

Barry made his address on behalf of the next of kin of the deceased Patrick Ahern. He asked the jury "who killed Patrick Ahern?" He answered his own question"they pretended they did not know who did it and at the same time had taken no steps to discover the criminal". He said it was reckless for eight constables to charge with bayonets on a crowd that had already dispersed. He asked the jury if all the people who had given evidence had entered into a conspiracy against the police. Barry concluded that there was malice aforethought in Creagh's orders that night and in the actions of the constable who killed Ahern.

Solicitor Seymour for the crown thought Creagh had only done his duty and Ahern had died through misadventure. Coroner Rice summed up the case for some time reviewing the evidence. Finally he asked the jury to clear their mind of passion and prejudice and find a true and honest verdict

The jury retired at nine forty five and returned to court after only fifty minutes deliberation. The foreman of the jury announced that the jury agreed unanimously. The verdict was read out, they found in favour of wilful murder against Constable Edward Swindell. The jury also said their opinion that the order to charge by Inspector Creagh was most unjustifiable. The coroner issued a warrant for the arrest of constable Swindell following solicitor Barry's request. The Saturday after the warrant was issued Constable Swindell was arrested and removed from the Midleton barracks. He was taken directly to Cork gaol and placed under the custody of the governor. Despite being arrested it was believed that he would be released again within a short time. It would have been disastrous for the government to have him convicted of this crime and would call in to question several more similar cases which were covered up.

A few days after the inquest several of the young men accused of assault on night of the 1st November made counter claims against the police. Their solicitor Mr Leahy managed to get a magistrate to sign several summons against the police while many others refused. Constable Callanan was summoned by Patrick Twomey for assault using a stick. McLean was summoned for assaulting and beating Patrick Mansfield and Head Constable Higgins for unlawful assault of Maurice Hennessy.

However on the 30th of November at the Midleton Petty sessions Creagh was to get his way. Judge Cadwell dismissed the cases against the police saying they were only carrying out their duties on the night. Delivering the judgement of the magistrates he said the whole affair was caused by the people of the town taking upon themselves the law and order. He said Patrick Mansfield was arrested for no reason and the people wanted justice and tried to rescue him. Patrick Knowles, Maurice Murphy and Walter Mansfield were sentenced to six weeks hard labour for assault and another six weeks for resisting arrest. Timothy Holland, John Walsh and Patrick Condon also received six weeks hard labour for riotous behaviour. Walter Mansfield went for Creagh and said "are you satisfied" but was restrained from doing anything further. The men were taken by train to Cork and transferred to the gaol.

The case against Constable Swindell wasn't called when the Winter Assizes sat in Cork early in December. The reason the Judge stated was the crown wasn't willing to prosecute and didn't send a bill to the grand jury. At this stage the accused had already been discharged from jail by an order from the High Court of Justice. This didn't stop the solicitors for Patrick Ahern's family from proceeding further; they then made an application to the Grand Jury.

By mid December it was brought up in the House of Commons when William Lane Member of Parliament for Cork questioned Chief Secretary for Ireland Arthur Balfour about the killing. Balfour gave the excuse that the matter was now under the consideration of the Attorney General Peter O'Brien. The Attorney General decided to have the case tried in court before magistrates and if a *prima facie* case could be found it would be sent to trial. Nobody except the police had any confidence in justice and the coroner's inquest had already returned a verdict.

In early January of the following year the principal witnesses of the case were being questioned again and a trial date was set for the 10th of the month. The case was to be heard at a special sitting of the Midleton petty sessions court and summonses were issued for the witnesses to appear. Rumours were rife in the town about Edward Swindell since he had been released and it was heard how he was in Kinsale with his father who was the Head Constable there.

The court sat on the 10th of January and was presided over by local magistrates. The police had brought in several representatives from the crown prosecution from Dublin. Magistrate Gardiner outlined the duties of the court explaining that it would then be sent forward to a trial by jury. Most of the remainder of the first day was taken up with hearing the evidence of Anne French and the subsequent cross examination. To go into it again would be a repeat of what was said at the inquest but Julian for the accused again tried to undermine her evidence by questioning her character. Despite him having prepared for the questioning and researched her past offences, Anne was unfaltering in her answers. Her story was convincing and had not changed since the inquest almost two months before. Several other witnesses gave evidence as they had done before at the inquest.

On the second day in Court Friday 11th Anne French was again cross examined by solicitor Julian. Also called were Dr Lawton and Justice of peace Mr Hallinan. While the court was sitting Maurice Murphy and Patrick Knowles arrived at the train station after being released from jail. A large crowd was waiting cheering when they arrived and accompanied them down the town. While passing the courthouse the cheering became louder as the crowd grew. They were then set upon by some of the police that were on duty outside the courthouse.

The court reconvened after the weekend on Monday January the 14th. Solicitor Julian said that Constable Swindell was innocent of the case against him and that every policeman in Midleton that night was also equally innocent. He went on to say he would exonerate not only Swindell but the whole body of police who were involved that night. He would call witnesses to prove his case who were none other than the police who were there that night. He called Creagh who repeated what happened like he did before. Much of the day was taken up questioning Creagh. Near the end of the day under cross examination he admitted that it must have been his men who stabbed Ahern. However he never admitted having seen it happen.

The next day in court was to be the last day of the proceedings; they had been as long as the inquest. Acting sergeant McLean described the events of the 1st November but denied seeing who stabbed Ahern. Under cross examination he admitted to using his sword on two occasions that night. First a charge down Church Lane he struck Maurice Hennessy who was alone on the shoulder. He recalled striking another man called Fitzgerald. On further examination he was asked "I suppose it would be nothing wonderful to strike a man if you saw him leaning against Tattan's railings?" McLean replied "if he didn't get out of my way I certainly would". If this wasn't evidence of the attitude of the police against the people nothing was. Several other constables were called but only corroborated the evidence already heard by their colleagues.

The evidence for both sides closed and Mr Carson representing the crown and the Attorney general addressed the inquiry and said Swindell wasn't on trial but the matter was under investigation. He asked the magistrates to consider the evidence on both sides.

The magistrates retired for a mere twenty minutes and quickly returned with a verdict. They then read out quite a lengthy sequence of events which they believed to have occurred that night. They made it impossible for Anne French to have seen Ahern being stabbed and said she would be capable of making it up to get her own back on the police. Their verdict was obvious that there was no evidence in the case against Swindell. Some of the magistrates made statements but James Penrose Fitzgerald made an unusual one. He said "I believe the public regard with as great detestation as the magistrates do the abominable plot against the life of Constable Swindell. I don't believe Mrs French invented the story but I believe there are others behind her and I would like to get to the bottom of it".

Mr Leahy who was a solicitor for Ahern's next of kin objected to the magistrates. He was ignored and one magistrate replied "I won't hear any more, I don't know who you are". They left the bench and the case closed.

It would be a long time before the people not only of the town but the larger area forgot the failure of justice. Constable Swindell was transferred out of the town to Belgooly, closer to where his father was. The case was so well known that when Swindell arrived by train at Kinsale he was instantly recognised before he even got off the train. A large crowd hissing and booing gathered around him.

Approaching the anniversary of the terrible killing of Ahern the police in the town got wind that something was going to happen. In November 1889 for almost two weeks the police watched the graveyard in Churchtown where Ahern was interred. They also patrolled the roads between there and the town in anticipation of a demonstration of some kind. District Inspector Creagh was still in the town and said to have been on the war path hearing it would be held on Sunday the 10th. He was only fed this information to confuse him while the planning went on in secret.

Police patrolling the graveyard

On the evening of the 13th the plan swung into action, scouts were posted on all surrounding roads and band instruments smuggled to the graveyard. Only a few hours before people of the locality were told and later a huge crowd gathered around the graveyard. After a ceremony there and speeches by local nationalists the crowd formed a procession towards the town and was said to number almost two thousand people. They were led into the town by a brass band and several torches. When passing Creagh's house the large crowd cheered defiantly of their success over him.

When near the police barracks the band played aloud *God Save Ireland* and everyone in the procession joined in. When they reached the Young Ireland Society building the crowd quickly and peacefully dispersed. The police were nowhere to be seen until it was over and then they all turned out of the barrack. Under head constable Higgins they made inquiries as to what all the noise was about.

There remained a great deal of bitterness towards the police in the town especially from the family of Patrick Ahern. Creagh and his constable's level of pettiness were shown when they summoned Patrick Ahern's mother

Catherine and sister Hanora for riotous behaviour on December 1890. The case was heard in January where a Constable gave evidence. He said the Ahern women had called him "Creagh's Murderer's" and threatened him right at their front door in Dickinson's' lane. The women where supposed to have threatened the constables that they would stick them with a pike. Defence solicitor questioned him and the Constable couldn't swear it was indeed Hanora. Another Constable gave similar evidence but when asked to identify Hanora Ahern in court, he could not. The case against her was dropped for lack of evidence but the attention then turned to her mother. Leahy argued on a legal technicality that the summons order was illegal much to the annoyance of Creagh. It was agreed that she would be fined 5s and costs. When it was read out the elderly woman said "thank god of it that we are not bound to the peace".

St. Valentine's Day Mystery
Midleton 14th February 1835

Love certainly wasn't in the air on Valentine's Day in Midleton in 1835. A fair had been held in the town during the day and afterwards there were the usual scuffles between men who had been drinking.

Two rival gangs of men in particular stood out from the normal occurrences with their violence. The leader of one gang was called John Noonan, a huge man of enormous strength. He thought he had gotten the better of his rivals, but was later in the night caught unawares. The five opponents got their revenge on Noonan but went too far. Details are sketchy but they barbarously killed him and fled.

It was obvious that it wasn't premeditated and the men knew their fate if murder could be proven against them. None of the five gave themselves up. Instead they went on the run thinking that it would all blow over.

Only one of the gang was apprehended and arrested. He alone faced the charges against him and was found guilty. The punishment was transportation for life to a penal colony such as Australia, which sounds bad but back then you could get similar for stealing a sheep.

Meanwhile, it was rumoured two of the wanted men had managed to escape to America and were living there. The search continued for the remaining two and went on for some time. It was later learned that one of the men who remained and evaded the police for years had since also left the country.

Many years after in the height of the famine, in June of 1847 one of the wanted men Patrick Tattan turned up in Midleton. He must have thought after all the years, twelve to be precise it may have been forgotten about or maybe he wouldn't be recognised. He was wrong and within a few hours of being in town he was behind bars.

It turned out Patrick Tattan had been only twenty miles away somewhere in the vicinity of Lismore working for a farmer for all those years. He had behaved himself and kept his head down avoiding detection as it was never thought he was so close to home. His reason for returning was that he had become sick and was no longer able to work. Tattan was bloated with what was then called dropsy an abnormal accumulation of fluid in the body. He was in no doubt that he was dying and now wanted to be back amongst his own people.

Shortly after being arrested Tattan was brought before resident magistrate Mr Knaresborough and charged with his involvement in the death of John Noonan. He was found guilty and sent for trial at the Summer Assizes but few believed he would survive till then. Afterwards in the county gaol he confessed to having been present on that Valentines night years ago. He denied being directly involved however saying he never struck Noonan.

Only two weeks later on the 22nd June 1847 Patrick Tattan died in County Gaol before he was tried at the Assizes. Now it would never truly be known what exactly happened that Valentines night in 1835.

Shoemaker murdered by one of his own.
Cross Lane, Youghal 1873

In the 1870's a shoemaker called John Dykes lived with his wife Margaret in Cross Lane just off Windmill Hill in the town of Youghal. Their grown sons Patrick, Thomas and Benjamin all seem to be still living at home.

In October of 1869 brothers Benjamin and Thomas are caught with stolen goods from a house in Youghal. They end up before the judge in court at the Cork Spring Assizes. Both were sentenced to twelve months hard labour in jail. Hard labour at the time really was hard, with jobs like working a treadmill, breaking stones or pounding hemp. They don't seem to learn from their mistake and about a year after being released they get themselves into similar trouble. In 1872 Benjamin and Thomas robbed a pawn brokers in the town and this time ended up serving 18 months hard labour in jail. All the while the other brother Patrick stays at home making shoes with his father.

Around Christmas of 1873 Thomas was again released from jail and returned home to work with his father. After a period at home, Thomas began to get violent and threatened to kill some of his family members. He always carried his shoemaker's knife which worried them even more. Fearing for their safety the family committed Thomas to the lunatic asylum and he remained there for several weeks. On the 5th of March John Dykes received a letter saying his son was now recovered and much better. Not long after he was discharged from the asylum and he returned home once again. At first he seemed to be better and went about his work as normal. But within days it was obvious that he wasn't quite so well, he displayed his old habits of being very irritable and threatening. He became more and more eccentric and abandoned his work wandering the fields instead.

On Sunday the 23rd Margaret noticed her son Thomas sharpening his shoemakers knife and was worried enough to mention it to her husband. That night they all ate dinner together and retired to bed not long after. It was nothing unusual back then for the whole family to sleep in one bedroom. Parents John and Margaret in one bed and the sons slept across the room from them in another bed. Sometime after the light had been quenched about one in the morning, Patrick complained that his brother had his knife under the pillow. Within seconds the brothers were rolling about on the floor in a desperate struggle. The father tried his best to intervene in the darkness and pull Thomas off his brother but couldn't. Meanwhile Patrick cried out for his father to save him. Knowing he could do nothing the father fled to raise the alarm and alert the police. All the time their mother was in the room listening to one of her sons beg for help at the hands of her other son. She fumbled about in the dark in panic looking for a light.

When she finally did get a light the terrible scene she had heard unfold was plain before her eyes. Patrick was thrown on the floor with a pool of his own blood around him. After murdering his own brother Thomas stood over the body saying "now he is dead and there is no more about him". As the police had not arrived with her husband she also fled the house and hid in fear for her safety.

Not long after the police arrived at the house and so did Dr Curran. The doctor couldn't do anything as Patrick was found to have been stabbed many times and was pronounced dead. Thomas was immediately arrested and taken into custody by the police. Patrick was only 31 years of age and his brother Thomas was a year older than him.

The inquest was held in Youghal on Tuesday the 25th of March. It was obvious the verdict considering that Thomas was found standing over his brother. Dr Curran told the inquest about the dreadful injuries he had found on the body of Patrick. Thomas had stabbed his brother many times leaving nine bad wounds. One stab wound was between the ribs and Patrick also had a broken rib. Another was in the thigh which had gone through a vein. There were three wounds in the chest near his arm pit and another on the neck. The doctor told how he found symptoms that showed Patrick had been suffering from consumption (now know as Tuberculosis) for years.

The jury of the inquest came to the verdict that Thomas Dykes was guilty of wilful murder. The question of his sanity and ability to plead was left for a tribunal before a jury. Again Thomas was sent back to jail this time under the coroners warrant.

The case was heard before the court at the Cork Summer Assizes on the 22nd July. Justice Morris presided over the case before a jury of twelve men. The case wasn't going into too much evidence and its primary aim was to assess whether Thomas Dykes was of sound mind. This would then determine his ability to plead or not. John Joyce told how he was the governor of the county jail for the last 24 years. He recalled twice having Thomas Dykes in the jail. Both times he was extremely troublesome and he didn't think the man was accountable for his actions. Two more doctors gave evidence saying they were in no doubt that Dykes was insane and unable to plead. However the physician of the County jail believed otherwise. He thought Thomas Dykes knew right from wrong and said he "was nothing more than an ordinary criminal". Doctor Townsend of the Cork lunatic asylum explained how just the year before Thomas was transferred there from jail. He behaved so well for a while the doctor was left with no other option but to discharge him. After hearing the witnesses the judge addressed the jury saying that the safest thing to do was to concur with the medical evidence. Of which it was three to one that Dykes was indeed insane.

The jury came to the verdict that Dykes was not of sound mind and unable to plead before the court. The judge sentenced him to a criminal lunatic asylum indefinitely.

Eglington Lunatic Asylum Cork where Thomas Dykes may have spent some time. By C.D Laing 1852 courtesy of Wellcome Collection

Why did you not get the right one!
Ballycotton 1921

In June of 1920 a battalion of Cameron Highlanders took up post in the town of Midleton. At first they patrolled the countryside on bicycles but after several ambushes in the area gave up the practice. They took to patrolling the area in convoys of lorries or *Crossley* tenders. Military from the same regiment were also garrisoned in Cobh. A party of these soldiers were sent to the barracks in Ballycotton to reinforce the R.I.C there. Regular lorry convoys arrived in the village to relieve the men holding the barracks. The Cameron Highlanders were also active in searching houses and rounding up suspected volunteers in East Cork.

With the War of Independence waging on and British administration was losing its grip on the situation. The military were unprepared for the guerrilla warfare they found themselves in. In December of 1920 Martial Law was declared in Munster. This was a last ditch effort to maintain control. Trial by a jury was now replaced by a military court martial. Coroner's inquests were also replaced by military courts of inquiry. The so called authorities were now free to do as they pleased and their own court of inquiry would justify themselves.

Early September 1920 the Ballycotton Barracks was abandoned for no apparent reason. The local IRA Company seized the opportunity and the barracks was burned to the ground a day later. Control of the village was then lost except for the regular lorry patrols. The following year to combat the patrols local volunteers were issued with orders to damage bridges and dig trenches in the roads. The trenches were cut in such a way to allow cars to pass but not the larger military lorries. This greatly impeded the military patrols element of surprise and gave the volunteers an opportunity to attack. As the guerrilla warfare intensified there was several ambushes in the area on the lorry patrols. Searches of known volunteers houses also increased and many went on the run. Several volunteers captured by the Cameron Highlanders in the Midleton area were subsequently found shot dead. Also in early 1921 another method was adopted in the Midleton area to curtail the military patrols. Landmines were planted on the roads and a group waited until the approach of the convoy.

One Sunday evening on the 3rd of July 1921 at 17:30 a convoy of Cameron Highlanders were on patrol near Midleton. A land mine exploded under the leading Crossley tender of the convoy and three Cameron soldiers were injured in the blast.

They continued their patrol with four lorries heading for the village of Ballycotton.

Along their way trenches were found several times on the roads to Ballycotton and the convoy halted until they could be filled in. It was recorded that in other locations the soldiers sometimes made locals fill in the trenches at gunpoint.

Approaching the outskirts of Ballycotton the convoy again came to a halt at the bridge on the border of the townland of Ballybraher to Ballycotton. Again they had to get out and repair the road before proceeding. While they repaired the road only a few hundred yards from the Protestant Church they spotted a local man nearby and thought he was acting suspicious. Maybe he was suspicious or maybe they just picked on the first person they saw. Anything would seem suspicious now especially after being mined only an hour or so before. The local man thirty six year old farmer Michael Whelan lived right across the road with his father. He must have tried to get away when shouted at. Wouldn't any one do the same in similar circumstances? The Lieutenant of the leading lorry pursued him and got him to stop by shooting him in the arm. Michael being wounded was easily apprehended and was marched back to the convoy.

When the convoy began to move again some of the British soldier's attention was drawn to several men running away at the top of a hill ahead. The number is unclear but by the fact that they had run the British thought this alone was suspicious. They afterwards claimed one was signalling but there was surely no need to signal as everyone would have heard the shots fired at Michael Whelan. The group of men on the hill were seen climb over a high wall and into a cornfield. They managed to make it over the top of the hill before the military fired at them.

A typical military convoy at the time
Image courtesy of the National Library of Ireland

Two men seem to be left on the hill who couldn't make an escape as fast as the group higher up. By now several of the British military were running towards the village to get a better vantage point. One of the men reached the wall near the top of the hill and got over it into a cornfield. There was nowhere to hide as the top of the wall was ground level of the cornfield. A shot was fired and the soldiers shouted at the man to halt but he didn't stop. As the soldiers came around the corner (by Higgins's house or near where the Silver Strand estate starts) they would have been able to get a clearer shot. It was from around here that several more shots were fired about 250 yards away from their target. Despite the distance one shot hit and the man went down in the cornfield. Having climbed the high wall he was only seconds away from being over the hill and out of their view. Had they missed maybe they would have taken aim on the other man.

The other man on the hill was his elderly father and he immediately followed into the cornfield to see how his son was. The soldiers then stopped firing as they had hit someone high above them in the field. A group of soldiers went up to the top of the hill to see what they had done. They climbed the wall and spread out in the cornfield to find their victim. They found Maurice Cusack lying in the cornfield and his elderly father John kneeling over him. They realised he was in a bad way and had been shot in the abdomen. Maurice's dog was there with him and barked at the soldiers knowing something was terribly wrong. The very people who had shot at him then tried to bandage up his wounds. Between them Maurice was taken down the hill to his house and a doctor was called. Maurice was put into bed and his dog stayed at his bedside. By the time the doctor arrived the man had died from his injuries.

Where Maurice Cusack was most likely shot, picture looking in the direction from where the soldiers approached

Maurice Cusack had joined the Royal Navy in 1897, rated as a boy 2nd class when he was only 17 years old. He remained in the navy for well over 20 years and was only discharged in October of 1919. Throughout the war years he served on the dreadnought battleship HMS *Colossus* as an able seaman. He saw action during the Battle of Jutland when the ship was hit twice which killed six of his fellow crew.

The very next day after the shooting on Monday the 4th a military court of inquiry was held instead of an inquest. The court was presided over by

Captain Gordon also of the 2nd Battalion of the Cameron Highlanders. It's like having an inquest where the coroner is friends with the chief suspect. It was never going to be impartial and the outcome was a foregone conclusion. The first witness called was sister of the dead man Bridget Sliney. She lived in the same house as her father and brother at the bottom of the hill. Also living there was her husband Michael and her five young children. She told the inquiry how her brother had only left the house three or four minutes before the shots were fired that hit him. From this evidence it's safe to assume Maurice only ran out to see what was going on hearing the first shots. Bridget heard the shots after her brother left the house and feared he had been hit. She then ran to his side at the top of the hill and subsequently ran to get the priest.

Doctor Hennessy told how he got to Ballycotton at quarter past eight on the 3rd. Maurice had died just ten minutes before he arrived. He examined the body and found the entry wound on his left side near the hip. The bullet had passed through his intestines leaving a corresponding exit wound on the right hip. He considered death had been the result of haemorrhage due to the laceration of the intestines by the bullet.

View from the hill of the same period showing the houses below

Several of the British soldiers also gave evidence at the inquiry. Lieutenant F Rankin said he saw someone signalling on the hill. He called after the man and thought he had been heard as the man crouched down. He saw him climb the wall and he admitted firing one shot as the man went towards the skyline. However to cover himself he said two other shots were fired at the same time. Nobody else admitted to firing a shot at this time.

Lieutenant Hannay told how he wounded Michael Whelan in order to get him to halt. Next he saw eight men disappearing over the top of the hill high above. After seeing Maurice fall in the cornfield he climbed up the hill. When he went to the cornfield the dying man said to him "why did you not get the right one?"

The finding of the court was never in any doubt but it wasn't told to the family at the time. In short it found that "the deceased was himself to blame in as much as he did not halt when called upon to do so, no blame attaches in the matter to the military authorities".

For some reason another court of inquiry was opened in Ballycotton on the 20th of July. This time the first witness called was father of deceased John Cusack. He was an elderly man of 75 years of age who had been a fisherman and in the Royal Navy reserve for most of his life. John's testimony told how he was out sitting on the hill that evening. He saw the convoy stopped on the road a few hundred yards away. He had seen his son Maurice come out of the house and climb the hill towards him. Shots were fired but he took no real notice of them. Minutes later more shots were fired and John believed one was aimed at him as it passed close by his face. The other hit his son Maurice. He didn't see this happening but was close enough to hear him fall. He rushed to his son's side but hadn't noticed anyone else on the hillside until the soldiers arrived. He also denied his son had waved a white handkerchief to warn others saying he didn't even have one on him. They had alleged that Maurice was using a handkerchief to signal, but even back then waving something white was a signal of cease fire as per the Hague Convention. The father told about his son being retired from the Navy and having taken no part in politics at all. John said he was at his son's side the whole time and Maurice didn't speak to anyone after he was shot.

The following day the inquiry reconvened at Cobh and several military witnesses gave evidence. Four of the soldiers who had climbed the hill told their own version with some trying to directly undermine John Cusack's testimony. Most of the evidence was the same as the first inquiry except for the following differences.

-One Lieutenant Roberts had seen what had happened but wasn't sure if John Cusack was there when he arrived in the field.

-Another Private was sure the old man was kneeling beside his son when he arrived.

-Lieutenant Rankin, who had previously admitted to having fired one shot at Maurice, said there was no old man there when he arrived despite arriving there at the same time as the Private who said the opposite. Rankin was sure he passed the old man standing outside his house at the foot of the hill. He then ran up the steep hill and claimed John Cusack arrived a minute or two after him.

Lieutenant Hannay was next to recount his version of events. He was certain there was nobody there except Maurice Cusack but again said he arrived at the same time as the others. He noticed a dog in the field but no old man.

It seems pointless relating the differences above but shows that even between themselves the soldiers were not telling the truth. After all they had every reason to alter the truth and make it look justified. John Cusack on the other hand had no reason to lie. He had lost his son, it couldn't get much worse. There was also no way John Cusack came up the hill behind the soldiers. A seventy five year old today would struggle to climb that steep hill quickly never mind nearly one hundred years ago.

The Brigade Commander admitted that the evidence was confusing and conflicting. Despite thinking Maurice wasn't involved with the volunteers he still claimed he was signalling to them. The inquiry again undermined the old mans evidence by insulting him saying he was illiterate and had difficulty giving evidence. This was not the case as his evidence is the most clear and concise of all at the inquiry. After this the court found the father's evidence didn't reflect what had happened and believed the conflicted story of their own men. The finding was similar to before but went slightly further.

"That the deceased himself was to blame in as much as he was signalling to unknown persons on the approach of the military at a time when he must have known such an act was highly dangerous to himself and also that when fired at he ran away and did not halt. That there was justification for opening fire and that no blame attaches to the military authorities".

If they believed their own finding John Cusack would not have still been writing to the military in October 1921 looking for the findings. Eventually GHQ in Dublin wrote to him with the finding but one can only imagine this only made the situation worse.

Maurice Cusack spent most of his adult life at sea and had never married. He had eight siblings in all; older sister Mary married John Murray. She lived nearby in Ballygeany and had a large family. Ellen married Frank Guess and lived with their family in Shanagarry. Hannah married local man Michael Power but emigrated to San Francisco with their family. Catherine married Edmund Naughton and ended up in Wales with her family. As already told Bridget married Michael Sliney and stayed at home in Ballycotton.

I didn't do it, five men broke in last night
Knockanenakirka, Dangan 1882

About four miles from Killeagh, close to Dangan Cross in the townland of Knockanenakirka there lived an elderly woman named Margaret Kelleher. She lived on a forty acre farm with her son-in-law William Hankard.

William's wife had passed away in 1876 and after the death of her daughter Mrs Kelleher who owned the farm made an agreement with her son-in-law. The tenancy of the farm would be put into William's name, he would manage it and she would be paid a sum of money every year. An unusual clause to the agreement was that William couldn't marry again until after she had died. This may had been for practical reasons as the farm house had only one large bedroom, which they both shared. He was on reasonably good terms with his mother-in-law but they quarrelled at times.

Some time in April of 1882, Hankard hired a young servant called Laurence Murphy aged twenty three to help on the farm. Murphy was to be paid 30s per quarter and would live on the farm in the small house even though he had to share a bed with Hankard. Young Laurence had also been talking about leaving for America.

On Friday 26th of May, William Hankard set off towards Cloyne to visit his brother and sister who lived at Tullagh beyond Cloyne. He was also going to stop off at Cloyne to purchase some seeds on the way home. That Friday he stayed at his brother Matthew's house near Cloyne.

Early the following morning Laurence Murphy ran to the nearby farmhouse of William Daly and said that Mrs Kelleher was in a terrible condition. He said four or five strange men had broken into the house sometime during the night and carried out a terrible assault on the old woman. Daly went with Murphy back to the house and found Mrs Kelleher lying in bed in a bad way. William Daly tried to rouse her but she was unconscious and didn't reply. She was still alive but only just. She had several serious head injuries and her face was covered in blood. Murphy said the old woman sent him out to attend to the cows and while there the attack occurred. The house was in a state of disarray with things thrown all over the kitchen. The front door was in an unusual position and was off the hinges inside the house. William Daly and Murphy then headed in the direction of Dangan to inform people of what had occurred.

On the way there they met Tom Daly and all three doubled back to where the crime had been committed. Tom went inside and saw the old woman lying there. He could see she was dying so he sent Murphy to get the priest. Both Tom and William Daly went outside and looked around for signs that the five attackers had left behind. They searched around the yard, haggart and the boreen but despite the ground being soft could find no traces of the footprints of five men. One of the Daly's found what appeared to be the murder weapon in the kitchen under the table. It was a hatchet and had blood on it but the handle appeared to have been washed.

It was about eight in the morning when Murphy arrived at Father Green's house and said that Mrs Kelleher had been brutally attacked. The priest did not comprehend what he was being told nor did he believe what Murphy had said. After a while he thought that maybe Mrs Kelleher was sick and went with Laurence to see how she was.

He found Mrs Kelleher in a terrible state in her bed with two brutal head injuries. After Murphy returned with the priest he told the Daly's several contradicting stories of the events that had occurred the previous night. One version was that he slept in the piggery while the attack took place. When he awoke he ran for his life through the haggart and then through a field called the red field. One of the attackers pursued him but he evaded him by jumping into a dyke. When asked how he spent the remainder of the night Murphy said he slept in the dyke until early in the morning.

Some time after the priest Rev Greene arrived he spoke to Murphy about what had happened and Murphy related a different story altogether. He said that during the night five men came to the door and drove the door off its hinges into the house.

It was nearly ten in the morning before news reached the police barracks in Killeagh of what had happened a few miles away. Once they became aware the police acted swiftly and it was only forty five minutes before the police arrived at the farmhouse, Constable Kelly got there about quarter to eleven that morning. When he got there Laurence Murphy was not there, he went to the bedroom where the old woman still lay in bed. Her forehead appeared to have been broken in, she was breathing very heavily and remained in an unconscious state. As the constable came out of the house he saw Laurence Murphy approaching from the direction of Dungourney. He asked Murphy what had happened during the night and the servant replied with a version of the story he had told earlier.

Constable Kelly noticed marks like blood on Murphy's clothes and asked him about a jacket in the kitchen which also had blood on it. Murphy replied that the jacket was indeed his and at this point Kelly must have been getting suspicious. Next the policeman examined the door and there appeared to be no signs of a forced entry. Nor were any signs of damage found on any of the windows. More police were now on the scene and two of them put the door back on its hinges. The two police tried to take the door off the hinges from the outside but could not. However they were able to do so from the inside. The police arrested Laurence Murphy on suspicion of brutally attacking the elderly woman. At this point the police would also have been aware that Murphy had previously been in trouble. A few years before he had broken into a public house in Dungourney and drank himself stupid with whiskey. While there he ran amok and was caught by the police. He had spent the last five years in Upton reformatory an industrial school in west Cork.

A doctor arrived from Killeagh but deemed that the poor woman's injuries were so bad it was just a matter of time before she died. Little could be done for her so she remained where she was.

During the day Murphy was held in custody at the farm house where he showed no sign of emotion for what had happened. He sat in the kitchen silently for the whole day while the police searched for evidence. They found two wooden boxes which appeared to be usually locked but were lying on the floor. The contents of letters and papers were strewn around the kitchen. The police gathered several items of clothing particularly those that Murphy had been wearing. A pair of trousers, a coat, vest and shirt which the accused had worn was sent for blood analysis by an expert. In the kitchen was an iron pot and a rag which it seemed had been used to clean the murder weapon. The police constables searched the "red" field across which Murphy had said he was chased. They could not find any footprints of the attackers despite the fact that dog prints could be seen in the field.

It was on Saturday evening about six pm when William Hankard was passing Mogeely heading for home that he heard what had happened to his mother-in-law. He met a man called John Kennefick on the road who told him she was close to dying. It was another hour later before he got home to find the police still at the house. Hankard was able to account for where he had been since nine the previous morning.

He told the police that he owned one and Mrs Kelleher the other of wooden boxes. They both hid them about the house and each used them to store their money in. Mrs Kelleher recently received a draft of £2, most likely from her son in America.

Later that night some time around eleven Mrs Kelleher died from her terrible injuries.

The following Tuesday the inquest was expected to be held by coroner Mr Rice of Fermoy but word was received at the last minute that he couldn't hold the inquest until Friday 2nd June. Many of the neighbours had gathered at the house for the funeral but the poor woman could not be buried as the post mortem examination had not been carried out. The police county inspector Mr Barry was present and requested twenty three of the farmers living in the area to view the body. These men would then have to attend the inquest as jurors later in the week. In the afternoon Dr Curran from Killeagh and Dr Sandiford from Castlemartyr arrived and carried out the post mortem examination. Shortly afterwards the funeral was held and the woman's remains were buried at the nearby graveyard.

Rumours were rife around the locality about the murder, Hankard who was not the most popular was said to be some way involved in it. It was said the rumours were spread by some of the murdered woman's relations who expected they would then get possession of the farm.

Nearby graveyard where Mrs Kelleher was most likely buried

The inquest was held on the 2nd of June in the house where the murder took place by Mr Rice. The main suspect Laurence Murphy was not present for the inquest. Neighbour William Daly gave evidence of being the first to see Mrs Kelleher on that morning before sending for the priest and doctor.

William Hankard next gave evidence at the inquest saying he was in Cloyne the night the horrendous crime took place. He said that only a few weeks before he hired Murphy at Dangan Cross to help on the farm. William did not ask where he worked before and noticed nothing peculiar about him. He confirmed that Murphy knew the old woman kept her money in the box and where she hid it. He told that the Sunday before the crime Murphy's father came to the house looking for some of his son's wages. Hankard refused saying it wasn't what they agreed but Mrs Kelleher intervened to keep the peace. She went to her locked box and got out money to give to John Murphy. Hankard stated that Laurence had seen the old woman take the money from the box.

Dr John Curran from Castlemartyr stated that he attended the dying woman. She lay on a pool of blood and was quite unconscious breathing very rapidly. After she died he carried out the post mortem examination with the help of Dr Sandiford. The doctor described the examination of the body where the first thing he found was two large head wounds. The first wound was above the left temple and the second wound above the left ear. The second wound was five inches long and penetrated the skull. The doctor said "it was amazing how she lived so long, I never saw a worse wound". He concluded that the cause of death was caused by compression of the brain from the fragments of the skull. He said the first incised wound was made with the sharp end of a hatchet while the other wound was made with the blunt end of a hatchet. He had compared the wounds to the hatchet found in the house and it matched exactly.

The coroner addressed the jury and said they must find a verdict based on the facts of the case. He said the duty of the inquest jury was to find an open verdict and not implicate any person directly. The jury found a verdict of wilful murder against some person or persons unknown.

Nearly a week later in Youghal on the 8th of June after the normal petty sessions concluded an inquiry was held into the murder. Since the crime had been committed Laurence Murphy had been held as prisoner in Youghal awaiting the inquiry. Many gathered outside the court house to catch a glimpse of the prisoner whom they had heard had committed the brutal murder. Captain Stokes presided as the resident magistrate while Inspector Cameron from Youghal represented the prosecution for the crown. The charge read out against the accused was "that on or about the 27th of May at Knockanenakirka, in the county of Cork, he did feloniously, wilfully and with malice aforethought kill and murder one Margaret Kelleher".

Several witnesses were called to give evidence. Father of the accused John Murphy was called. He said his son came to his house at five on the morning of the 27th May. His son told him the story of five men coming to the house and thought that Mrs Kelleher was dead but said it was at nine or ten the previous evening. John Murphy told his son that if he did not see how the woman was and report it he would be hanged for it. Laurence Murphy was crying at this point but ran off to inform the neighbours.

Dr Matthias O'Keeffe was a lecturer of medical law and carried out medical analysis for such cases. He had received two parcels of items relating to the case and carried out an examination on them. He could prove that despite being washed the murder weapon had been contaminated with blood. He was also able to find traces of blood on the clothes which could not be seen to the naked eye.

The accused who had not taken much notice of the proceedings in court said he had no statement to make regarding the murder. The judge returned the case for trial at the next Summer Assizes on the capital charge of murder. This meant that there was to be no bail and the accused could be sentenced to death.

On the 25th of July Justice Barry resumed the business of the Cork Summer Assizes. The first case called that morning was the brutal murder near Dangan with Laurence Murphy in the dock. From a very early stage in court Murphy was seen to view the proceeding with a great deal of indifference. Sergeant Sherlock with solicitors Mr Green and Mr Moriarty appeared for the crown prosecution while Mr McNeil defended the accused.

Once the jury was selected and sworn in Sergeant Sherlock addressed them. He was quite confident that the prisoner would meet with justice by the hands of the jury. He outlined at length what had transpired on the night in question and again said the jury would have no hesitation in finding Laurence Murphy the perpetrator of the brutal murder.

Like the inquest William Daly was the first to give evidence. He said how Laurence Murphy came and woke him early that morning. He went with Murphy to the farmhouse where the crime took place and saw Mrs Kelleher lying in a pool of blood. William Daly stated in court that he had not noticed any blood marks on Murphy that morning.

Constable Kelly stated that he arrived at the crime scene about eleven on the morning in question. He told how he arrested Murphy after listening to his far fetched story and noticing blood stains on his clothes.

William Hankard told how he left the Friday morning to go to Cloyne. When he returned on Saturday night his mother-in-law was dying and he found both money boxes forced open on the floor of the kitchen. He said how Mrs Kelleher kept her box locked. William told the court how he kept his box in his own room under the window but Murphy would have known this as they shared the room. He said that his mother-in-law kept hers in the settle in the kitchen. Murphy knew where she kept it as the week previous she was seen to take money from it for his pay. Two days before the murder William Hankard had given the accused a chisel to sharpen and put lead into the gudgeon of a roller. After the murder the chisel was found back in its normal place on the clevy. In a traditional farm house shelves high on the wall were often called a clevy.

Constable Martin Fleming was called and examined by Sergeant Sherlock. In court he produced the same chisel that Hankard had referred to earlier. He produced the box belonging to the deceased Mrs Kelleher and showed to the court how it had been opened by this chisel. The marks on the box corresponded exactly to the size of the chisel. This didn't seem like much but in the case of the crime being carried out by several intruders they were unlikely to have found the chisel. Unknown intruders were also more unlikely still to carefully put it back in its normal place. Whereas Murphy was now known to have had the chisel just before the murder and also knew that there was money in the house. Dr John Curran gave medical evidence about the death of Mrs Kelleher.

Professor Matthias O Keeffe explained how he had carried out analysis on several items found in the house including the clothes of the accused. The hatchet he stated had been in contact with a lot of blood before being washed. All the clothes had several stains of blood but the shirt also had stains of blood on the inside.

Mr McNeil defending the prisoner tried to explain the blood on the inside of the shirt saying a man could be scratching himself. However Dr Curran was called to the stand again and explained that he examined the prisoner after the murder. He had not found any marks on Murphy's body that would explain the amount of blood stains on his clothes. Afterwards the prosecution closed the case for the crown saying they would call no more witnesses.

Mr McNeil expressed his astonishment to the judge that the prosecution had not called John Murphy father of the accused. Solicitor Greene told the jury that the prosecution would not call a father to give evidence against his son. The defence then asked to call John Murphy under the impression he would add to their case. The man said before the court he had known his son to be a little out of his mind since he was five years old. He described the events on the morning in question when Laurence came to his house at an early hour. He also said his son began to cry that morning before setting off to Daly's to raise the alarm.

It was obvious that McNeil's case was to plead for the insanity of his client to get a reduced sentence. The next witness would help his case. Dr Moriarty surgeon at the county gaol described how he observed Laurence Murphy since he was incarcerated. He said how he immediately noticed how Murphy had a defective intellect and said "he was an imbecile". The prosecution objected to Murphy being called an imbecile and said he sometimes shows shrewdness in his answers. They said he was quiet capable of being coherent at intervals and understands the charges against him.

Rev J Wilson was next sworn in saying his father was the rector in Dungourney. He said that five years ago he knew Laurence Murphy very well and "always thought him to be a sort of fool". Around this time Murphy had broken into the church there, he played with the organ and rung the bells. Murphy tossed everything about the place before leaving. However he left behind his cap and pipe in the church. The rector didn't have him prosecuted because people of the locality knew what he was like and seemed to have accepted it.

Dr Alcock of the Upton reformatory wasn't able to make it to court but had sent a telegram of his opinion of Laurence Murphy's state of mind. The judge however said such evidence could not be allowed. Other doctors were called to give evidence to strengthen the case for the defence but none could really recall Murphy and added nothing to the case.

When the court reconvened after lunch Mr McNeil addressed the court on behalf of the accused. He made an argument saying the evidence of the prosecution was of a completely speculative nature. He went on to say that the story his client told was consistent and believable, that the murder was carried out by five intruders. Then he made an unusual statement to the jury. He said if the jury felt that Murphy had committed the crime he relied on an acquittal on the grounds of insanity.

The judge Justice Barry addressed the jury and said the case had little controversy but was there enough evidence. He told the jury that the accused story was totally incredible but was Murphy capable of knowing what was right or wrong. Before finishing he asked the jury "did the prisoner when he committed the act know he was doing wrong".

At quarter to five in the evening the jury retired to come to a verdict. Three quarters of an hour later the foreman of the jury returned and said to the judge "my lord we all believe the prisoner killed the woman but we think he should not be hanged for it". The judge replied to the foreman that it was a matter that they would have to decide upon one way of the other. Again the jury retired to come to a verdict.

Mc Neil for the defence of the prisoner saw an opportunity when the jury were indecisive. He applied to the judge to further examine Laurence Everard of Upton reformatory to determine the accused mental state. The jury was recalled to court to hear the evidence of the curator of the industrial school. Everard questioned by McNeil stated that Laurence Murphy was confined to the school for five years. He had daily contact with Murphy throughout those years. He went on to say that on the 11th June 1881 Murphy was removed from Upton and sent to the lunatic asylum as he had become dangerous. He had on several occasions tried to kill some of the other inmates of the school. Everard also said that while in the school Murphy was a confirmed kleptomaniac. He was always stealing things and hiding them under his bed and always items of no value. He said that to the best of his opinion Laurence Murphy did not know the difference between right and wrong. The judge seemed to be annoyed with the lack of progress and replied that this evidence had not advanced the case but the foreman said we can't agree my lord.

The jury retired again and returned to court at nearly seven with a verdict.

Murphy was convicted of wilful murder but the jury strongly recommended mercy on account of Murphy's mental state.

The judge justice Barry seemed to have his own view of the case but replied to the foreman that the verdict was a good and proper conclusion. The judge addressed the prisoner directly at length and told him what he really thought of the case. He told Murphy "you murdered cruelly and for the basest of motives to take what money may have been". It appeared the judge had only one sentence in mind despite the jury's plea for mercy. Next he said to the prisoner "if you are capable of such an effort, I would recommend you to endeavour to make peace with god whom you have offended by your extreme wickedness". All that remained was for the judge to announce the sentence but before he did he warned not to hope for a change in sentence as it would not happen. He announced to the court," the sentence and judgement of the court which I do hereby adjudge and order is that you Laurence Murphy, be taken from the bar of this court where you now stand , to the common gaol of the County of Cork, and that you be taken on Tuesday 22nd of August next in the year of our lord 1882, to the common place of execution, within the walls of said prison in which you were last confined , and that you be then and there hanged by the neck until you are dead, and that your body be buried within the precincts of the prison, and may the lord have mercy on your soul".

During the long deliberation of the judge Murphy seemed to be far removed from what was going on in court. He appeared to be incapable of appreciating what had transpired and the implications it would have. While the judge spoke Murphy rocked to and fro in the dock and stared vacantly into the crowd.

Despite the judge's insistence on the death sentence some time in August the sentence was changed more in line with that of the jury. Murphy was sentenced to penal servitude for the remainder of his life.

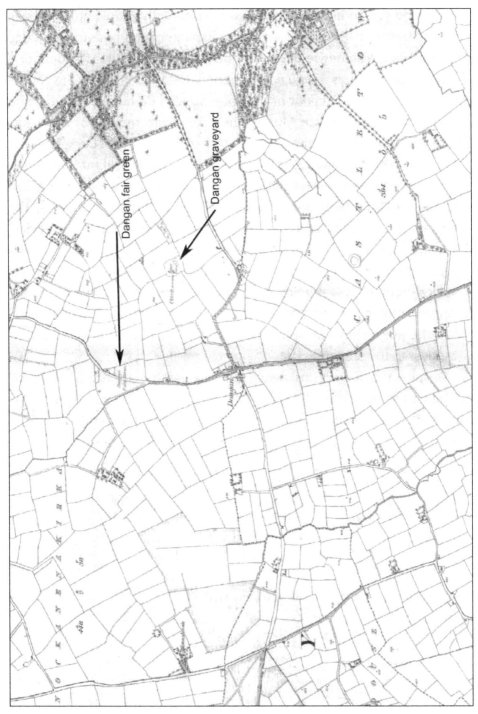

Map Showing Dangan Cross with townland of Knockanenakirka to the north

A day at the fair gone wrong
Near Dangan Cross 1865

Dangan is now only a crossroads but was once considered a small village on the road to Tallow only three miles from Castlemartyr. It had a history of being a quiet peaceful place where there was neither a need for a police barrack nor a magistrate. The small village only consisted of a handful of houses. However the tiny village became well known for holding an annual fair in the month of August. The fair like all country fairs at the time was attended by large numbers of country people and was for many the highlight of their year. As was often the case when the men at the fair had too much to drink arguments broke out between them resulting in fighting. The police were always in attendance at the fair to prevent things getting out of hand.

At Dangan fair on the 7th of August 1865, a body of seven police were on hand should anything happen. The police were from several local barracks, two from Killeagh and two from Castlemartyr all under the command of Constable Jacques from Castlemartyr. All was quiet at the fair until six in the evening when some fighting broke out and a man called John Connery was arrested for being drunk. Several of his friends followed the police and asked for him to be released but the police refused. As a result of this stones were thrown at them and a crowd soon gathered around them. The seven police used their bayonets to fend back the crowd but became separated and had to beat a retreat. Four of the constables with Jacques in command kept hold of the prisoner and took cover in a nearby cottage that was being used as a temporary barrack for the day. Meanwhile the other three constables ran to a nearby field to get away from the angry mob.

Terence Ahern said to be the leader of the angry mob got up onto a ditch and encouraged the others to follow. He said the Irish were good fenians and would prove they could fight for their freedom. The crowd then threw stones at the house the police were sheltering in and threatened to burn it down. Despite the attackers being unarmed the constables in the house fired into the crowd as did the three in the field. Some of the police

**Roughly the area where the Dangan Fair
was held north of Dangan Cross**

fired several times and one didn't fire at all but within minutes seven locals had been shot. The crowd quickly dispersed and there was no more trouble. The four police had managed to retain their prisoner and made their way to Castlemartyr. The other three police made their escape to Mount Uniacke and then went to Youghal to inform the authorities what had occurred.

It was later learned that one man Laurence Kelly was in a critical condition after being shot in the thigh. Three other persons were seriously wounded by the attack; William Carey received a large flesh wound from a bayonet. Sullivan was lucky he had just been shot in the ear; with the upper part of his ear gone while a third man Andrew McAuliffe was shot in the arm. None of the police had received any serious injuries at all.

The door was taken from the house and Kelly put on it as a makeshift stretcher. He was carried off to a farmhouse in the nearby townland of Coolcap where he was attended to by a doctor. Kelly a labourer of about thirty years of age, was then taken to Midleton hospital to be treated. Doctors there found the shot had broken his femur from behind and the ball was still lodged in the flesh. They managed to extract the ball hoping Kelly a powerful man in his prime would recover. The next day it was realised he was deteriorating rapidly and he was not going to survive. A statement was taken from Kelly while he was still able. He said that he heard no fenian speech but was walking away from the place when shots were fired saying "I had my back turned to the peelers when I was shot". Medical evidence showed that he was indeed shot from behind. The evening of the 9th August a little over forty eight hours after the shooting took place Laurence Kelly died at seven pm in Midleton Hospital.

The police were intent on getting their own back at the rioters and rounded up some of those involved. It was to their advantage to call the mob a fenian revolt. On the 17th August Ahern was arrested and charged with having addressed the crowd at Dangan. Ahern who was only twenty two years old had been employed as a clerk by a Midleton shopkeeper but was planning to immigrate to Australia.

The day before on the 16th of August an inquest was held at Midleton Courthouse into the circumstances of the death of Kelly at Dangan. It adjourned shortly afterwards because several people had made an attempt to intimidate one of the witnesses. After the adjournment the witness Margaret Walsh and her father William were chased down the street by an angry mob. They were threatened by the mob and called paid informers. The pair became separated with William managing to get away but Margaret had to take refuge in a house and the police came to get her. There was no doubt that locals were wary of William Walsh as he had allowed his cottage to be used as a temporary barracks for the day of the fair and obviously had been paid for it. This would have given rise to the idea that he was being paid by the police to give information.

The next day the inquest was resumed at the courthouse by coroner Mr Henry Barry. All sides of the case were represented - Mr Julian for the police, Mr Wallis for the family of Laurence Kelly and Mr P O'Connell for the Crown. It was thought the inquest was going to sit for several days as there were forty five witnesses to hear in court.

The coroner addressed the jury "you have to inquire how, when and where the deceased came by his death. I presume it will be admitted that the man died by gunshot wound which was inflicted by the police and that

Typical scene of an Inquest in Ireland at that time

being so, it will be for you to say whether the police were warranted, in the execution of their duty, to fire on the assailants".

Dr James Foley was sworn in and said he attended to Laurence Kelly about four in the morning after the shooting. He said that he removed the lead ball without any great difficulty but realised the man was in a critical condition and would likely die. He told the jury that the ball passed through the femur and also damaged his hip bone. After removing the shot he sent the patient directly to Midleton hospital. The doctor told the jury that from the direction of the shot in the thigh that Kelly was stooped when he was shot.

The inquest resumed on the 18th with Margaret Walsh called to give evidence. She was in her father's cottage the temporary barrack for the fair when the trouble broke out. Margaret was questioned before the jury by both sides of the case and described how stones were thrown through the windows before the police fired. Next called was Margaret's father William and when he took to the stand it caused a great commotion in the packed courtroom. He refused to be sworn in when handed the bible until he was paid for his loss of earnings. He said he was a tailor by trade and it was agreed to give him 1s per day. Walsh reluctantly took the bible and was sworn in to give evidence. As he did the proceedings in court became more comical like a scene from the Irish RM. As Walsh took the stand he came upon the glass of sherry that was put there for his daughter, to steady her nerves while giving evidence. He took up the glass at the stand and tasted it but shook his head in disgust; it was not what he was used to. He began telling Mr Julian that his cottage was used as a barracks and when Connery was brought there, a crowd gathered outside. He told that the police were outside the cottage trying to fend off the mob but eventually took refuge in the house. Walsh hid under a table but was hit by a stone before hiding in the chimney.

An inspector from Youghal called Fanning, read the relevant regulations of the constabulary to the jury despite Mr Wallis's objections. The inspector was cross examined by Wallis who asked in detail how many shots each of the police had fired that day. They had each fired between one and three shots Wallis made light of this in court calling Jacques "the hero of the battle of Dangan" but was called to order by the coroner. Despite this Wallis went on with his questions and caused a sensation in court when he was told that Jacques had fired the shot that killed Kelly. It was heard that he aimed particularly at Kelly but tried to shoot him in the legs. It also transpired that Jacques shot Andrew McAuliffe in the arm and that it was also Jacques gave the order to open fire.

Next it was Constable Jacques who gave evidence. He recalled stopping John Connery fighting in the field of the fair. He sent him home but ten minutes later he was found fighting again. He arrested him and they made their way to the temporary barracks. The crowd gathered outside the gate. At this point the police had left their guns inside. After the crowd pushed their way through the gate Jacques ordered his men to get their weapons and warned he would fire if the crowd didn't disperse. He heard one of the crowd reply "Fire away we don't care about you it would be as well for us to be dead as eating potatoes and salt". He said the crowd continued to be pushed forward from behind and he ordered his men to retreat before they stabbed someone with their bayonets.

They drove the crowd back but as they did were attacked with stones.

Jacques took cover behind a cart in the yard while three others had made it to the safety of the cottage. Jacques shouted the order to fire on the crowd but only one shot was fired. There was a lull in the stone throwing and Jacques used this opportunity to run to the cottage. He immediately loaded his gun and fired out a window. He saw Kelly at the front of the group throwing stones. Jacques said he fired at him as he stooped down to gather another stone. After several shots were fired the constables remained in the house for some time despite hearing shouts that the place would be burned.

Jacques said he got no assistance from the three constables in the field and had afterwards reported them for their conduct. The hearing was adjourned until the 23rd of August.

When it did sit again more of the constables gave evidence, Mr Julian for the police said the jury was tired of hearing more of the same. The coroner couldn't even recall who he had summoned to give evidence. After this no more were called to the stand.

Wallis spoke to the jury saying the police wanted to turn this ordinary country fair riot into something political and Fenian. He said the police were not justified in firing but left it in the hands of the jury to decide. The inquest was again postponed for another day when it would finally be concluded.

The inquest sat again on Thursday the 24th and the jury retired to come to a verdict. When they returned to court they gave a verdict that Kelly was indeed killed by a gunshot fired by Jacques. But the jury said the verdict was an open one meaning they couldn't reach any other conclusions. The jury was discharged. Wallis objected strongly to the verdict and asked the coroner to place Jacques in custody for wilful murder. The coroner refused several times and told him the court was over.

As a means of justifying their behaviour the police took action against people present at the riot. They were not going to be left unpunished. On the 12th of September at the Castlemartyr petty sessions twelve men were charged with having taken part in the riot at Dangan. Ten of the twelve men charged were farmer's sons from the locality.

It was suspicious that the main witness a man named Lynch against the accused had himself been involved in the affray. Under cross examination

Lynch admitted to being previously convicted of sheep stealing and twice for assaults on women. When asked in court was he known by the nickname Sooty Jack, he confirmed he was but in his next breath denied getting the nickname after climbing down a chimney to steal bacon. In addition to this questionable witness several constables identified some of the men at the fair. The six who could not be identified by the constables were acquitted. The remaining six were all bailed on payment of sureties of between £10 and £20.

The case dragged on until the following year and came before the Cork Assizes. John Smiddy and David Connery both got 6 months hard labour. The other 4 men all got 3 months for their part in the riot.

As a result of the riot and the notoriety Jacques had gained he was transferred from Castlemartyr to somewhere else in the country. It was also to prevent any attempt at revenge for the death of Kelly. Coincidentally Laurence Kelly's brother Thady was said to have also left the area around the same time. For many years the story was told in the local area and folklore says Jacques came to a violent death. Thady Kelly returned to the area and locals suspected that he had avenged his brother. However Thady denied this to the last.

A tiny article in the Cork Constitution late in 1866 gives us more information about Jacques. It announces that Jacques had been promoted to rank of Head Constable and was going to Belfast. Certainly throughout the next year and into 1868 Jacques was very much alive and arresting fenians in Belfast. Years later in 1899 a William Jacques dies aged 69 in Lurgan of natural causes. His occupation is given as a retired District Inspector, could this be the same one and Thady was indeed as innocent as he claimed to be.

William Walsh who was known locally as Liam Ruadh became the villain in the story as the informant. Even when he died he was hurriedly buried in an unmarked grave. Very little remains today of the Dangan fair green or Walsh's house.

Final Destination
Harbour Row, Cobh 1889

Alexander Queery was found leaning against a wall at Harbour Row in Cobh and seemed to be just another drunken sailor. His ship was sheltering from a storm and he was allowed ashore on leave. Nothing looked unusual, it was assumed he was drunk and had run into a wall causing himself a head injury. Reports said he was running away from his shipmates at the time. A doctor was called and arrived on the scene quickly. Alexander was taken to the nearby General Hospital but had died by the time he got there.

Alexander was from Belfast and only twenty five years of age. His new wife was now a widow; they had been married just eight months. His ship the *Zuleika* was a Liverpool brigantine that was en route from Glasgow with a cargo of coal for Tralee.

Harbour Row. Image courtesy of the National Library of Ireland

The following day Friday the 20th September 1889 the post mortem was carried out and the findings of that suggested something more suspicious. The police were quickly on the case and made inquiries as to what had happened. Shortly after several arrests were made of those who were suspected of being involved in the death.

First arrested were Julia Saunders and sisters Norah and Kate Donovan. Later the same day William Collins a shop porter and Cornelius Foster a shoemaker were also arrested. When in custody Cornelius made a statement telling the constable "well I suppose I am sold". After hesitating he said "but I will tell you the truth anyhow. Collins and I were walking up Harbour Row between McCall's and Banon's. I saw the man strike Julia Courtney (recently married to Saunders) and run across the road. Collins and I ran after him and he fell when he reached the footpath. I saw one of the women strike the man with something she had in her hand. I and some other people tilted him up against the wall". He heard one of the women say when the man was on the ground "come away out of that". Collins however was quite the opposite, when arrested he made no statement at all.

Zuleika was still in Cobh on Monday the 23rd when the magisterial enquiry was opened at the town courthouse. Early in the morning crowds of townspeople gathered outside the barracks where the accused were held. District Inspector Ruthven was in charge of the crown prosecution. He told the jury he merely wanted to prove the five accused were connected with the death. Then he would apply for an adjournment until the inquest concluded.

One of the first witnesses called was seventeen year old David Drinan. He gave his occupation as a Billiard Marker which was a common job for a young man back then. He told how he had seen the three girls standing outside a shop and saw Queery approach the girls. He was walking away at the time but looked back to see the two accused men running after the deceased. After Queery fell Julia Courtney struck him on the head with something she had in her hand. Julia was still often referred to as Courtney as she had only married George Saunders not three months before. When she married back in June, the other accused Nora Donovan was her witness.

Isabella Ahern also saw what happened on Harbour Row that evening. She watched three men running and one fell on the footpath. The other two caught up and one of those kicked the man on the head. Next the three girls arrived and one of them struck the man on the ground. She said once the man fell he never got up again.

After hearing several more witness statements the judge felt there was enough evidence to prove all the accused were involved with the mans death. All five were refused bail and remanded in custody until the following Friday. By then the inquest would have sat and found a verdict on the cause of death.

On Tuesday the 24th an inquest was opened in the town hall by coroner Richard Rice. A jury of fourteen local men were sworn in with John Ireton an undertaker from Harbour Row acting as foreman. Also on the jury was Joseph Sessarego, it was near his drapery shop on Harbour Row that Queery had died. Another juror was Edward Murphy a publican at 4 Harbour Row and Edward O'Farrell an auctioneer from King's square. A solicitor Mr Blake appeared for the family of Alexander Queery. The three women accused had a solicitor between them, Mr Alan Gray while the two men accused also had their own legal representative Mr Allen.

Dr Hodges had assisted in the post-mortem and explained to the jury the cause of death. He described an injury at the back of the head and how it had not fractured the skull. In his opinion the cause of death was a rupture of a blood vessel in the brain which was caused by the physical injuries.

Again young David Drinan takes the stand and is questioned by Mr Blake. He accuses Drinan of being friendly with one of the Donovan girls but he denies she is his sweetheart. The coroner intervenes and asks "what is the character of these women? Are they always in the habit of walking out at night?" But Drinan still denies he has been keeping their company, despite one of the other girls saying otherwise.

Isabella Ahern was also called again, she told the same story she had before. This time she added that while Queery was being beaten on the ground she heard the cry "give it to him boys" but thought it was a man's voice.

At the end of the first day of the inquest the jury were very much divided in their opinions. One juror John Costello remarked "in my opinion it's not a case of such great gravity altogether" but the coroner disagreed reminding him a life had been lost. Costello still wasn't convinced and said the man died as a result of heart disease. The coroner again replied saying the doctor had not gone as far to say that at all. The inquest was adjourned until the following day.

When the jury sat again on the second day, Isabella Ahern was recalled as she had not finished the evening before. She now told the jury how she had seen a man fall on his face and hands. While on the ground two men kicked him in the head. She was questioned by Mr. Allen the solicitor for the accused men but said she was sure it happened.

From her evidence the case seems to be quite obvious but more witnesses were to tell contradicting stories. Charles Barron a clockmaker living at 11 Harbour Row was next examined. He was standing at his door on the night in question. He saw a man pass on the other side of street, when another man approached him from behind and struck him on the head. One man fell to the ground while the other fled the scene. He saw three women approach, but couldn't tell if they hit him or not.

Harbour Row from the other end
Image courtesy of the National Library of Ireland

To further complicate things Eugene McCarthy a pawnbroker's assistant was called and told another version. He claimed to see a sailor running up the other side of the street. The sailor in his haste ran into a ladder according to McCarthy. His chest hit the ladder and the sailor fell to the ground. He saw no men around when the sailor fell nor did he witness anyone kicking him. Shortly afterwards three women arrived and one hit the sailor with something behind the left ear. Eugene ran out and intervened telling the woman to stop but she fled with her friends. When questioned by the District Inspector, the witness admitted Collins was there when he stopped the woman. He heard Collins say the sailor deserved it as he had insulted one of the women.

The coroner summed up the case telling the jury they must simply find a verdict according to the facts. John Costello again asked a question about the man dying as a result of heart disease. The coroner however said the jury's verdict was not to mention the man suffered from heart disease as it was clearly not the cause of death.

After only a few minutes of deliberation the jury returned the verdict "that the deceased died at Queenstown on the 19th day of September 1889 of injuries inflicted on the same date by a person or persons not produced before us".

Sometime in early October the *Zuleika* finally weighed their anchor and set sail out of Cobh harbour to finish their voyage. The ship was obviously missing one of their crew and the remaining five onboard must have had mixed feelings leaving the town. The ship made its way around the south coast of Ireland and the voyage was a difficult one as a gale sprang up again.

Back in town the five accused were brought to court again on the 2nd of October before resident magistrate Mr Redmond. Solicitors for the accused applied on their behalf for bail. The judge replied he was inclined to give bail to all five and the prosecution didn't object. Bail was set for the Donovan sisters at £20 each, while the remainder were set at £50 each. All witnesses were bound over to attend the next Winter Assizes where the case would be heard before a jury.

While this was going on the remainder of the crew were battling the elements at sea. On the evening of the 6th October the *Zuleika* was seen heading north towards the Blasket Sound. Later in the night the wind changed direction to the west and increased in force. During the night the ship succumbed to the storm and was dashed ashore against the rocks. All the crew were lost and the cabin was found on a beach north of Cahirsiveen.

The Winter Assizes were not held in Cork in December as usual. That year they were held in Nenagh and no record of this case being called has been found. Nor was it heard at the next sitting of the court in the spring.

It's possible the case was never called, the crown dropped the case and those accused were all acquitted. Either way Alexander Queery's faith was sealed, if he didn't die on the streets of Cobh, he would more than likely have drowned off the coast of Kerry.

For a small plot of land.
Ballingarrane, Shanagarry 1901

Approximately 2 miles from the village of Ballycotton and close to Shanagarry lived two families, the Dwyer's and the Crotty's.

Patrick Crotty was a farmer of about 60 acres living in the townland of Ballingarrane, with his wife Nora and adult children. Their children still at home were John, Michael, Timothy, Elizabeth, Hanna and Mary. Patrick had by 1901 been married for 45 years during which time Nora had given birth to 15 children. The Crotty's were one of the largest farmers in the townland and let the land from the landlord Peter Penn Gaskell of Shanagarry.

William Dwyer on the other hand was a labourer and had built his thatched cottage 15 years previously on a small plot that had been abandoned. Before the Dwyer's lived there, a man called Colbert who worked for the Crotty's had occupied the house. Colbert had paid rent to Patrick Crotty while living there. Crotty made the mistake of letting the Dwyer's occupy the plot and rebuild the house without paying rent. Over time the Dwyer's became squatters and assumed right to stay there. The small plot was at the most northern end of Crotty's farm and on the boundary to the townland of Shanagarry South and Monagurra.

William Dwyer lived there with his wife Mary, daughter Bridget and three sons Maurice, John and Michael. Maurice Dwyer was a Stoker in the Navy and happened to be home on leave from his ship HMS *Black Prince*. William Dwyer was said to be an industrious man who had a horse and a sow with a litter of pigs. The Crotty's however were unhappy with their neighbours, who they said had a habit of trespassing on their land and knocking down the boundary fence on several occasions.

On the evening of the 18th November 1901, Patrick Crotty and his son Timothy were out walking in their own field when they saw William Dwyer and his son John building a little piggery and encroaching on their land. Crotty immediately confronted the Dwyer's and told them to stop building the piggery. He said he would come back in the morning and rebuild the boundary fence. Despite an altercation between the men, William Dwyer

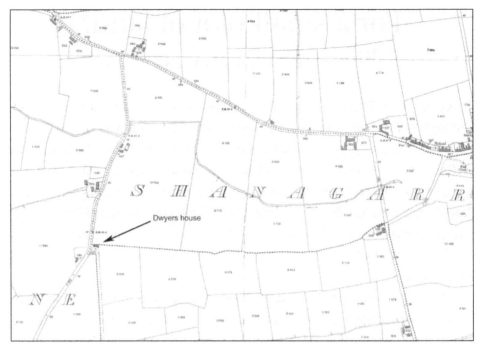

Map showing the location of Dwyer's in relation to Shanagarry

had no intention of stopping the building. He told the Crotty's that he had an old spite for them for a long time.

The following morning at nine o'clock the three young Crotty's approached the area in dispute to repair the boundary fence. They carried with them implements to carry out the repairs including a spade and a powerful adze-shaped instrument known as a graffawn. The Dwyer's had been watching their approach and Maurice Dwyer was seen taking off his coat and tying his braces around his waist as if preparing for a fight. Mary Dwyer was also heard to shout encouragement at her sons. Before the Crotty's could begin to repair the fence the entire family of the Dwyer's rushed out upon them armed with implements. Maurice Dwyer had a four pronged pike and his father carried a graffawn.

A fight occurred between the families and Maurice Dwyer made for Timothy with a pike and wounded him in the throat. John Crotty was struck by William Dwyer and fell into a nearby dyke with his body lying on the road. Timothy and Michael Crotty fled and took refuge in a nearby cottage leaving their brother on the ground. Maurice, John, and Michael Dwyer along with their mother and sister pursued the Crotty's. Maurice called after the brothers while they sheltered in the cottage saying he would murder them and hang for it. He also told them he had a sting for them for over 20 years.

However, William Dwyer realising what he had done remained standing over the body of John Crotty. Michael and Timothy attempted to return to the scene to discover the fate of their brother but were again chased away by the Dwyer's. The Dwyer's were then said to have passed by the body and retired to their cottage.

When he got the chance Michael made for Ballycotton to alert the police and get a priest for his brother who he knew was dying. On the way he met the acting sergeant Sexton who returned to the scene with him.

News of what had occurred reached Ballycotton, more police, the priest Fr Browne and Dr Murphy quickly set off. By the time the doctor arrived it was too late to be of any help. Not long after William Dwyer and his three sons were arrested. The prisoners were taken to Cork jail that day but Mary and Bridget Dwyer were allowed to remain at home. Some time in the evening Mary Dwyer set out for Ballycotton leaving her daughter alone. Not long after Bridget, uneasy being alone in the house, set off after her mother. While walking along the road she looked back to see their cottage on fire and a crowd of spectators watching. The crowd grew in numbers as the house burned but no one had any intention of putting it out. The house was burned to the ground and afterwards the Dwyer women were arrested.

On the 20th of November an inquest was held at the house of John O'Brien in Ballingarrane by coroner Richard Rice from Fermoy. Several men from the locality formed the jury for the inquest including foreman John O'Brien a farmer in Ballybraher, Timothy Fenton and Maurice Whelan from Ballycotton, Robert Garde from Ballynamona, Martin Fennessy and Robert Fitzgerald both farmers from Shanagarry and Garret Stack from Ballymaloe. Several witnesses including the Crotty's were called to give evidence of what had occurred that morning. Last to give evidence was John Guess a farm labourer from Shanagarry. Guess said he had been working in a nearby field that morning. He saw John Crotty retreating with all six of the Dwyer's after him. Crotty was not carrying anything while the pursuers were armed. He saw one of the Dwyer's strike Crotty as he approached the road and he fell. As John Crotty lay on the road with his head in the dyke William Dwyer was seen to strike him three times more.

The Dwyer's did not appear at the inquest but were held in custody at the time. The coroner stated "they were not there to vindicate any person or bring home guilt but to find the facts of the case". The jury's verdict simply agreed with the medical evidence and added that they believed the Dwyer family inflicted the injuries that killed John Crotty.

The abandoned plot close to where John Crotty was killed, with Shanagarry in the background

The entire family was tried before Mr. Justice Andrews at the Cork Assizes in December 1901 and was found guilty of manslaughter. The policeman who arrested them said that he considered them hard working industrious people before the incident. However, a Navy official who was called to give evidence at the trial said that Maurice Dwyer's conduct and character in the service had been very bad.

The judge caused a sensation in court when he sentenced the entire family.

William, Mary and Maurice Dwyer were sentenced to fifteen years penal servitude each. Michael Dwyer received eleven years while John and Bridget got a sentence of ten years each.

In April of the next year the Dwyer's brought a case for compensation before the court in Midleton claiming their house had been maliciously burned down. Huge crowds turned out at the court to see the Dwyer's who had been brought from Mountjoy jail on the train. When William,

Mary and Bridget appeared in court dressed in jail issued hooded cloaks it caused a sensation with the onlookers. They sought compensation of £130 for the malicious burning of the house. Representatives appeared for both Midleton district council and Cork county council opposing the claim for compensation. They made the case that the fire was accidental so the Dwyer's should not get compensation. A local builder from Cloyne gave evidence of having inspected the house and said it could be put right for £30. He heard further evidence regarding the contents of the house. After hearing the evidence of several people including the Dwyer's the judge made the decision that the burning of the house was indeed malicious. The judge assessed damages at £64 13s to be levied from nearby electoral divisions Ballycotton, Ballintemple, Cloyne and Ightermurragh.

Early the next year an appeal fund was set up locally for the Crotty's as they must have suffered financial troubles since their son was killed. The fund was well subscribed by over 200 people from the area with single donations from £2 to 1s totalling well over £50. This would roughly be equivalent to €5,000 in today's money.

Unfortunately for the Crotty's the well intentioned generosity of the public doesn't seem to have been enough. By 1904 Patrick Crotty had fallen into debt and had several creditors. One of those owed money was Coppinger's a merchants in Midleton who ironically had been the largest subscribed to the appeal giving £2. They were now owed £38 and Cork Distillers £44. The largest sum owed was to a local farmer closely related to the Crotty's who in the past had lent them money. In June of 1904 the farm was advertised as being put up for public auction on the 20th of that month. It was described as a compact farm of 67 acres with an excellent house and outhouses.

By September of 1904 the creditors had received a writ from the courts to recover the money owed to them. Crops were seized by the bailiffs and guarded until the day of the auction Friday the 23rd of September. Early on that Friday morning before the auction could take place some excited exchanges took place on the farm. Luckily it was kept under control by the police and didn't become a repeat of what happened three years previous. Their biggest creditor a local farmer and nephew of old Patrick Crotty arrived to see if a settlement could be reached. He had loaned money to his uncle some years previous but was never repaid as promised. The Crotty's now seemed to resent their cousin for wanting his money and defended their farm as they had against the Dywer's. They threatened to take the life of their relation rather than see their crops sold off but several police were again in the thick of it keeping both sides apart. Right before the auction was about to start Nora Crotty junior made for her cousin and would surely have hit him but for the instant response of the police. Norah despite being restrained protested at the auction calling out "you will never take a sheaf of it you bastard".

Despite this the auctioneer got started but with all the hassle nobody was prepared to bid. The Crotty's were confident nobody would buy it and they would be left to thresh the barley and pay their debts. Seventeen acres of barley was offered for sale and it was their cousin who offered £50 for it. The Crotty's protested that it was worth £200 but nobody else was willing to intervene in the feud and bid. A huge row broke out after the auction and as before would have become a struggle but for the police. Old Mrs Crotty tried her best to keep her sons and especially her daughter Nora under control but emotions were running far too high.

Later in the afternoon it flared up again when it came time for the barley to be removed from the farm. The Crotty's felt even hard done by as before the auction they had gone to the trouble of cutting and binding the barley. Now it was sold for very little and only needed to be threshed before being sold. The Crotty family stood their ground and made their best efforts to prevent the barley being taken. Armed with blackthorn sticks and anything that could be used they blocked the gap to the field and prevented their cousin from entering their land. On several occasions they made for him and like before a serious assault would have been likely but for the police. The Crotty's were eventually surrounded by the police and attempts to take the barley were abandoned till a later date. Later two of the Crotty's were arrested and taken to Midleton.

Things must have gone back to some kind of normality and the Crotty's must have somehow found the money to keep their creditors at bay and keep the farm. The farm remained in the Crotty's possession as they are still living there in the census of 1911. Not a few months later in July of 1911 Patrick Crotty died aged 87 and his wife was left to run the 60 acre farm. In February 1914 after all the fighting over land and money they were evicted from the farm. It seemed the rent on the farm had not been paid for several years. The land was on the estate of Penn Gaskell an absentee landlord residing in London. The farm had recently been purchased under the land acts and the eviction was carried out by the Sherriff's Balliff's who were protected by a large body police.

To this day the spot where John Crotty was killed is marked on the side of the road by stone marked with a black cross.

Stone that is said to mark the spot where John Crotty lay on the road

Who killed my wife?
Pound Lane (now Devlin Street), Fermoy 1891

During the day on Monday the 14th of September 1891 Patrick Hogan and his wife Mary were seen quarrelling in what was then known as Queens Square, Fermoy.

She asked him for some money to get her petticoat out of a pawnshop because she wanted to go visit her brother in Castletownroche but Patrick wouldn't give it to her. The fight intensified and he struck her whilst on the street. Later on they went closer to home and ended up drinking in John Murphy's public house at the cross on Cork road. On their way home from the pub a fight between them broke out again. They were said not to have been drunk but having had drink taken. Mary refused to go home with him and ran off to a neighbour's house. He pursued her from one house to another and eventually got hold of her in Mrs McGrath's house. She threatened to go home to her brother's house in Castletownroche over eight miles away that night. She didn't get away from him and he dragged her home to their house on Pound Lane, now called Devlin Street. Before even getting her in the front door neighbours saw him hitting Mary on the face.

A few women heard the row inside the house and plucked up the courage to go round when it had seemed to settle down. They were shocked to find Mary Hogan thrown on the floor on a pile of straw. She looked to be in a bad way but at first they thought she had fallen and was just unconscious. They quickly realised though that Mary was dead and one of the women said to Hogan "oh she is dead I will go for the police". At first Patrick hadn't realised what he had done and was sitting there holding their young child in his arms. He replied to the women "who killed my wife?" It must have dawned on him and he asked one of the women to hold the child. He asked for a razor to cut his throat. He didn't get one and ran off across the fields. Before he fled he called his sister-in-law saying "Nancy I depend on you for my life."

The Square, Fermoy where Patrick Hogan was seen arguing with his wife. Image courtesy of the National Library of Ireland

The neighbouring women on the street gathered at the Hogan's house but were all shocked and screamed when they looked inside. The alarm was raised and the police were quickly on the scene.

Head Constable Whitfield arrested Patrick Hogan and cautioned him but he made no statement. Later when he had been brought to the barracks, Hogan was willing to talk and told him a story of what happened. "I gave my wife two pints of port in Murphy's, Cork road. She came home before me and when I came to the cross some woman told me she was in a weakness. I thought they were humbugging me and I told them to go about their business. I went inside and laid my hand on her lips and found her stone cold. I wish to god it was I took the lead of her before she took the lead of me".

The inquest was held on Wednesday the 16th by Coroner Byrne from Castletownroche. The coroner stated the inquest was merely to find the cause of death and no evidence of an incriminating nature was to be given. Doctors Dilworth and Byrne both gave testimony of having carried out the post mortem. They found injuries on the hands, legs and face with swollen lips. There were several marks on the skull which had caused a large loss of blood internally. Marks on the back of the head had been caused by a blow to the head or a fall. There was an injury to the spinal cord which also caused bleeding. The doctors said that the injuries were such that they couldn't have been self inflicted. The medical cause of death was internal bleeding on the brain and upper spinal cord.

Upon hearing the evidence the jury didn't take long to find a verdict. After a short deliberation the jury found that death was caused by concussion on the brain but didn't refer to by whom.

A special court was held in Fermoy on Monday the 5th of October by resident magistrate Major Hutchinson. Despite there being a great deal of interest in the case the proceedings were kept private. It was not held in the court room but in the magistrate's room. Only the accused, the police and the press were allowed attend the proceedings. Patrick Hogan was undefended while District Inspector Ball conducted the case for the prosecution.

Doctor Timothy Dilworth a dispensary doctor in Fermoy was again called to give medical evidence. Doctor Byrne had attended the scene that evening and carried out a superficial exam within an hour of death occurring. Dr Byrne told how he had assisted with the post-mortem and corroborated the testimony already heard from Dilworth.

James O'Brien from Ballingarry told how he saw Patrick Hogan on Pound Lane that evening. He saw Hogan drag his wife back to the house and he didn't hear them speaking to each other at the time. Later he heard the commotion on the road and went to the house where the women had gathered. Mary Hogan was seen stretched on the ground with marks on her. O'Brien said he hadn't seen these marks on Mary earlier.

Patrick Hogan's sister-in-law Anne Hogan was called to the stand. She told how she had seen the couple earlier that day after three in the afternoon. They were outside Cudmore's on the corner of King Street now called McCurtin Street. The couple were quarrelling on the street, Patrick headed for home and his wife followed behind scolding him. Anne said how the next time she saw her sister was later that evening. She went to her sister's house with some other women and saw her lying dead on the floor. Her husband was still there at the time holding the child.

Head Constable Whitfield related how he had arrested the accused near Pound lane on the night of the murder. When in the barracks he took a statement from Patrick Hogan who claimed to be innocent of murdering his wife. Whitfield produced a hat in court which he had found under Mary Hogan's head. Patrick Hogan claimed that the hat was indeed his property.

District Inspector Ball said in his opinion the body had been moved around the house that night to the place he found it. Some person dragged it until the head and shoulders rested on a pile of straw and Ball alleged the hat had fallen from whoever dragged the body.

Once the evidence for the prosecution concluded, Patrick Hogan was asked if he had something to say. He again denied murdering his wife saying she had got a weakness. Seeing her on the floor he went over to help her and when he stooped over his hat fell off. After this the Judge returned the case to trial by a jury at the next Cork Assizes.

The case was heard before Justice Holmes at the Cork Winter Assizes on the 10th of December. This time the accused was represented by Solicitor Robert Powell while several queens counsel solicitors prosecuted. A jury of twelve men were sworn in to decide on the case. When the prisoner was charged with his crime before the jury he entered a plea of not guilty.

Solicitor Wright for the crown addressed the jury and described the facts of the case. He said nobody had seen what occurred within the house that night but said the case was clear. The only question he said was whether the crime was murder or manslaughter. Once he concluded his statement Mr Powell addressed the bench.

He applied to withdraw his client's plea of not guilty and enter a plea of guilty to manslaughter. The application was heard and the prosecution agreed with the plea.

Patrick Hogan was sentenced to twelve months jail with hard labour.

Devlin Street, Fermoy

Mother-in-law murdered
Little Island 1843

In rural Ireland when the sons of a widow got married they would often bring their new wives to live in their house. Houses were much smaller and all the occupants may have had to sleep together in a single room. Under these conditions living in such close proximity it would be of no surprise to find that relations sometimes became strained between the in laws.

One such case was in Little Island in 1843. Catherine Tuohig was on bad terms with her mother-in-law Margaret. Matters got worse when Catherine had a miscarriage and she blamed it on her mother-in-law who was said to be old and feeble. Early on the morning of the 18th May 1843 Catherine Tuohig's husband left to go to work. Later in the morning Margaret's grandson came to the house to fetch something. Catherine was coming out of the house with a large basket on her back but she doubled back to the house when she saw him. She told him she was going to her mother's house with some things but would not go now. Catherine placed the basket in a room with her cloak under. The young boy should have realised that something was wrong when Catherine began to tremble. He didn't however as he was afraid of getting into trouble at work and hurried away. Before leaving he asked where his grandmother was and accepted the answer that she was out.

Meanwhile Catherine's husband returned for his breakfast and was surprised to find it was not ready. He was more surprised when neither his wife nor mother was anywhere to be seen. He wasn't too alarmed but by evening however the family grew worried and began to search the surroundings. Margaret had now been out since early in the morning and Catherine was also now nowhere to be seen. It was about six in the evening when a family member in desperation searched the cottage to find clues of the missing women. She opened the settle bed in the kitchen to find a shocking scene. Inside was the body of the old woman Margaret doubled over.

It was suspicious that Catherine had fled the scene. Margaret had terrible injuries to her face and body and it was obvious that she had been beaten to death. An inquest was held the following day by which time Catherine Tuohig had not yet been found despite a large search by the local police. Her husband told the inquest that his wife had previously tried to poison him and had often threatened his mother that she would settle her.

The jury of the inquest reached a verdict that the deceased, "to the best of their belief came to her death by the wounds inflicted on her by Catherine Tuohig".

The day after the inquest on the 20th of May, Catherine Tuohig was tracked down and arrested near Killeagh seventeen miles from home. At first she gave false names and denied knowing anything. She was immediately taken into custody and gave a statement to a magistrate in Glanmire. It was obvious to the magistrate that she was suffering from insanity but had formed a plan to escape to Bristol. Fearing she would take her own life she was taken to the lunatic asylum.

She must have spent many months in the lunatic asylum as the case was called before the court in August 1844, over a year after the murder, at the Cork Summer Assizes. Catherine was charged that she did feloniously maim and kill Margaret Tuohig. Solicitor for the defence applied to have the case postponed claiming they were not expecting the trial and some witnesses were not present. His client Catherine was allowed out of the asylum that morning having been there since being arrested.

The judge asked Dr. Osbourne from the asylum was Catherine Tuohig quite sane. The doctor replied "perfectly my lord and is so for the last nine months."

After debating for some time the judge eventually relented and allowed the prisoner out on bail which was most unusual in cases of murder. Bail was set at £20 in addition to two sureties £20. The case was set to be called again at the next assizes but it was not called again until 1845.

At the Spring Assizes in March of 1845 the case came before a jury in Cork.

Lawyer for the prosecution Mr Bennett explained to the jury how the crime had taken place nearly two years earlier. Since that time he said the accused had been out of her mind and unable to be charged with the crime. It was only recently that she was in a fit enough state to attend a trial.

Bennett told the jury, it was up to them to decide was Catherine Tuohig insane or not when her mother-in-law was killed. He asked the jury to decide was she guilty or not and was the crime manslaughter or murder. One fact the lawyer also related to the jury was that Catherine Tuohig had just given birth shortly before her mother-in-law was killed.

The first witness was Thomas Tuohig, the grandson of the dead woman. He had arrived home that day and enquired where his grandmother was. Catherine had absconded after he left.

Fanny Tuohig was next called and told how her mother was in good health the last time she say her alive on the evening before she died. She described before the court how she found her mother's body hidden in a settle bed. The body was bent over to fit in the settle and had the signs of a violent end.

As there were no actual witnesses to the murder the statement Catherine Tuohig had given after her arrest was all the prosecution had. A magistrate Nicholas Marshall Cummins was called to the stand as he had taken that confession from her in Glanmire in 1843. Catherine had told him that she had a row with her mother-in-law that morning. She merely pushed the old woman who banged her head on a dresser. Catherine hid the body and tried to destroy her bloody clothes but as we know met Thomas when leaving the house. She hid the clothes under the bed and when the house was empty went on the run hoping to escape to England.

The final witness was a doctor from Cork city Daniel Cantillon who would prove the mental state of the accused. He had seen her professionally several times before the murder had taken place. In that time he said her mental health suffered as a result of a bad lying in period. At that time lying in was a period after childbirth where the mother was confined to bed to rest. The confinement could vary from 2 weeks to 2 months. The rich could afford professional care but for the working class it was left to female relatives, the mother-in-law in this case. Dr Cantillon was of the opinion that many women suffered madness after a "bad confinement". Six weeks before the murder the doctor sent for Catherine's husband and informed him of his wife's condition. The doctor warned him that there was danger approaching and his wife was likely to do something irrational with the slightest provocation. Her family were warned to remove anything likely to trigger it as she was most irritated at the time.

After hearing the evidence especially that of the doctor the jury came to their verdict. Catherine Tuohig was acquitted of murder on the grounds that she was insane at the time.

Ballycrenane Mystery
Ballycrenane, near Garryvoe 1865

In the 1860's on the shores of Ballycotton Bay, east of Garryvoe, in the townland of Ballycrenane, there lived a farmer called William Walsh. On the surface he seemed to have what most wanted, a large farm and a much younger pretty wife. He was a farmer of 100 acres of good land and had it on cheap rent. He was aged about forty eight years and was married to a younger woman Ellen who was thirty four. Ellen was said to have been very good looking and looked much younger. The couple had been married about thirteen years; Ellen was a widow when she married Walsh and had one child with her first husband. During the thirteen years six more children were born. For the first years of marriage they lived happily together being the most comfortable farmers in the area.

Some time in 1863 William Walsh enlarged his farm by buying another plot of land nearby. He paid £200 for the extra land and this caused a lot of jealousy and bad feeling in the area especially from other competitors for the farmland. A few years before when Griffiths Valuation was carried out Walsh held only 40 acres. This was let from the landlord John M Praed who had bought 842 acres there in 1854

On the 3rd on November 1863 a fire broke out in Walsh's haggard. It was presumed to have been malicious as it started in a hayrick furthest from the house but nobody was seen doing it. The fire spread quickly and before long four stacks of oats, five of barley, two barrels of wheat as well as straw and hay were destroyed. The total damage was estimated to be about £140, a very considerable sum at the time.

However this wasn't Walsh's only troubles, for the previous three years he and his wife lived on very bad terms. It was common knowledge amongst the servants and neighbours who often witnessed their bitter quarrels. The source of the rows was the jealousy of an ex servant boy, Joyce. Despite being fired he often returned to the house but was turned away by the husband William.

On the 20th November 1865 William Walsh went to Cork to sell a calf. On his return journey he stopped off at public house in Ladysbridge and had a glass of whiskey. He left and continued his journey home arriving there about eight. He had his supper and went to bed some time around nine. The children were already in bed at this time as was his wife in another bed in the same room. At six the next morning James Curtin was one of the first up. He let a tenant farmer Patrick Lynch into the house and went to his master's chamber to get Lynch a match.

The wife replied the second time Curtin called and upon entering the room he was horrified with what he saw. To his horror there was William Walsh hanging out of his bed. His legs were still in the bed but his face was lying flat on the wet clay floor. Curtin cried out something like "I fear he is dead". Ellen Walsh only a few feet away in the same room got up from her bed. She was said to have clapped her hands and made to attempt to get the body of her husband into his bed. She did not bother to ask those that helped her if her husband was alive or not.

Marks were found on his neck that showed signs of strangulation. Not long after Ellen Walsh was arrested in suspicion of being involved in the murder. Joyce, the ex servant boy, was suspected of having assisted her but wasn't arrested as there was no evidence he was in the house on the night. None of the windows in the house could be opened and the door had been bolted from the inside.

An inquiry was held into the suspected murder at Castlemartyr petty sessions court on Dec 1st.There was a huge interest locally in the case and the courtroom was packed. One of the first called as witness that day was servant boy Robert Kenny. He slept in another room in the house that night. He said he heard choking in the night coming from the other room. He said he was afraid to go and investigate because if he did the murderer would kill him. Another servant told him that Joyce had previously come to the house tried to kill William Walsh by choking him and tired to throw him into the fire.

The next witness was eldest son of the murdered man, Daniel Walsh 12. He said it was six months since Joyce tried to choke his father and throw him into the fire. He said his mother was present and looking on but did nothing.

Another servant Thomas Geary was called as witness. He stated that three months previously William Walsh called him into a room with wife

Modern view of Ballycotton from close to where the murder took place

Ellen Walsh. William asked her in his presence to give up Joyce and go with him to the parish priest Fr Fagan. William said that they could then live on better terms but his wife refused.

John Moore solicitor from Midleton appeared for the accused Ellen Walsh who was held in custody. Another solicitor from Midleton Mr Mackay represented the next of kin of William Walsh.

The third day of the inquiry 6th December was held in the Ballycrenane School house only a short distance away from the scene of the crime. One of the first witness called was father of the murdered man 84 year old Edmund Walsh. He said about a year ago the accused denied to him having anything to do with the servant Joyce. He went on to say that his now dead son William had even doubted that he was the father of the last child born.

The brother of deceased gave evidence next; he said a few months ago he found Joyce hiding in the barn with Ellen Walsh. The witness said his now dead brother had come to him not long ago. He said he was sorry he paid the rent as he was ashamed of his wife. He said that money was no use as he was unhappy. His wife had said to him she would "sooner be in hell for seven years than sleep with him". This was damning evidence indeed as at the time Ellen Walsh was seven months pregnant.

For the defence Mr Moore didn't have any witness to call but proceeded with a long speech. He accounted for the marks on the dead mans neck by him falling on the floor. The marks on his windpipe could be caused he said by wearing tight collared shirt. He said his calling out in the night could be the cause of a fit.

The jury after deliberating for an hour returned a verdict that William Walsh died by strangulation in his own bed. The inquiry said it was carried out by a person unknown to them but aided by the wife Ellen Walsh and that she did choke strangle and kill her husband. Ellen Walsh wasn't bothered when she heard the verdict.

She was held in custody until her trial before a jury in court.

It wasn't until March of the next year that David Joyce was arrested and taken to the county gaol. New witness statements gave further suspicion to his involvement. The first was James White who slept in the same room as Joyce on the night of the murder. White said he went to bed at nine and Joyce wasn't there. He awoke later as Joyce returned and the accused told him he had been asleep in a ditch. One of the children also came forward at the time saying on the night they heard their father say "Oh Davy, don't murder me".

The trial was to be heard at the Cork Spring Assizes held in the county court late in March. There seemed to be some delay, probably in getting evidence and the trial doesn't seem to go ahead but both the accused were still held in custody. The defence solicitor applied to the court to have his clients discharged under the Irish Habeas Corpus Act. This act made a provision that if prisoners were not indicted for the charges they were held for, in the same sessions that application could be made for their release. Legally it was very complicated and led to much debate before a judge.

For the crown Sergeant Barry made the case that more evidence would be found and time was needed. It seems neither of the accused were discharged and the case was postponed until summer Assizes which would be held in July.

The case was heard before Cork criminal court starting July 25th 1866. Ellen Walsh and David Joyce stood alongside each other in court both indicted for murder. From the onset the judge decided to separate the indictments against the accused and said Ellen Walsh should be tried independently. The couple were separated in court and they had not been together since being arrested in November last. After being rearranged in court Ellen Walsh pleaded not guilty.

Sergeant Barry in his opening statement for the prosecution made what would now be unusual remarks. He said the case "exhibited features of an unusually painful and appalling character". He went further and said "the labouring class of the country had their failings, it was true but those failings did not comprise the perpetration of such crimes." Ellen Walsh he said "disclosed a record of blood and lust which but rarely defiled the history of Irish peasantry". The prosecutions case was going to show how Ellen Walsh's shameless adultery led to the murder of her husband.

The prosecution's speech went on for some time and detailed the case, saying how painful it was taking statements from the deceased's children. A model of the cottage was shown and described in court. Walsh's house was described as being typical of a farmer's house of the time. It was long and low only having a ground floor divided into three rooms. It was thatched and the floors were merely clay. The kitchen was the central and largest room with a room off the kitchen on either side. In the room to the right of the kitchen that night slept two farm servants and Daniel Walsh, the eldest son. The room at the other end of the house had two beds. In one bed slept William Walsh and a younger son Ned. The other was occupied by wife Ellen Walsh and her three daughters. Ellen had long refused to occupy the same bed as her husband.

The prosecutions case was that Ellen Walsh sent her daughter to retrieve Neddy from the bed after the crime had been committed. She had a conversation with the children the next morning as to what they should and shouldn't say when asked. This alone the prosecution held was evidence that Ellen Walsh was so close to the crime without being involved in some way.

Dr Fowke of Cloyne first gave evidence and stated that he had examined the body on the 22nd of November. He had found two cuts consistent with finger nails on the wind pipe and several other cuts on the neck. The next witness called was servant Robert Kenny who slept in the house that night. He had been in service with the family for seven months and during this time the couple quarrelled a lot. He said Ellen Walsh had gone to bed before her husband that night. When William went to his bed Kenny heard the wife speak to him in an angry manner. During the night Kenny heard a screech from Walsh but he didn't get up to investigate it.

The other Servant in the house James Curtin was called to give evidence in court. He had not heard any noise while he slept that night but woke when Kenny called him. Curtin was the first up in the morning and opened the door for Patrick Lynch who was outside. The door had been bolted but could be opened from the outside with an instrument. However the door could not be bolted again from the outside. Lynch entered the house that morning and asked for a light. Curtin led him to the other bedroom to get a match from his master only to find him dead. He found him with his legs still in the bed but his right cheek was on the floor.

Patrick Lynch in court corroborated this evidence saying he followed Curtin to the bedroom that morning and said it was daylight at the time being six in the morning. He went on to say that Ellen Walsh was clapping her hands after hearing her husband was dead.

The next witness to be sworn in court was Edward Walsh only nine years old; he had been in the same bed as his father the night in question. Before being sworn in he told the judge "I know that I am bound to tell the truth and I will go to hell if I don't". He said he recalled his father coming from Cork that night but he was in bed asleep before his father came to bed. In the middle of the night he heard his father screech out in Irish "oh fie Davy don't" after that his father was dragged out of bed. He heard footsteps around the room of a person with no boots, on the wet floor. The floor was wet because rain was getting in between the thatch and the wall. It was pitch dark and the young boy couldn't see who was there. The boy was struck in the eye by a hand. He called out to his father and managed to catch the hand he thought had struck him. The hand was pulled away suddenly and shortly after he heard his mother tell his sister Ellen to get him from the bed. Obviously the boy was very frightened and wouldn't leave the bed but his sister said "come out you blather". When he did he saw his mother on the floor. As the questioning continued in court the boy said his mother had told him not to tell Kenny or the Police what had happened that night for his life would be in danger.

Ellen Walsh's daughter who was about ten years of age was up next. She said that on the night in question she didn't sleep like her younger brother. She was in her mother's bed awake and she heard her parents arguing, which it seems was quite normal. She lay awake in the bed and the clock in the room struck eleven, she heard a sound like footsteps in the same room. After that she heard her father cry out "Robin Robin" followed by "Fie Davy don't" the same as her brother had heard. At the time her father was making a noise in his throat. Ellen stated her mother got up from bed. The next morning young Ellen was questioned by her mother if she had heard anything during the night. She said she had heard noises in the night and her mother said she would have her life is she was to tell anyone. Young Ellen also recalled hearing her parents talking two weeks before; William told his wife she was in the family way by Joyce. He asked her to leave the house but she said she would only leave for 7 shillings a week.

Daniel Walsh next gave evidence, he was thirteen years of age but he slept in the other room and heard nothing during the night.

A woman from the locality Catherine Nell who had been in service in the house twelve months before gave some of the most damning evidence. During her time there Joyce used to sleep in the house and she once caught Ellen Walsh in bed with Joyce. She also caught them in the stables and said "their position was an improper one". Catherine recalled being employed by Walsh's when the haggard was burned down. Sometime after the burning she overheard Ellen and Joyce talking about it. Joyce remarked that "Willie Walsh was making a great many enemies for himself". But Mrs Walsh wasn't impressed with the burning and replied "Devil crack their necks that would not knock satisfaction out of his own bones and not be burning my crops". She was heard to say to Joyce "devil break your neck that would not do this and that to him, and have cows and horses afterwards for yourself". Joyce asked "are you giving me liberty" to which she replied "yes I am". The court was adjourned before Mr Waters spoke for the defence.

The beginning of the second day Mr Waters got his chance to address the jury for the defence. He said the prosecution's case was based upon suspicion and presumption. He was going to make the case that the evidence shown was insufficient to support the charges. He asked the jury how a murder of a man in the prime of his life takes place in a house full of people and nobody had come to his aid. A terrible struggle must have taken place yet only one cry was heard. The defence spoke at length about the case and went on to doubt the medical evidence. Waters said that the body was inspected two days after the death had occurred. At this stage Dr Fowke would have heard stories and been predisposed to find evidence that matched what he heard. The defence asserted the story that Walsh succumbed to some sort sudden illness such as an epileptic fit or seizure and asphyxiated. The injuries he said were caused by the man himself gasping for air. He concluded that young Neddy was struck by his father while he struggled in the same bed with that unknown and sudden illness.

The defence went over the evidence of several witnesses at length and found any inconsistencies however small in their evidence. He addressed the jury directly and said before the accused can be tried of murder the jury must satisfy themselves there was no other rational conclusion.

The prosecution replied for the crown that the evidence was indeed circumstantial but the facts were consistent. The prosecution stated that if William Walsh was found to be murdered it was immaterial by whom. For if he was murdered the wife was aware of the fact and guilty of being involved.

The judge finally addressed the jury and said the case was ten times darker than an ordinary murder case. He asked the jury now to take great care in considering the case but was confident they were in a position to make a calm conclusion. The murder if it was a murder was carried out with audacity and recklessness. The case for the crown was that someone caused the murder but it was obvious it was not Ellen Walsh herself. She was at the time seven months pregnant and had give birth since the murder. She alone would not have been unable to carry it out. However she was capable of helping and letting the assailant in and out of the house on the night. The prosecution said this was enough to find her guilty of conspiring to have her husband murdered.

The judge stated "God Forbid they should have to find her guilty of murder because they are satisfied she committed adultery". The judge summed up the case and again reviewed the evidence, it was regrettable he said that the post-mortem was not more careful and complete. The experienced judge gave several scenarios of where guilt could be found or not. The big question he said was "did the accused procure the death of the deceased? If not she would not be liable for his death and even though she knew of it".

After the judge finally summed up the case the jury retired to consider all the facts and come to a decision. After deliberating for about three quarters of an hour the jury returned to the court room with a verdict of not guilty. Suddenly there was a murmur heard in court and one person began clapping but it ceased instantly when nobody else joined in.

Despite being found not guilty the prisoners were not immediately released from custody. The authorities it seems did not know what to do and could not decide whether they should be released or not. The counsel for both sides and the judge met again on August 1st to decide what course of action should be taken next. The defence again relied on the Habeas Corpus Act and assured Justice Fitzgerald to release the prisoners was well within the act. Sergeant Barry asked the judge to hold the prisoners in custody unless he felt the act forced him to release them. Ellen Walsh he said would not return to her home but committed to leave the country.

There was still another indictment against Ellen Walsh and the judge said it was better if such an arrangement could be made. Justice Fitzgerald went on to say for the woman's safety, moral and physical steps should be taken so the pair would never again meet. All parties agreed to this course of action as they feared for the safety of the prisoners, Ellen Walsh it was said didn't have a friend in the country. On the night of the acquittal bonfires were lit in the neighbourhood but suppressed by the police.

It was eventually decided to discharge both prisoners on the conditions they would immediately leave the country and never revisit nor meet each other again.

Ellen Walsh was to give up all her claim to her husband's estate in exchange for the sum of £80. She was being sent to America and Joyce was sent to Liverpool.

Period map showing Garryvoe and Ballycrenane

Did he or didn't he?
Garryvoe 1843

(WARNING – Pregnant woman murdered, some readers
may find this upsetting. Gruesome details.)

On June 18th 1843 in the vicinity of Garryvoe a christening was held with a
party afterwards at Mick Ahern's farm. Several people stayed up all night
and didn't leave until early in the morning. A young woman of the locality
called Mary Donovan stayed nearby that night at a house belonging to
Frances Walsh. Early in the morning Mary got up and said she was going
to see the parish priest Rev Egan. She headed off at the same time as
people were going home after the christening. Mary was seen on the road
but went missing and was not seen again. She was unmarried but was
pregnant (or as they said then was *with child)* at the time she disappeared.

It wasn't until the 28th of June that local Timothy McCarthy found a
leg in widow Beausang's wheat field. He went to inform his neighbours
and they continued to search the field that evening. It wasn't until the
following morning that the badly mutilated body was found. He didn't
immediately recognise the body as being Mary Donovan as the face was
beaten so badly it could not be identified. What they found was a shocking
scene - the torso was badly mutilated, the woman's womb cut open and
the unborn child exposed. They ran to inform the police of what they
found and a larger search was conducted of the area to find the other
missing arms and legs. A pit about four feet long was found to have been
dug nearby. The ground was rocky and the hole was not deep enough to
conceal a body.

A man who had been seen talking to Mary on the road the morning
she went missing was the chief suspect. An inquest was held not long after
the body was found but no one came forward with information. There
was no doubt however that the inquest could return only one verdict and
which was that Mary Donovan was murdered.

The parish priest announced from the altar that there was a reward
of £50 for anyone who had information about the terrible crime. Shortly

afterwards a local called John Hennessy came forward with information, not for the money he said but for Rev Egan the parish priest.

A local farmer William Barry was arrested on suspicion of carrying out the dreadful murder. His house was searched, a large pistol found which was thought to be the murder weapon and blood was found on a waistcoat of his.

It was not until the Cork Spring Assizes on the 27th of March the next year 1844 that the case was heard. A jury of twelve men were sworn in before Chief Justice Baron. William Barry was charged with wilful murder of Mary Donovan on the 19th June the previous year but he pleaded not guilty. Barry, 32, was said to be dark faced. He was described in court as a respectable looking fellow and decently attired of the farming class of society as opposed to a labourer.

Mr Bennett for the crown prosecution opened the case to the jury and outlined the circumstances surrounding the case. He said it was a charge that could not be reduced to manslaughter owing to the brutal nature with which it was carried out. He said William Barry went home from the christening that Monday morning alone on a horse. His wife and family went home separately with a horse and cart driven by a servant. Barry was seen talking on the road with the deceased Mary Donovan. William Barry went home and changed his clothes. He left again and said he had to borrow a horse from Mackey's. This Mr Bennett said was untrue as Barry didn't go there at all. This was when Barry was supposed to have carried out the murder and arrived home about an hour and a half after leaving. Bennett said these events would be proved in court and said the jury must find a verdict of guilty.

Mary Donovan's sister Johanna took the stand and recalled the day of the christening. She met Mary that day and told how she was crying. She was able to describe in detail what clothes Mary had been wearing as she had made some of them. Johanna also told the court that her sister "was lame and had a turn in her neck". Another sister Elizabeth was called next but was too weak to give evidence. It was feared she was about to faint and she had to be removed from the court.

Frances Walsh, better known as Fannie, told how Mary had stayed in her house the night before and had often stayed there. Mary had told

Frances that she "was in the family way" and was going to see the parish priest. Catherine Mullins spoke to the court in Irish saying she saw the accused William Barry riding after Mary on the road that morning.

Another local Ellen McCarthy gave similar evidence but had seen and heard more that morning. After William Barry's wife had passed she saw William riding side by side along the road with Mary Donovan. She heard Mary say to the accused "you know very well that I did not do that" but didn't hear the reply.

A young boy of about twelve years of age Patrick McCarthy was called next. He was at the christening as he worked for Mick Ahern. Patrick told the court that he drove Barry's wife and family home that morning. On the way he saw William Barry up the hill talking to a woman. He saw Barry go home and change into work clothes telling his wife he was going to Mackey's for a horse. Patrick saw William return about an hour and a half later and fell asleep on the settle.

Another servant Catherine Walsh was called next, she was fourteen years old and in service with William Barry. That morning when the family came home she was sent to Mackey's for milk but did not see William Barry there. She said that after the body was found her master William Barry hadn't been living at home on the farm for some time. She couldn't recall in court how long he stayed away for but said he was away between Michaelmas (29th September) and Christmas.

John Hennessy's evidence was going to be the most controversial. This witness said he knew both William Barry and Mary Donovan for many years. That morning he went to a clover field which he rented to see how the clover was getting on. While there he saw Barry and Mary enter a nearby field. He told the court this made him curious. He thought Mary was an "airy girl to be out in such a lonesome place so early in the morning". Hennessy moved closer but was behind a furze bush and wasn't seen by the others. The pair were talking when Barry struck her on the head with something he took out of is coat. He heard Mary screech as she was struck and fell down. The witness said "I knew he was murdering her with the strokes he gave" but Hennessy then doubled back and ran in the direction he had come from. Hennessy said he had not been seen as Barry had his back turned to him while he committed the dreadful crime. Running home he met more neighbours on the way but didn't say anything about what he had witnessed. John Hennessy didn't attend the inquest or inform the police. Eventually after the body was found Hennessy told the parish priest what he had witnessed who told him he must inform the police.

Before the case for the prosecution closed Edmond Mackey gave evidence. He recalled how William Barry never came to his farm after the christening for a horse.

After the case for the prosecution closed, Solicitor O'Hea made a case for the defence. He spoke at length and asked the jury to acquit his client, while he spoke Barry cried in court. He went on to say "the points of enquiry of the case were three in number". Number one he said was identification, there had been none except the clothes. The second point was the murder; there was no doubt that she was cruelly murdered. O'Hea spoke about the third point, who had carried out the murder, this he said was the greatest consideration. He moved on to talk about the evidence that was putting the guilt on his client. Addressing the jury he asked was the story told by Hennessy one on which they could rely on. He asked what John Hennessy doing there at such an hour in the morning to see clover he saw every day. Undermining Hennessy's evidence was clearly what the defence was attempting. He questioned the conduct of Hennessy on that morning saying he was a coward knowing she was being murdered and not coming to her rescue. Even after he fled the scene he did not raise the alarm to neighbours he passed. The defence claimed that Hennessy had not said a word until the reward "thirty pieces of silver" was offered. He asked what sort of man Hennessy was, who came forward for claimed religious reasons yet witnessed a murder and kept it secret. The defence asked the jury to consider the case carefully and referred to past cases where the accused was executed and later proved to be innocent.

The defence called Barry's landlord Robert Penrose Fitzgerald to the stand. He stated that William Barry was his tenant for the last nine years and during that time was a quiet peaceful man who was never in any trouble whatsoever.

Finally the judge addressed the jury before asking them to come to a verdict. Summing up he said the entire case rested on the evidence of John Hennessy. He told the jury if they believed Hennessy's testimony they should find Barry guilty, otherwise they should acquit him. The judge asked them to retire to come to a verdict. After a mere ten minutes they returned to the court with the verdict of not guilty. Friends of William Barry in the gallery began to cheer loudly and clap their hands but were stopped quickly by the sheriff of the court. The court instructed Barry to be discharged.

Ashore on leave
Ballinacurra 1841

For many years Ballinacurra was a thriving port serving the nearby town of Midleton. The village grew on the banks of the Owenacurra River where quays and storehouses were built. Coal, iron, wood and slate were imported from places like Liverpool, Bristol and London. The fertile land in East Cork was always good for growing corn and Ballinacurra became the centre for malting. The finished malt was shipped for brewing, mainly to Dublin. Over the years many sailors arrived from far off places and came ashore to visit while waiting for their ship to sail again.

In 1841 one such sailor, James Connell, was on shore leave while his ship the *Lydney Lass* was in port. On the 18th of February he walked into the nearby town of Midleton and went to Fitzgerald's pub. While there a disagreement broke out with John Neil, a labourer who worked in the area. Neil better known in these parts as Sean Bawn was drinking with a friend called McCarthy. Both men were originally from Clonakilty.

Connell was alone and outnumbered by the West Cork men so he left the pub. While walking back to his ship in Ballinacurra he met a woman on the road. They were both going in the same direction and talked while walking along. Suddenly half way to Ballinacurra Sean Bawn and his friend came up from behind the pair. The men knocked Connell down on the road in front of the woman. Sean Bawn set upon him and struck him on the head with a big stone. James Connell's skull was fractured and he lay on the side of the road unconscious. Nobody did anything to help him until the regular coach service to Cloyne came along. It was the following morning before James Connell died from his shocking head injuries. Sean Bawn was tracked down by the police and arrested. However his accomplice McCarthy managed to make his escape and remained at large.

On the 23rd of February an inquest was held by Coroner Geran in Midleton, but was postponed until the 3rd of March to gather more witnesses. The finding of the inquest was obvious, that he died as a result of a stone being thrown at him.

Despite the fact that John Neil had been arrested the case against him was postponed and was not called before the Cork Spring Assizes. It would be many months later before the case came before a jury at the Cork Summer Assizes in August that year.

Now John Neil (Sean Bawn) stood charged on two indictments. The first, that he killed James Connell. The other that he killed an unidentified person, this was to cover the case that the sailor's name was not in fact James Connell.

When called in court solicitor for the Queen's Counsel Mr Bennett addressed the court first. He was in no doubt James Connell had been killed but questioned the identity of whom had done it and also asked could the charges be reduced to manslaughter.

The first witness sworn before the court was Midleton publican Edmund Fitzgerald. He recalled seeing a James or John Connell dressed like a sailor in his premises on the night he died. To the question "was John Neil there that night" he replied to be best of his knowledge he was. The jury was having none of his doubt and asked was the man charged in his pub that night or not. The publican now relented and said he was sure Neil was there and so was John McCarthy.

He clearly recollected when the sailor left as he paid his bill and shook hands before going.

It was half an hour later before Neil and McCarthy departed which the publican said gave the sailor plenty of time to reach Ballinacurra. Another half hour later the pair returned again to the pub but made no mention of where they had been. Edmund had no recollection of there being any trouble between the men that night before leaving his premises. He mentioned how he knew John Neil for some time and he was a quite respectable man.

While Fitzgerald's testimony was somewhat unclear the next witness was much surer and could put the three men together that night. Honora Flahavan once sworn first told how she knew Sean Bawn. That night she worked in Fitzgerald's helping her sister Mary who was sick. She told that the three men all sat at the same table in the pub. The sailor she said was there from four to six, in that time ate his dinner, drank two pints of port and a glass of punch.

Honora revealed she had witnessed an altercation between the sailor and McCarthy that night. It happened she said as three women selling goods got up to leave.

Both McCarthy and Connell helped one of the women put a basket of eggs on her back. Connell tried to take an egg from the basket without the woman seeing it. McCarthy however told her and he grabbed the sailor by his collar and shook him. Connell tried to defend himself but was clearly going to be out numbered and knew it. When McCarthy threatened to follow him and break his nose he made to leave without another word. She said when McCarthy and Neil returned to the pub that night they were laughing and only stayed 15 minutes.

Despite being sick that night Mary Flahavan had an even clearer recollection of that night's events. She was sure the deceased man's name was John Connell but heard a boy call him James. When Connell got up to leave that evening Mary heard John Neil say to his friend "by god almighty, I'll have his life before morning or either he will have mine". Mary said her sister Honora had not heard this exchange as she was at the back door at the time. She heard McCarthy reply to his friend" hold your tongue; I'll give him a bloody nose before morning". According to Mary it was only about 15mins after Connell left that the other pair went.

A woman Mary Mansfield was called to give evidence of having met the sailor that night. She knew he was a sailor by his dress and first saw him going towards the distillery. He asked her how to get to Ballinacurra saying someone had sent him astray. Mary was about to give directions and put him on the right track when she saw Kitty Mulloy. Mary knew Kitty lived in Ballinacurra and enquired was she going home. Kitty Mulloy agreed to take him to Ballinacurra saying she would enjoy the company walking there.

Catherine Mulloy was called to describe the events that occurred that evening as she walked home with Connell. She seems to have enjoyed walking along with him and took his arm. Before reaching the village of Ballinacurra two men caught up with them from behind. Mulloy didn't know them but described one being much taller than the other. The men greeted them in a friendly manner saying "god save you couple". The sailor returned the greeting before the two when overtook them and walked on.

Just before coming to the village the men ahead doubled back and came against them. As they approached the greeting was far from friendly this time around. The smaller of the two men took off his hat and pulled a stone from it. He angrily said "god blast you is that you" before striking the sailor on the temple with the stone. The sailor slipped from Catherine's arm and fell to the ground. She identified John Neil as the man who threw the stone that night and seemed sure of it. She had never before seen any of the three men before that night. When Connell was on the ground Catherine admitted she fled but later returned when she felt it was safe.

The defence lawyer Prof Butt proceeded to question the witness trying to drag her character down. At first she didn't seem to understand what he was trying to say when he asked about her modesty. He got straight to the point "on your oath are you a prostitute". The questions kept coming "are you a woman of the town" to which she clearly replied "I am not". He pressed her again saying "do you swear that positively" she replied "I do". Catherine explained her business in town that evening saying she was on an errant for her master who lived in Ballintubber.

The intentions of Prof Butt were quite obvious. If he could show Catherine to be disreputable then doubt could creep in of other plausible ways the sailor could have died. He was in no doubt that her evidence could be enough to see his client hang.

However the case for the prosecution continued and had several more witnesses to call. Next to take to the stand was Elizabeth Horgan whose testimony fitted with than of Catherine's as she had passed all four on the road that night. A little time afterwards she heard a scuffle between two or three men. Elizabeth said this was near the cross road to Bailick. As she looked back she clearly saw John Neil and another man run off down the new road to Bailick.

The driver of the Cloyne carriage Timothy Mahony described how he had come on the man lying on the road that night. It was one of the passengers who alerted him that there was a man on the road as he said he was going pretty quickly at the time. He stopped and with the assistance of a passenger lifted the sailor onto his carriage. He was still breathing at the time according to Mahony but was clearly unconscious. They took the sailor to a house in Ballinacurra to get help for him.

A local woman Mary Rohan from Ballinacurra was called to take the stand. She told that it was in her house that the sailor was brought in a bad way that night. He had black eyes and a cut to his temple. Mary stayed up tending to his injuries until after eleven that night and someone else than stayed with him during the night. She said it was not until eight or nine the next morning that he died. That morning the captain of the *Lydney Lass* arrived and identified the sailor as James Connell.

Instantly Prof Butt objected to the witness calling him James Connell. His argument was that it was secondary to the case and the captain himself was not present to identify the deceased. After much debate the prosecution relented allowing Butt's objection to be sustained saying "I think we have enough without it".

The prosecution was confident as they still had several more witnesses to call. They called John Twomey who was employer of the Neil for two years. Twomey recalled clearly that night saying Neil had gone to town to get his shoes mended but was home about half seven or eight. When Neil returned home he told his employer he had been to Fitzgerald's pub and had five pints of porter. Neil also told him that night he met his cousin McCarthy and encountered "a rogue of a sailor from England". Twomey had heard his servant had tried to take a pipe from the sailor's pocket and an altercation occurred between the pair in the pub. When asked by Butt to describe his servant Twomey said "he was fond of drink and did his work very well".

Finally Dr Barry described the injuries he found on the body of the deceased sailor. The wound he found on the left temple was small when compared to the larger fracture of the skull. Replying to a question the doctor said the whole left side of the skull was bashed in and nothing would have saved him. Death was as a result of an accumulation of blood on the brain. This concluded the evidence for the crown prosecution who felt they had a perfectly good case.

Prof Butt spoke for the defence but he didn't call a witness or give a long speech about his client. Instead he took an unusual course and asked the judge did he think the court had proved the name of the sailor. At first the judge didn't think much of it saying it was now too late to make that point. Butt however was not backing down and argued his right to question in great detail. He asked the Crown prosecution to elect which of the indictments they were going to charge his client with. The judge said this was going to leave the crown in a most embarrassing position.

Butt continued saying the evidence before them proved that John Connell was murdered and not James as detailed in the indictment. It caused great debate in court but Butt clearly had formed a plan and was sticking to it. The prosecution and the Judge argued that there was evidence of both names. However Butt argued only a boy said the name was James and he was not produced as a witness so therefore it was not evidence to go before the jury.

The judge went back over his notes of the whole case and seems to realise that Butt was right. He addressed the prosecution saying there was no evidence of James Connell being murdered. One of the prosecutors seeming desperate said "sure that the woman Rohan swore the captain called him James". Only to be reminded that they had allowed that statement to be excluded so it was no longer legal evidence.

The judge made it clear that they were not going to be allowed to go back and call the witness again. The judge told to the prosecution to proceed if they could but they were caught short and felt there was nothing to be done.

After more likely exchanges the judge began to address the jury. He told them they must acquit the accused on a point of law that it was not James in the evidence given. The jury began to leave the room to decide their verdict, it was clear the jury were not happy with the predicament they were left with. One juror spoke up to the judge saying the foreman did not agreed. The judge now was getting annoyed and gave a speech saying "you must not hang a man because you believe or know him to be guilty, it is the law that tries him, it is the law that hangs him if he be guilty".

The jury now left the room but shortly after another juror appeared back in court saying "the jury are of the opinion, that Mrs Rohan proved the deceased's name to be James". The judge again clarified that this evidence was now illegal. Three of jury now remained in court and obviously did not want to participate in finding the verdict.

The judge warned that they had better find a verdict or another jury would have to be found. One juror emerged saying we are all agreed except the foreman. The remaining three were not forced to join the others and a few minutes later they returned with the verdict.

Now even the foreman agreed but it was obvious he was not happy with the situation. At last the verdict was called out "not guilty". The prosecution asked that the prisoner not be released immediately and they agreed before moving on swiftly to the other cases. The prosecution must have felt that he had slipped through their fingers. They never thought for a second that the name was going to be such an issue. The evidence of Mrs Rohan could have been pressed further at the time or the boy called to court. Had they not been so confident in their case justice may have been carried out.

The port of Ballinacurra
Image courtesy of the National Library of Ireland

The Tailor of Ballyrobin.
Ballyrobin, Cloyne 1926

Edmund Donovan was born in the townland of Ballyduff south of Ballymaloe in February 1872. Records show he was baptised in Cloyne on the 11th of February. His father was Florence Donovan who was a farm labourer and later on a thatcher, his mother was Bessie Fennessy. The surname Fennessy was a common name around Ballymaloe at the time. Life was very tough back then, Bessie gave birth to fifteen children but only eight survived. As Florence was not well off, all the children had to go out and make their own way in the world. Edmund became a tailor and we presume apprenticed to another tailor in the locality.

In 1898 aged 25 he married a local woman from Churchtown South called Mary Roche and started a family. Edmund was living in Ballyrobin before getting married. Mary Roche was a dressmaker by trade and was well able to help his tailoring business. After marrying the couple lived in thatched cottage in the townland of Ballyrobin North near Churchtown South. How exactly Edmund acquired the cottage is not clear, he may have inherited it. Records show a William Donovan born in Ballyrobin in 1810; this could have been his grandfather.

The only land Donovan had was about an acre that went with his cottage. Two years after getting married Donovan took on eight acres from a local farmer to supplement his income. It was located opposite the tailor's cottage across the road in Ballyrobin North. The land was taken under what was then called the eleven month system now better known as conacre. The eleven month system was common and gave the tenant no legal right to the land. At the time the tailor was paying £4 a year rent.

By 1901 Edmund must have been doing quite well and had other tailors also residing with him. The census of 1901 shows that his brother-in-law Martin Roche residing in the same house and also working as a tailor. In addition he also employed at the time an apprentice tailor Patrick Leary who also lived in the house. To keep three tailors employed in such a rural area Donovan must have been good at his trade and was getting business from more than just his neighbours. He would have been travelling the locality to people in need of his services, making measurements and coming back when the suits were ready. It's known that he walked the cliff path to Ballycotton delivering suits. His payment was said to have been part money part salted fish. By this time Edmond had a very young family with three children less than 2 years of age.

Ten years later the census shows Edmonds family has grown to seven children aged between one and eleven years old. He now no longer has room to have other tailors residing there but he continues his trade as a tailor. Also living with them was his elderly father-in-law James Roche. Their eldest son Florence had died aged only eight in 1907.

Living nearby, the next house on the census was James Walsh. He was married only five years and had no children. He was obviously a reasonably well off farmer and could afford four farm servants all residing in the same house.

After a few years Mrs Kennefick a widow wished to sell part of her farm. So she needed to get Donovan out of the land he rented. She was said to offer him alternative land elsewhere. However Donovan wouldn't give up the field right across from his cottage for another which was offered. Sometime around this the tailor stopped paying the rent but remained in possession of the land. The acre plot on which the tailor's farm stood, was once part of Kennefick's farm. In 1846 as part of the outdoor relief work £50 was granted to build a road from Churchtown to Ballyrobin passing the graveyard. This new road in Ballyrobin North went through Kennefick's farm leaving an unusually shaped acre to the south of the new line. It was this plot that later came into the Donovan's possession. The field across the road that all the trouble was over was therefore once part of the same field the tailor lived on.

Things were about to change in 1916 when Mrs. Kennefick of Ballycatoo herself only a tenant farmer put up for sale her interest in a 52 acre farm, which included the eight acres Donovan had use of. The 52 acre farm was subject to £9 18s rent half yearly. An auction was held in early 1916 and the tailor was present at the auction. There was a great crowd said to be present that day taking a keen interest in the proceedings.

Among the many bidders and despite strong competition the farm was purchased by another local farmer James Walsh. Walsh had an agreement with another local farmer Smyth for part of the farm. Between them they paid £600 for the 52 acre farm which was equivalent to about 12 years wages for a normal worker at the time or several hundred thousand in today's money. The tailor did not protest at the auction or when his neighbour Walsh purchased the tenancy. By now the tailor's family had grown to nine children and this put added pressure on the family, the older ones could now begin the family trade. Sometime after the auction Donovan objected to the field being bought and tried to assert a right to the eight acres. This gave rise to a lot of trouble in the locality with people taking sides.

AUCTIONS

BALLYROBIN NORTH
CLOYNE, CO CORK.

EXCEPTIONALLY FINE FEE-SIMPLE FARM
FOR SALE BY AUCTION.

WM. G. WOOD & SONS

ARE favoured with instructions from the Owner (who is reducing her farming operations) to Sell by AUCTION, on TUESDAY, 1st FEB., 1916, the Valuable Interest in this Choice Farm, containing 52a 2r 18p very Prime Land, subject to the very Low Annuity of £19 16s 0d (£9 18s 0d Half-yearly).

The Holding is situate within 7 miles of Midleton, 3 from Cloyne, and ¼ mile from Churchtown, and will be found a very tempting investment, being easily worked, laid out in five level fields intersected by public road, and well fenced. It is noted for its heavy cropping qualities, and being close to the sea, sand and sea-weed can be had in abundance. Twelve acres highly-manured Tillage, 16 acres Stubble, remainder in Pasture, including 16 acres after first crop hay.

Annuity paid to last Gale Day.
Sale on the Lands at 12 o'Clock noon. Immediate possession.
Further particulars from
Messrs. PHILIP WILLIAM BASS and CO., Solicitors having Carriage of Sale, 9 South Mall, Cork; or

WM G. WOOD & SONS

AUCTIONEERS, VALUERS AND FARM SALE EXPERTS, 79 SOUTH MALL, CORK, BANDON AND SKIBBEREEN.

Notice of the farm sale in 1916, image with thanks to Irish Newspaper Archives and Irish Examiner

After buying the farm Walsh must have thought he would easily deal with the issue of the land Donovan was laying claim to, after all he was a justice of the peace and member of the Board of Guardians. Walsh was also an active member of the county council and prominent public figure in the area. Only two years before in 1914 he had been the Home rule candidate for the area and carried out an election campaign all over east Cork.

The tailor had a cow, a calf and a pony grazing in the field in question. When Walsh became the owner he was said to have turned the animals out of the field. One of the first signs of trouble in the area was in March of 1916 when a haggard belonging to John Smyth in nearby townland of Tullagh burned down. It occurred at four in the morning and was thought to have been caused maliciously. There were thirty eight tons of straw and forty tons of hay destroyed in the fire.

Trouble between Walsh and Donovan quickly escalated into disturbances in the area. A few months after the farm sale on the 16th of May 1916 both Donovan and Walsh were in court at Cloyne petty sessions. Walsh had summoned the tailor to court on three counts that his pigs had trespassed on Walsh's land. Donovan was fined £3 6s, bound to the peace and remanded on bail. The tailor refused to pay the fine and instead went to prison. On his way home from court Walsh must have felt he was getting somewhere. With the tailor in prison he would have to give in. However before he got home he met one of the tailor's sons who accosted him on the road and called Walsh a "grabber". He told Walsh "you think you have done a good days work today but you will pay for it and soon". The next morning two cows belonging to James Walsh were found with their hamstring tendons cut and completely immobilised. It was obvious who the suspects were and the next day Sergeant Grace from Cloyne carried out an investigation. All he found was a billhook at Donovan's house with blood on it. As no other evidence was found nor any witness it didn't go any further. One of the cows recovered and the other had to be killed. Later that year in November Walsh was awarded £37 10s in court as compensation paid for by the tax payers of the local electoral divisions. At that same court appearance Donovan appealed the earlier decision that his pigs had trespassed on Walsh's land. He claimed that it was only once and not three times and succeeded in getting the fine reduced from £3 6s to only 3s.

Eventually James Walsh who lived only a few hundred yards from Donovan became the sole owner of the farm after he bought Smyth's interest.

Sometime in March of 1918 James Walsh was driving a horse and cart home from Midleton with his wife when a shot was fired at them. Walsh reported it to Sergeant Grace in Cloyne and Donovan was subsequently arrested. The tailor was brought before the court in Midleton but later released. Some time before 1921 Donovan was again arrested for firing at James Walsh. At the trial he was freed because of lack of evidence that he had shot James Walsh in the mouth. By July of 1921 Donovan was arrested again and charged in Midleton with firing at Walsh with intent to kill. He was later released on bail and committed for trial. A trial was looming and Walsh was giving evidence that this time he saw Donovan fire at him at close range. Sometime after this the tailor proposed arbitration suggesting the Rev Lynch parish priest in Cloyne as arbitrator. Both parties signed an agreement to arbitration and promised to abide by the parish priest's decision. Lynch PP investigated the case and interviewed both parties. His decision was that Donovan had no right to any claim on the land but a Free State Land court may find otherwise. The tailor on hearing the finding refused to accept it and was said to have renewed his threats. In the presence of the parish priest Donovan told Walsh that "I fired at you and I am not sorry, but I am sorry I missed you and will try again".

In the 1920's there was a general slump in the tailoring trade in Ireland. Costs had risen in the last ten years and the price of a tailor made suit had doubled in that time. Also drapers were selling ready made suits much cheaper. Money was scarce and few could afford new clothes and less still the more expensive tailor made option. It was in this climate that Edmond Donovan had to raise a large family and this may have influenced him to continue what he believed he had to do. By now the tailor's family had grown to ten children, nine sons and one daughter.

The situation did not get any better, Walsh's cattle were maimed and difficulty was experienced in getting corn threshed. It was suspected that the tailor had threatened the owners of threshing machines not to thresh corn for certain farmers. Friends of James Walsh were also being boycotted which included the Manning's of Ballylanders. In 1922 in order to get the corn threshed the farmers appealed to the Free State troops in Midleton for help in the matter.

Again in April of 1923 Donovan was in court for threatening violence against James Walsh. He had not been called to court on the usual days but arrested on a warrant just 30 minutes before a special sitting of the court. The judge bound the accused Edmond Donovan to the peace on a surety of £50. The money was forthcoming and the tailor was released.

In September of 1923 straw and hay belonging to William Smyth who now resided near Castlemartyr was burned. This was presumed to have been malicious and connected with the boycotting of threshing machines. Previously a man named Daniel McCarthy from nearby Ballymacandrick had threshed for James Walsh who was at the centre of the feud. Some time after Donovan received £50 from McCarthy so he would be free to thresh for who ever he wanted. Fifty pounds was a significant amount of money at that time when the average labourer's wages was 16 shillings a week.

The feud continued on for several more years, Donovan was again in court and this time was bound to the peace. He refused to be bound to the peace and said he would be tormented by Walsh. So instead he was sentenced with one month in jail and when he returned home after the situation didn't get any better. He again sent out more threatening letters warning others not to thresh for Walsh and his friends Higgins and Manning.

The tailor's family had started to move out of home but Ireland in the 1920's didn't offer many opportunities. One of the first to leave was John despite not being the eldest. He immigrated to America in September of 1924 moving to Hartford Connecticut and becoming a tinsmith. He gave his occupation as tailor at the time of emigration showing he had worked with his father until then. Just over two years later his older brother James joined him in the states arriving in mid September.

On the 18th September 1926 a few days after James had left Ireland, Sergeant Shore who had only been stationed in Ballycotton a few weeks arrested Michael Manning. Sergeant Shore had received a report that Manning had fired a shotgun into the house of O'Keeffe. Manning was marched to the barrack in Ballycotton late at night but refused to make

The tailor's sons who all emigrated to America

a statement. Sergeant Shore locked him in a cell for a few hours and tried several times to get a statement from him. In the early hours of the morning at 5 am he released Manning on lack of evidence. Despite only being stationed in Ballycotton since the previous June Sergeant Shore knew of Manning, Donovan and Walsh because of all the hassle going on. On numerous occasions that summer he had been to the area following reports of trouble.

Later on the 27th of September 1926 friends of James Walsh, the Manning's from Ballylanders, approached a man named Charles Power from Midleton to contract his threshing machine. Power gave them an evasive answer saying he would let him know later as he knew the situation only too well. The next day while threshing in a nearby farm Power received a threatening letter. It stated "don't thresh for Manning or you will be boycotted too quick". The letter was shown to the Manning's and we can only guess that this exacerbated the situation further.

On Sunday the 3rd of October Edmond Donovan went to 9:30 am mass at Churchtown and from there he travelled to Ballinrostig and Whitegate. After that he went to Cloyne to see a hurling match between Aghada and Ballinacurra. When he wasn't home for his dinner his wife wasn't worried as he often journeyed around on Sundays getting orders for his tailoring business. But this day she was worried as earlier while feeding a calf at the back of the house she had been fired on. At 7:30pm his wife went out as it was getting dusk and she saw some men near the house only a few yards away. When she went out they went around the back of the house, she unleashed the dogs. At the same time their daughter Mary had passed her father at Ballyonane hill 2 miles from home, he had a puncture and was pushing his bike. Mary arrived home first and this must have reassured the tailor's wife who had now become worried for his safety.

When the tailor arrived home he told his wife he was being watched. He went into the house and told her he had bought a cow. At the time some of the children were playing cards in the kitchen with Daniel Cronin, Matt Brady and a man named Fitzgerald. She went out to close the front door and saw three men out on the road. Two of the men she didn't know, but one she recognised as Michael Manning who she later described as wearing a grey cap and a grey coat. A few minutes after Donovan asked his wife to come out to the gate to talk about the cow and not disturb the card playing. No sooner had they stepped through the wicket gate and taken a few steps towards Churchtown when a shot was fired. The first shot hit its intended target and her husband yelled out in agony. She held him by the arm when another shot was fired he again screeched out and this time fell to the ground. The children who had been inside ran out to the door when another shot was fired. Mrs. Donovan ran inside to encourage the children in but came back out again straight away. She later said "I did not care whether I was shot or not, I went out to see if he was dead or alive". The shots had been fired from behind a hedge across the road, she saw men jumping over the ditch and making their escape into Walsh's land not 5-6 yards away. Again she didn't know who two of them were but for a second time saw Michael Manning.

The tailor was bleeding very badly and lying in a pool of blood but was still alive. With the help of some of her children she pulled her husband into the kitchen. His injuries were such that he died in a few minutes.

While the poor man was lying dying in his kitchen not 200 yards away in James Walsh's, a dance was going on. Many of the young people of the locality had been invited to the "party". Walsh had never before been known to hold such a dance in his house.

Donovan still had six of his children living with him in the house. William aged twenty, Martin nineteen, Mary eighteen, Michael sixteen, Philip twelve and Pat aged only ten. The three older boys James, Edmund and John had moved out at this stage. Surprisingly the tailor's parents Florence and Eliza were still living near Ballymaloe both in their early eighties.

One of the tailor's sons Michael cycled to Cloyne get a doctor. He also informed the authorities that his father had been shot and had been wounded on the face and head. Around quarter past nine Dr Murphy dispensary doctor in Cloyne arrived at Donovan's cottage. By the time they arrived on the scene the tailor had died from his terrible shot wounds. The doctor made an examination of the body and found the right side of his face and neck covered with shotgun pellet puncture wounds.

At about quarter past ten the guards arrived and so did Superintendent Dineen. When the Superintendent went to the neighbouring house of James Walsh he found dancing to be still going on.

The tailor's wife must have told Superintendent Dineen she had seen Michael Manning on the road before the shooting and he became the obvious suspect. The Superintendent proceeded to Manning's house in Ballylanders accompanied by sergeant Shore and arrived there before eleven. The house was in darkness and Manning appeared to be in bed. When he emerged they informed him Donovan had been shot and he was expected to account for his movements that evening. They questioned Manning who refused to make a statement replying "I won't answer any questions or make any statement". They searched the house and in the kitchen found empty cartridge cases. An armed detective was sent to Manning's house in Ballylanders and remained there throughout the night. A few hours later, in the early hours of the morning of the 4th October Superintendent Dineen with Chief Supt Brennan took the accused Michael Manning to the scene of the crime where Edmond Donovan was still lying dead. The accused kept his cap on in the presence of the dead man and the superintendent asked him "have you any sympathy for the dead?" Manning replied "no I have not he never had any sympathy for me". He asked Manning was there any reason he would have been shot and the accused replied "there were often many men better than him shot". Manning was taken into custody and held in Midleton barracks for several days.

The investigation was directed by Chief Supt Brennan from Cork and Supt Dineen from Midleton. A large number of guards swarmed the area making enquiries about the murder. Twelve men were arrested and all but Michael Manning were released. The same day an inquest was opened at Churchtown. The deceased was identified by his twenty year old son Martin Donovan. The inquest was adjourned for two weeks to allow for evidence to be collected.

The evening following the murder Dr William O'Riordan from Ballycotton accompanied by Dr Murphy from Cloyne conducted a post mortem examination. Lead pellets had punctured through the victim's skull and also shattered his jaw bone. The gunshot injuries to his neck had lacerated the jugular veins and carotid artery. The examination found he had died from haemorrhage of the gunshots wounds that totalled seventy.

The searching of the area for the murder weapon continued for days. Teams of Gardaí cut furze and ditches searching for clues, bloodhounds were also used to assist the search. On the 7th of October on Michael Manning's farm the stock of a single barrel shotgun was found. Sergeant Mc Quaide found the barrel of a shotgun in a neighbouring haggard near the graveyard. The barrel was hidden in a rick of straw along with two live shotgun cartridges.

Despite the large scale investigation the Gardaí failed to identify the three men who were in the field across from the tailor's house that night. The wife identified one as Manning but didn't know who the other two were. Manning never admitted to being there and gave nothing away. The guards had their own ideas who the other two were but had absolutely nothing to go on. One suspect was a complete outsider who worked as a labourer for a local farmer. The Gardaí watched him round the clock for weeks but never witnessed him put a foot wrong. They were even said to have watched him working in the fields for days on end hoping he would do something.

During the investigation a surveyor from Youghal was employed to measure the distance between the house of the accused and Donovan's. This was measured to be 1908 yards and walked by the Gardaí to prove the timing of the crime. It took the sergeants 14 minutes to walk from Manning's house to Donovan's. Sergeant Harney from Cloyne walked from Ed Roche's house to Donovan's a distance of over 600 yards it only took five minutes to walk.

The Friday following the murder, Manning was still held in Midleton without being charged. He requested a solicitor and that evening the 8th

**The graveyard in Churchtown, the barrel of a shotgun
was found nearby. This was on the route between Manning's
and the tailor's house**

October he was charged with murder before a peace commissioner. On the 30th October Michael Manning was charged at a special sitting of Midleton court. The charges against him were *that on the 3rd October at Ballyrobin he did feloniously, wilfully and with malice aforethought kill and murder one Edmond Donovan.*

The court went on for weeks into December and several witnesses were called to give evidence. Mr D Casey state solicitor was for the prosecution while Mr J Ronayne defended the accused Michael Manning. Each day the accused was driven from Cork jail to court in Midleton and returned to jail every evening. Many people of the locality were called as witnesses to recount the evening of the murder. Charles Terry of Ballymacotter gave evidence that on the night of the murder he was waiting at Flynn's cross for his brother and sisters to return from Churchtown between seven and half past. During this time the accused passed by with Thomas McGrath coming from Churchtown heading towards Ballylanders. At half seven his siblings returned with John Ivers, William and Thomas Higgins and all proceeded to Michael Higgins house nearby. After delaying on the road the group went on to Michael Higgins house passing Donovan's seeing

EAST CORK MURDER.

...shows the scene of the crime which was enacted on last Sunday night, when Edmond Donovan (tailor), aged 55, was shot dead. The spot marked X shows where the victim met his doom.

This small picture was in the Cork Examiner the Saturday after, image with thanks to Irish Newspaper Archives and Cork Examiner

nothing unusual. They walked to James Walsh's where the dance was held arriving there around eight. In the house at the dance when they arrived was James Walsh and his wife, John Hyde a labourer of Walsh's, Michael Higgins, Walsh's brother-in-law and a Mr. Moore from Midleton.

Later in court Thomas McGrath of Ballyandreen gave evidence that he walked home with Manning that evening. They parted company at Ballylanders cross but he was unsure of the time, it could have been between half seven and quarter to eight.

More evidence was given that the accused played cards in Edmond Roche's house in Churchtown; he left there about seven and returned again about nine. The accused when he returned to Roche's house was alone.

James Prendergast a farm labourer from Ballycatoo also gave evidence. He stated on the night in question 3rd of October he played cards in Ed Roche's house in Churchtown. When he got there Jeremiah Cronin, Denis Hassett, Edward Motherway, David Kennefick and Daniel McGuire were present. Prendergast arrived around eight and they continued until about nine. As the game broke up and he left the accused Michael Manning entered Roche's house alone.

In court the widow of the deceased was cross examined for over 3 hours on one occasion. She admitted to the long standing dispute with James Walsh and also knew her husband had sent threatening letters. She said she didn't try to stop him and had not interfered with him in the matter. She also said she was bitter towards her neighbours the Walsh's and his friends. Her husband she said stood alone and had no backers. She went on to say "there was no one who would do anything for him" but Walsh had friends who backed him.

By the 10th of December, the hearing was coming to an end the last three of 33 witnesses were called before the court. Mr Ronayne for the defence stated that the whole case hung on the evidence of the widow which he stated was "not worthy of belief". He claimed the widow's times were incorrect and claimed it happened later. He also called in to question the evidence of the people in Donovan's house that evening and cast doubts as to why the third man Fitzgerald did not give evidence.

The case did indeed hang on the timing of the murder, Manning was seen around half seven and not seen again until nine except by the widow outside her door after the shooting. There is no record of what the accused did between these times and whether he gave any statement of what he did or who he was with. The prosecution had achieved its objection of

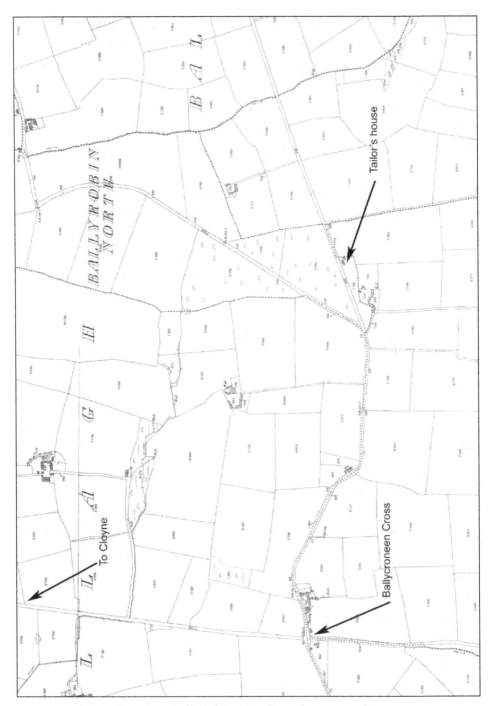

Map showing Ballyrobin North and surrounding area

proving a prima facie case, which meant it was accepted as correct until proved otherwise.

Despite this in December the District Court in Midleton returned the case for trial to the Central Criminal Court in Dublin. The case was sent for trial in the Dublin Central Court in 1927. By the end of February 1927 the Attorney General entered a nolle prosequi which means will no longer prosecute. Michael Manning was released from custody afterwards.

In May of the same year Manning took a case against Supt Dineen in Cork Circuit Court. He alleged wrongful imprisonment by Supt Dineen between 4th October and 9th October until he was charged. He sought damages of £300 for being held against the law. However it was shown that Dineen had reasonable grounds and suspicion to arrest Manning. By refusing to give a statement he had given Dineen further suspicion. It was also found by the jury that the arrest was not unlawful. The farmer's case for damages failed.

The dispute in Ballyrobin still didn't come to an end but continued for some time. Threatening letters were still being sent to people in the neighbourhood.

In March 1927 Mary Higgins a sister-in-law of James Walsh was arrested on the charge of sending threatening letters. She was charged with sending several letter's to farmers in the area. She was said to have written to James Hoare of Tullagh and Peter Hegarty of Ballinvoher demanding the dismissal of James O'Flynn, John Brady and his son William Brady who they employed. They ended with "this is no idle threat. Don't get into trouble when you can avoid it". This seemed to be linked to the murder case as both Brady and O'Flynn had given evidence against Manning.

Later in the month of June on the 30th a sudden fire broke out in the yard of Michael Higgins, Mary Higgins brother. The fire caused damages of several hundred pounds. Injured by smoke from the fire was a valuable roan filly that was exhibited shortly before at the Midleton Show.

In Midleton District court early in July the case against Mary Higgins was heard, again Mr J Ronayne defended for the accused. Samples of hand writing had been obtained and compared to the letters in question. A handwriting expert was called who stated that the writing was similar to that of the accused but could not swear in court it was written by the same person. In just a few days the judge thought the case should be investigated further by a jury and returned for trial to the next Cork Circuit Court. In October almost exactly a year after the tailor was shot, Mary was in court pleading not guilty to the charges. Again samples of handwriting were examined and compared before the jury. After seeing the evidence the jury found her guilty but pleaded for mercy. Hearing this, the judge decided to reduce her jail sentence from six months to three.

The story of the tailor continued to be talked about for many years throughout the neighbourhood and many versions of the story have been told. Some people say that Manning shot him alright and walked home the road that night in plain sight of anyone to see. The murder weapon was carried away by somebody else.

Others claim to know more and say Manning wasn't even there that night. This was despite the tailor's wife saying on two occasions she saw him on the road. Manning was rumoured to be meeting a woman that night somewhere else while the party was on. The reason for him being the chief suspect was the feud between him and the tailor had been particularly bitter. He had also in the past on more than one occasion threatened to kill the tailor

It's claimed by some the man who shot the tailor was a well known republican marksman from Midleton who had gained experience during the troubles. However nobody had seen him there or at least nobody was willing to say they had. Some reckon he was the man who fired the shot but nothing was surer if you wanted it done he wasn't going to miss.

Over the years both sides had become so entrenched that neither was going to give the other an inch but what the tailor didn't realise was it was going to cost him his life.

Christmas Tragedy
Kilva, near Cloyne 1843

We expect Christmas to be a peaceful and joyous time of the year when even the bad people in the world behave for a day. Anyone of us with this naive view would have been even more shocked in Cloyne on Christmas day 1843.

Early on Christmas morning Ellen Fitzgerald walked from her place of employment to Cloyne to spend the day with her friends and family. Ellen was originally from Cloyne where her father was a butcher. She worked as a domestic servant for an officer who lived some distance away. She was approaching the village of Cloyne on the road from Midleton when she must have been set upon. Ellen's body was found dead thrown at the side of the road. It was immediately known foul play was involved as her face had been beaten and seriously disfigured. Her body was covered in mud and whoever killed her had pulled off some of her clothes. The exposed body also bore the marks of the violence that killed her.

The chief suspects were some sailors who had been seen about the town the previous evening. As one could imagine, this caused quite a stir in the area and locals were on the look out for strangers that stood out in the area.

Within days local man Michael Cashman was arrested for the murder, he was actually a cousin of Ellen's. He was normally employed as a foot runner to convey the bags of mail between Midleton and Cloyne. The police searched his house and found a handkerchief with marks of blood on it.

An inquest was held by Coroner Geran in Cloyne on the 4th and 5th of January.

The details of the inquest are unknown but the verdict of the jury was reported.

"We find that on the morning of the 25th December last, at Knocknamaderee in the county of Cork Ellen Fitzgerald was found exposed and dead, with certain contusions of the body. The jury do unanimously

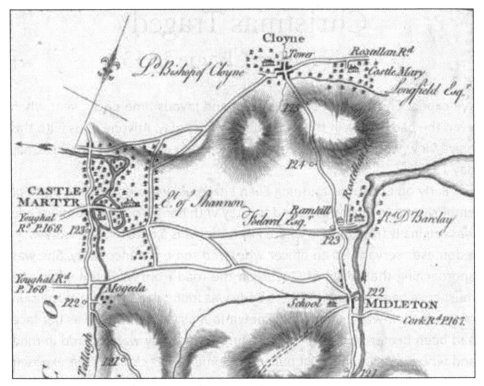

Map showing the road from Cloyne to Midleton from Taylor and Skinner road maps of Ireland 1777

find that Michael Cashman postman of Cloyne was accessory to the death of said Ellen Fitzgerald".

By March with the Cork Spring Assizes looming Michael Cashman was still in custody awaiting trial by jury. However there is no record of the case being heard at the Assizes this year.

It was the Cork Spring Assizes in 1845 before the case came before judge and jury. 15 months after the crime had taken place. Cashman was charged with the wilful murder of Ellen Fitzgerald on the night of 24th December 1843. As the evidence was mostly circumstantial it was not going to be easy for the jury to decide.

As was normal the prosecution opened by giving a brief outline of the case and calling witnesses to support it. Wife of Midleton postmaster Mrs Brabazon was called as she had encountered both Cashman and Ellen on Christmas Eve. The witness clearly recollected that evening saying a woman was with Cashman before he set off for Cloyne. She was crying in the post office, she heard her son ask why the woman was crying. The reply from Cashman was "she is in dread to come home with me tonight and sure she need not". The pair left the post office at eight heading for Cloyne. Mrs Brabazon did not see Cashman again until seven the next morning. Clearly, there was no day off for Christmas and post still had to be delivered. He came back again that Christmas day at four in the afternoon with more mail. This time she asked why he had left his cousin on the road the night before. His reply was "damn her, she got drunk and weak on the road and I had to leave her behind". Mrs Brabazon was quite clear though that she could not identify the woman crying in the post office as Ellen Fitzgerald, as she had not seen her face or heard her name called. At the inquest though, she identified a torn bonnet as being the one worn by Ellen that night.

When questioned by the defence, the woman explained how Cashman had to be regular delivering the mail. He was allowed one hour and ten minutes to go from Midleton to Cloyne and had been doing the job well for the last three years. The postmaster Joseph Brabazon gave a similar account to what his wife had provided.

As the case went on the prosecution tried to build a case and convince the jury that Cashman had indeed killed his cousin. As nobody had seen the murder carried out many witnesses were called giving mostly circumstantial evidence.

A publican from Ballinacurra John Neil described Cashman being in his premises on Christmas Eve. He served him a half glass of whiskey and said Ellen drank most of it. The publican however found it curious that Cashman returned to his pub two days later St Stephen's night. This time Cashman asked the publican not to mention he had been there on Christmas Eve.

The prosecution called a Ballinacurra man David Coleman to take the stand.

David could clearly recall seeing Cashman go into Fenton's pub in the village on Christmas Eve. While he was in the pub a woman was waiting outside the pub door. A little later he saw the pair on the road heading towards Cloyne. Coleman could hear them talking and the woman was reluctant to go on saying she would go back to Midleton.

The man insisted saying "come along" but she said no for a second time. He heard the man cursing at her saying he would take her life if she didn't go on. He had a hold of her and dragged her on up the road to Cloyne. The witness explained how he now followed the pair to see if the man was going to injure her. Further on the road he lost sight of them but in the distance heard the screams of a woman's voice.

By far the best witness the prosecution had was Patrick Carroll who encountered them on the road to Cloyne that night. Patrick was near Bowles Gate on the road about nine that night when he heard a woman cry out "I won't allow it, I will tell mister in the morning". He stopped to hear what was going on and heard a man and woman arguing. The man accused her of being drunk but she said she was not. Next Patrick met Cashman on the road walking towards Cloyne. After passing him he came on a woman lying on the flat of her back at the side of the road. She struggled to get up and said she would remain there until the morning. Patrick called Cashman back and told him off for letting the woman at the side of the road. Cashman returned to her and helped her up off the road. That was the last he saw of the pair as they went on to Cloyne and Carroll said he headed towards Ballinacurra.

Several members of the Heney family were present in court as they had met Cashman at their farm in Knocknamaderee near Cloyne that night. Ellen Heney saw Cashman at their door that night; he called for a candle to light his pipe. Her father was out at the time but it struck Ellen that Cashman's clothes had blood and dirt on them.

Ellen said that Cashman later called when her father had returned. She heard her father say to him "Mick I thought that you had gone down before to Cloyne". Cashman told her father that he had delivered the post but had left the woman on the road. As he couldn't wait he told her to go back to Kennedy's house where he now went to fetch her. Ellen said that Cashman's reason for calling a second time was to get a candle as the night was dark.

Ellen Heney's father Jeremiah was called as a witness and corroborated his daughter's account. Jeremiah told how Cashman returned to his house on Christmas Day. The post boy told him how the woman was found dead on the road exactly where he had left her the night before. That day

Cashman also remarked how he would be obliged if he would not mention him being there the night before.

Another member of the Heney family Mary came forward to give evidence. The accused said to her "my soul upon your soul, don't hang me by telling I called at your house for a bit of candle last night". She met him again on the road on St Stephen's day and again he asked her not to say a word about him. A third time she met him he said "do you put up your little girl not to be mentioning my name".

Sarah Collins postmistress for Cloyne told the court how Cashman arrived at half past nine that Christmas Eve, twenty minutes late. She recalled his clothes being covered in mud and she remarked to him "Cashman you're late". He however had the excuse that he had fallen on the road which seemed to account for both his clothes and lateness.

Anne Terry who lived at Kilva Cloyne told how she was up before sunrise on Christmas morning 1843. On the road near her house she came upon woman lying there. Anne's first reaction was to run to wake some neighbours who found the woman to be dead. They informed the police in Cloyne.

Daniel Browne a police constable in Cloyne recalled seeing the body on the road that Christmas morning. The teeth were loose and she had several cuts to her head. Brown told how after arresting the accused man he searched his house and found a handkerchief under the bed with spots of blood on it. He produced it in court but the judge examining it said he could see no blood on it.

Doctor Robert Travers examined the body of the woman on the night of the 28th December 1843. He found closed injuries with bruises on several places of her head. The largest wound was in the centre of the forehead. There were also similar injuries to each temple and one at the rear but the skull was not fractured. All her teeth on the lower jaw were stove in but the remainder of the body had very little marks of violence.

In his opinion death was as a result of concussion on the brain as a result of the large injury on the forehead.

When the prosecution had rested, Solicitor O'Hea spoke for the defence. He had no witnesses to call, nor anyone to give an alibi for his client. Instead the solicitor gave a long speech comparing the case to similar ones in the past. He said Cashman was a man of good, honest, upright and impeachable character. He asked what motive had he to do it saying men of good character needed a good motive to do such a thing. Would this man now desert his good character and do such a thing out of impulse. He argued that in a case such as this, with only circumstantial evidence a man's good character should affect the case greatly. O'Hea proceeded to pick over the case finding fault in the evidence given where he could.

Finally the judge charged the jury and sent them out to arrive at a verdict. It took them well over an hour before they returned with their decision. The foreman came back and read out their verdict of not guilty. Michael Cashman was discharged and the court finished for the day.

What really happened on the road to Cloyne that Christmas Eve? Did Cashman actually go back for his cousin afterwards or not? The prosecution was very restricted in this case as they could not put the accused under oath and question him. This was seen at that time as forcing the case and would not be allowed for another fifty years.

Had the prosecution the ability to question Cashman, some of the serious doubts may have been cleared up, although he still may have been found not guilty.

Don't take a lift from strangers
Between Midleton and Carrigtwohill 1833

Transport in Cork in 1833 was not easy by any means. It would be another decade before rail transport reached the city and horse drawn carriage was the most popular method of travel. Charles Bianconi was the founder of Irish public transport and his coaches connected many towns. However many relied on private operators known as car men, they earned their living with a horse and carriage. The word car back then had a different meaning than today and was used to describe the carriage.

It was in this setting on the 17th January of 1833 that Edmund Cotter had arranged a car to take him home. Sometime in the afternoon, strolling across Patrick's Bridge he met twenty one year old Thomas Cashman who he already knew. Cashman was a car man who plied his trade between Cork and Midleton. He was feeding his horse but told Edmund he would take him home for nothing. Before setting off for home the two men went to a nearby public house and drank a half gallon of porter.

It was there that they met Ellen Leary who was heading for Midleton. Ellen drank two glasses of porter with the men before leaving as it was growing dusk after four. It was dark when the three arrived at the village known then as New Glanmire, now called Glounthaune. It was between five and six pm and Ellen had been complaining how slow the horse was. She said it was getting late and forced Thomas to drive the horse faster. As late as it was they still stopped in the village and went to Ahern's public house. Here they had another drink or two and Cashman asked Edmund to go on with them to Carrigtwohill. Edmund however said he wasn't going home that night and had some work to do in Glounthaune.

The pair left Ahern's and headed on towards Carrigtwohill which was only about three and a half miles away. It was sometime between eight and nine when they stopped in Carrigtwohill for more refreshments. There they met a servant called Irwin who was looking to go to Midleton. After Irwin bought Cashman two pints they again left for Midleton. By now they were nearly four hours after leaving Cork having travelled less than 10

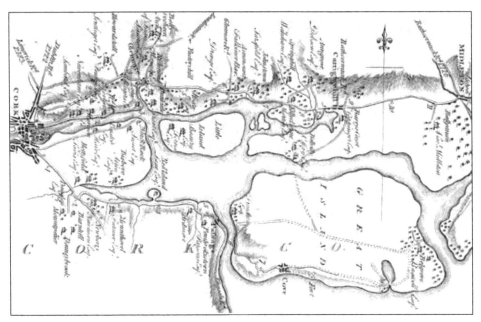

Map showing the road from Cork to Midleton at the time from Taylor and Skinner road maps of Ireland 1777

miles. It was a far cry from the journey by car today which would take less than 15 minutes.

When they were about half way between Carrigtwohill and Midleton, Ellen was only about a mile from home. Ellen enquired what Cashman was doing turning off the main road and he replied "you know". It was then that Irwin jumped off and said he would walk away before them.

Nothing was heard from them again and nobody could say what happened next. It was later that night about ten when Cashman turned up at Ellen Leary's house. He had with him in the carriage Ellen's body. He told her sister that Ellen had only fainted and taken a fall from the carriage. You would think he would clear off as fast as he could but he didn't and stayed there half the night. He must have believed it himself that she was still alive or his guilt would have been hard to disguise. It's impossible to imagine him being there with the grieving family when they discovered she was dead. There were several marks on her body that pointed towards a violent death but this must not have been discovered at the time.

The inquest was held in Midleton on January the 26th and by now Thomas Cashman had been arrested. During the proceedings the deceased

Ellen Leary was described as a good looking unmarried woman of thirty five years of age.

Evidence was given that Ellen had died from strangulation and there were also signs of a struggle. It was clear from the marks on her neck and bruises on her body that she had indeed suffered a violent death. After hearing from several witnesses the jury came to their verdict. They found Ellen Leary had died while in the company of Cashman, who was since in custody. The jury also found she had been strangled after she had been raped. The accused Thomas Cashman was held in custody until a trial before a jury.

The case came before Judge Jebb at Cork Courthouse on Thursday the 21st of March 1833 with a jury of twelve men. Before the case was called there were two separate cases of stealing a mare and a sheep. Both cases were dealt with swiftly and sentenced to be transported for life for such petty crimes.

Thomas Cashman was called and charged with the much more serious crimes of rape and murder. He must have been well aware of the severe sentence he would receive if he was found guilty.

Medical evidence was given by Dr Joseph Barry who had examined the woman's body the morning after her death. He had found marks all over her legs and thighs which indicated violence. There was a mark all round her neck showing how she had been strangled by someone. He concluded by saying "her person bore the marks of recent violation"

A publican named Joseph Nagle told how the pair had entered his pub between eight and nine that night. He clearly recalled how Ellen sat on a stool by the fire while Cashman sat on a chair nearby. Shortly after Irwin came in enquiring about going to Midleton. The publican said Irwin bought two pints for Thomas Cashman before going outside with Ellen. He thought that Ellen had some drink taken but said she wasn't too bad and would have been able to walk home.

The publican's wife Elizabeth was also called to the stand. She told how Ellen had bought a penny worth of whiskey earlier in the day. Neither did she think Ellen was drunk but merely jolly.

Edward Irwin who was one of the last to see Ellen alive was next questioned. He recollected entering Nagle's pub that night and said it was Joseph Nagle who referred him to Cashman when he enquired about going to Midleton. He recalled buying two pints of porter but said he and Cashman drank one each before setting off.

When they turned into the boreen a mile before Midleton Cashman told him he needed to go to a house. He suggested if Irwin walked on he would pick him up again on the road. Not suspecting anything being amiss Irwin said he walked away thinking they would be along the road again shortly.

Another witness Thomas Keeffe told how Cashman had come to his house about ten the night of the murder. He asked for a drink of water saying it was for Ellen Leary who was drunk. Keeffe told the court that when he went out he saw Cashman shake the woman but when he let her go she fell down again.

Cecilia Geary also said that Cashman came to her house that night. He told her Ellen Leary was ill and wanted her to light a fire to warm her up. Geary however didn't get involved and told him to take her home.

When the prosecution had called all its witnesses the defence called publican James Byrne. He claimed that Ellen Leary had bought whiskey in his pub in Carrigtwohill on the morning of the 17th January and also in the evening.

The defence called several more witnesses who gave accounts of Cashman's good character.

After hearing all the evidence the jury still didn't know what had happened from the time Irwin had left to the time Cashman turned up with her dead body. Nobody had come forward with information so circumstantial evidence was all they had to go on. Cashman as the accused would not have been allowed to give his own account in court. The jury had to decide if it was reasonable to think that as the last person seen with her he had killed her.

The judge charged the jury and gave his own opinion of the case.

He said "I think that the homicide was committed by him, not with the design of concealing the act but in a struggle with her while endeavouring to defend herself and prevent the violation of her person". The judge didn't leave much for the jury to question and finished by saying "homicide unintentionally by a person in the perpetration of a felonious crime, which rape is, is murder". Afterwards the jury retired for fifteen minutes and returned with the verdict guilty of murder.

The judge put on his black cap and all in court knew what it signified. He addressed Cashman and explained he had been found guilty of two of the worst crimes possible. He told him "you have but a short time to remain here. Before two days are elapsed you will be numbered with the dead". The judge implored him not to waste what little time he had left getting the sentence changed as it wasn't going to happen. He explained that the law must take its course and "a dreadful example must be made in order that men may not indulge their passions". Before then the death sentence was often passed for lesser crimes but by the 1830's it was reserved for very serious crimes. For some crimes judges passed the death sentence and afterwards changed to transportation but not for the capital crime of murder.

The judge concluded by saying "the sentence of the court is that you Thomas Cashman be taken from the place where you now stand to the gaol and thence to the place of execution , and that you there be hanged by the neck until you are dead and may the lord have mercy on your soul." Hearing the sentence Cashman was said to have been shocked but was immediately taken from the dock.

And so it was as the judge said, two days later on the Saturday morning Cashman was taken out in front of the County gaol to face his punishment. Back then there was obviously no opportunity for an appeal nor any hope of the sentence being changed.

At the last minute he called for the sheriff and told him he had neither murdered her nor intended to murder her. He said that he had fallen victim to his passion and was guilty of violating her but claimed she had initially consented. According to him she changed her mind and resisted his intentions. In her struggle trying to get away the string of her cloak got round her neck and she was strangled. There was no way to verify this story and there is no other record of Cashman giving a statement until then. In those days the justice system was harsh by modern standards, as the judge had said to prevent others from doing similar crimes.

Cork County Gaol where Thomas Cashman was executed

No matter what he said, it wasn't going to change anything at this point. He was led to the scaffold and the noose was put round his neck. Executions were then held in public and a large crowd would have gathered to see the hanging.

Let go of the net
or we will pop you
Carrigaloe, Cobh 1911

On the night of Tuesday 16th of May 1911, Patrick Murphy set out from the Passage side of the river for a night's salmon fishing with three others. He was a fifty year old fisherman living in Tooreen near Monkstown. Patrick had been a fisherman all his life and had for many years been taking out a licence to fish salmon on his boat. The licence number 33 was painted on the boat but he actually had two boats numbered 33. One was only used at a time if one required maintenance, he fished the other. That year however he had not taken out a licence to fish salmon. This wasn't unusual, most likely not having the money for the licence. Many would be allowed to fish by the bailiffs, knowing the licence would be got later when they had earned enough to pay for it.

That night he was joined by his cousin William Murphy, George King and Michael Walsh. The boat rowed across the river and anchored their net close to the shore on the Carrigaloe side. The men beached the boat about half eleven and waited for salmon to strike the net. After nearly two hours the shadow of a boat was seen approaching in the moonlight. It had five men aboard it and came from the direction of Cork.

The fishermen watched as the boat went to the end of their net and started to take it on board. They rowed towards the outer end of the net and called out to the men taking it. The answer they received back was "bailiffs". The fishermen began to haul in the net to prevent the bailiffs getting it. Meanwhile the bailiffs were also hauling in the net from the shore side. With both boats hauling as quickly as they could they rapidly grew closer toward the middle of the net. However the boats never came in contact with each other and were always a boats length apart. The fishermen were unarmed except for a few oars.

The general area today looking in the direction from which the bailiffs approached

When they were about fifty feet or two boats length apart the bailiffs called out, "let go of the nets or we will pop you, you sons of bitches". The bailiffs were heard saying amongst themselves "get ready the revolvers and pop them". Without another warning a shot was fired but it passed over the fisherman's heads. They scrambled to let go of the net but it had become snagged on the boat. Seconds later two more shots were heard in quick succession. Patrick Murphy who had been leaning over the side trying to free the net cried out "Michael I'm shot" and fell against the gunwale. The fishermen let the net free and frantically rowed away towards home.

The shots had also been heard on the other side of the river and when the fishermen reached the shore there were people there waiting. Amongst them was the local police constable Casey. Seeing Patrick Murphy lying in the bottom of the boat it was obvious to them what had occurred. The injured man was helped out of the boat and taken home to be looked after. He was still bleeding badly and was very weak. Constable Casey sent word for the local doctor and the priest.

The bailiffs soon realised that they had shot one of the fishermen. They kept hauling the net and took it all on board and went back towards Cork. They saw two more boats coming towards them and fearing it was more fishermen out to get revenge they turned about. The bailiffs landed at Monkstown where one of them called Bulman got out and reported the occurrence to the police. Afterwards the boat rowed to Cobh where statements were given to the police there. The head constable cautioned both the men who carried revolvers in the early hours of the morning but was unsure what course of action to take and so didn't arrest them. The bailiffs returned to Cork under a police escort still fearing revenge from the local fishermen.

Later that day Patrick Murphy was taken to the Cork District Hospital where his condition was described as critical. It was realised that the third shot fired that night had hit him in the lungs. The shot hit on the left side went through the lungs and chest exiting under his right arm pit. After a few days he had improved a little but was still in a very bad way.

Meanwhile both the bailiffs who carried revolvers that night, William Bulman and William O Neill were arrested. They were charged before magistrate in Cobh and remanded in custody to the county jail on the 19th.

On the evening of the 26th Patrick Murphy died in hospital and his death was recorded as septic pneumonia caused by the gunshot in the lungs.

An inquest was held in Cork on Monday the 29th of May by Coroner J Horgan before a jury of fourteen men. Both Bulman and O'Neill were in custody at the time and didn't want to attend the inquest. The bailiffs were not represented legally at the inquest while Coroner Murphy stood for the deceased.

Detailed medical evidence was given by several doctors about the injuries Murphy sustained from the bullet wound. One told how the bullet entered between the ribs passed through both lungs and exited the body.

It also emerged in court that before he died Patrick Murphy had given an account to justice of the peace Edward Fitzgerald. However Fitzgerald was a justice under the reign of King Edward and had not been sworn in during the reign of George V the year before. Therefore his evidence could not be heard in court.

Abel Hawkes, who was in charge of the bailiff's boat, was next called. He told how he didn't have a revolver that night but had previously cautioned the men for using their guns. The revolvers he said were only to be used when one was in imminent danger.

He was questioned at length due to his poor answers and made to look like someone who was not in control of the situation that night. When asked why he didn't do something after the first shot was fired Hawkes claimed to have no authority. This was not true as he was 61 years old and had been a bailiff for many years. Bulman on the other hand was only 23 and O'Neill a similar age and they didn't have the experience of the older man. However Hawkes was repeatedly caught out with his answers but continually denied knowing which of them fired the shots. He claimed the shots were only fired to frighten away the fishermen and allow them to seize the net. Both the coroners seem to struggle to hide their opinion of the case when questioning Hawkes.

After hearing the evidence Coroner Murphy spoke for the next of kin of the deceased. He said while the fishing was illegal Patrick Murphy was still entitled to go home with his life. He said if the bailiffs were allowed to shoot like this then a police man could shoot someone for cycling away without having a light on their bicycle.

Summing up the coroner said he believed there was abuse shouted between the boats that night but that was all as the boats didn't come within striking distance. What he said next was very unusual for a coroner but showed his frustration with the case. He said Hawkes evidence was of little use and believed that he should not have been in charge of the boat. It was obvious from the way the inquest was going that there was a strong feeling against the bailiffs.

The jury returned the verdict that "Patrick Murphy died from septic pneumonia caused by bullets making a perforation in the lungs". The jury also remarked they believed the use of revolvers in this case was totally unnecessary.

Within days of Patrick's death on May 31st the case was heard at Cobh petty sessions court before resident magistrate John French. District Inspector Toppin was prosecuting the case while a solicitor Mr. Donegan appeared for the defence of the two accused.

The first witness called was the bailiff who was in charge of the boat that night Abel Hawkes. Aside from what was already heard Hawkes claimed the fishermen said that night "back into them, sink them, you won't get a single mesh of it". He said the bailiffs threatened to shoot fearing for their safety. The remaining bailiffs James Duggan and Charles Arnold also gave similar testimony. None of the men admitted to having seen who fired the shot that hit Patrick Murphy.

Statements given to the police in Cobh by Bulman and O'Neill were read out in court. These statements were evidence that the accused were indeed the bailiffs that had fired the shots. O'Neill's statement admitted he fired the first shot high over the heads of the fishermen, he fired another shot but the revolver misfired. He said that Bulman fired two shots at the boat.

The reading concluded and the accused were further remanded in custody to await a trial by jury. What was obvious from the inquest was any jury in Cork was going to be against the bailiffs due to the case being well known. The local parish priest had set up a fund for Patrick Murphy's family. Many of the wealthy locals supported the cause and instalments were to be paid weekly to the widow who had seven children to keep.

The bailiffs were well aware that public feeling was seriously against them in Cork where everyone knew Patrick Murphy and that he left behind a large family. His widow now cared for their seven children which ranged in age from thirteen to baby Patrick born in March the same year as his father's death.

At the Summer Assizes in Cork the case was called but adjourned to a later date. The defence for the two accused asked for the trial to be moved from Cork. They felt that a fair trial was no longer possible in Cork due to the ill feeling against them.

By October bail had been granted to the accused at £100 each but they must not have had the money because they remained in jail. By November both the accused men were transferred to Mountjoy jail. They were awaiting their trial which was fixed for the 20th November in Dublin.

On November 20th the case was heard in Nisi Prius court No2 at the Four Courts in Dublin before Mr Justice Dodd. Both were charged that "on the 17th May they feloniously, wilfully and with malice aforethought killed Patrick Murphy".

At the trial, Michael Walsh told his version of the events that night. He said the closest the boats had come together was about 25 feet or a boats length. He said the fishermen never got any chance to use violence or defend themselves as they were unarmed. Walsh admitted to the court that the fixed net was illegal and that the mesh size being used was also not allowed.

William Murphy said the fishermen never raised an oar or threatened anything. William had left go of the net when the bailiffs threatened to fire but it had fouled the gudgeon pin at the aft end of the boat.

Again the bailiffs gave their version of what had happened, all saying that the fishermen were threatening to sink them. Hawkes now claimed one of the fishermen had said "scuttle their boat, drown them". To this O Neill was said to reply "if you come nearer I'll fire". The bullet found in the boat was produced in court and proved to only fit into Bulman's revolver.

When all the evidence was heard Mr Lynch kings counsel solicitor gave a speech for the defence of the bailiffs. He claimed the fishermen were going to sink the bailiff's boat. Lynch stated if the fishermen were not going to attack, why else did they remain after realising it was the bailiffs. He said the shot had only been fired at the other boat not at the fishermen. Lynch believed that the verdict should be one of misadventure and both the accused acquitted.

Justice Dodd summed up the case before charging the jury. In his opinion the case could not be claimed to be one of self defence. If a man fired at a boat with men in it and hit one of them he was responsible the judge said.

At twenty minutes to eight in the evening the jury returned with their verdict, "we find William O'Neill not guilty. We find William Bulman guilty of manslaughter under strong provocation and we strongly recommend him to mercy". After reading the verdict O'Neill was discharged from court.

Hearing the verdict Lynch for the defence spoke about Bulman's good character and how he supported his mother. The judge however cut him short and interjected "what about the murdered man's family".

Justice Dodd needed to pass a sentence on Bulman. The judge used the opportunity to air his own view of the case. He blamed the fishermen saying they were high handed and violent. However he went on to say the bailiff exceeded his duty and the law was brought into disrepute. The judge sentenced Bulman to eighteen months imprisonment from the date he was first arrested. He had already served six months in jail. The judge stated that only for the jury the sentence would have been one of penal servitude.

It was clear that the judge and more importantly the jury in Dublin believed the bailiffs evidence over that of the fishermen. If the case had been heard in Cork it may have been the complete opposite.

I knew it was you father.
Shanagarry 1839

On the morning of the 1st of February 1839 the normally quiet village of Shanagarry was plunged into horror and shock when a man called James Forrest turned himself in at the barrack. While Forrest told what he had done he at no time tried to account for his actions.

The previous Friday night James Forrest an elderly farm labourer had been drinking in Cloyne but left there early and made his way home to Shanagarry. When he arrived home about six in the evening he knocked at his own door and was answered by his fifteen year old son. His son Michael said to him "I knew it was you father, I knew your knock, I knew your step". His son ate his supper while the father sat by the fireside. Once the son was finished his supper James Forrest for no apparent reason seized a spade and attacked his own son. He struck him on the back of the head fracturing the skull behind the ear and caused an almost instant death. Between then and Sunday morning he tried to conceal the body of his son by digging a hole by the wall in the clay floor of the house.

By the Sunday morning Forrest must have come to realise what he had done and could no longer live with himself, he told some of his neighbours what he had done. He went to the closest barrack in Cloyne and made a statement to the head constable Henry Roche. The constable immediately sent for the local magistrate Francis Rowland of Kilboy house Cloyne to witness the statement. They took a statement from Forrest who said his son's body would be found buried under a bed in the house covered with straw. The spade used as the murder weapon would be found hidden in the chimney.

When Rowland and the Constable went to the house they found it was as Forrest had said and found blood still on the spade. The confessed murderer was taken to Midleton barracks and held there until after the inquest. The reason he gave the police for his terrible deeds was that he had fallen out with two of his neighbours. He had decided he was going to kill these neighbours for whatever thing they had done to him. He was worried nobody would be left to look after his son when he was in jail. As far as we know he never got around to killing the two neighbours but said he was ready to suffer the consequences of the law for killing his own son.

James Forrest's wife had died some years previously and he was living alone with his son. He had an older daughter but she was said to have left the house and went into service elsewhere on account of her father's harsh treatment of her. A post mortem examination was carried out by local doctor Dr Cashman.

An inquest was held by county coroner Mr Geran on the 12th of February. It returned a pretty obvious verdict that young Forrest had died as a result of wilful murder. The case came before Justice Baron Richards at the Cork Spring Assizes in the Cork criminal court on the 18th of March. The accused James Forrest was called before the court and pleaded guilty to the charge of murder. The clerk of the court addressed the jury saying the case was an extraordinary one and led them to believe that the accused was suffering from insanity. Forrest was convicted and sentenced to jail.

A few months later in Cork County Gaol James Forrest was again in trouble. He stabbed one of his prison wardens named Harding in the stomach with an awl. He was transferred to the lunatic asylum for the protection of everyone in the jail.

Suspicious circumstances
Bailick, Midleton 1903

Early on Sunday morning 1st November 1903 Eugene Heffernan of Bailick near Midleton went to his neighbours and told them his mother had died during the night. He asked one woman would she come around and help to prepare his mother for her burial. The neighbours were not at all surprised as Bridget Heffernan was 75 years of age and had not been herself for some time. She often wandered aimlessly and her son had to go looking for her at all hours of the day or night.

Eugene seemed to be quite upset that his mother had died especially as he lived alone with her. He was 37 and a labourer working nearby for Bennett's who malted barley for the brewing industry. He told the neighbour that he would soon go and get a coffin for his mother and wished to have her waked that day. However finding several injuries on the old woman's body, the neighbour began to question him. He claimed she had got out of bed early that morning and fallen over injuring herself. The neighbour woman advised him to inform the police saying if he didn't people would only talk later on.

He did go and get the police about ten that morning, the police came back with him to the house. The sergeant searched around the house and examined the old woman. During the search the sergeant noticed blood and things out of place. His suspicions became aroused and it wasn't long after that Eugene was arrested by the sergeant. Later that day he was charged before a magistrate and remanded to custody. Several friends of his heard what had happened and went to visit him in the barracks. One of the friends was overheard advising him saying "shut your mouth the less you say now the better for yourself, it will be nothing don't be fretting".

The inquest was held the very next day at Midleton Courthouse on the evening of the 2nd of November. The coroner was Mr Richard Rice, while district inspector Webster represented the crown prosecution.

Bailick Road

First witness called was a neighbour and distant relation Anne French. Anne had not seen Bridget since the Friday before the occurrence when she was standing out at her gate. She said how on the morning before the inquest Eugene came to her at 8:20 in the morning and told her his mother had died. The pair walked to Heffernan's house and along the way Eugene said she had died about six that morning. He also related how she had been a good mother to him and he was going to miss her.   When   Anne saw Bridget she was in bed under the bedclothes and it seemed plausible enough that she died in her sleep. They proceeded to wash her but had to cut the clothes off as the body was stiff. As they did this Anne noticed her wrist was discoloured and broken. Anne became more concerned when she found another wound on the head with clots of blood around it. She said "Eugene look at that wound" but he seemed to disregard it saying "that is the first I saw of it". Anne told the jury how she next asked Eugene why he had not called a doctor. His reply was that Dr Lawton was not available but Anne asked why not Dr O'Brien? At that point Eugene said Dr O'Brien would have only sent his mother to hospital. He also told her that as soon as his mother was washed he would go to get a coffin. She was going to the chapel to be waked. Again Anne questioned him saying when anyone died suddenly it should be reported to the police to be investigated. He replied that he had already reported it to the police but left the house and returned with Sergeant McSweeney. Anne heard Eugene tell the sergeant that his mother came out of the bed while he was sleeping. She fell against the table which collapsed and fell to the ground. Hearing this Anne told the inquest she noticed a heavy stick which was cracked on the floor, it was produced before the jury. Finishing her testimony Anne told how as a neighbour it seemed "there was no better son to a mother or no better mother to a son". She did recall seeing Mrs Heffernan with a black eye a month before but assumed she got it when out wandering about.

Dr Patrick O'Brien was next called before the inquest; he had been Bridget's doctor. He had examined the body the evening before and found her to be dead with about 12 hours. Under his instructions the body was removed to the workhouse where a post-mortem was carried out with Dr Lawton. Describing the post mortem he listed the injuries they had found. There were injuries to the right shoulder elbow and arm. Both bones had been broken at the wrist. In addition there were several wounds to the face, two of which were deep cuts. These he said were caused by a blow of a stick like the one which had been produced. The skull had been fractured at the forehead and several other wounds were found on the head. All of these the doctor said could have been caused by a round implement such as a stick. Addressing the coroner the doctor told how the injuries could not have been caused by a fall and were also not self inflicted. Death he said was caused by compression of the brain and shock as a result of the injuries.

The coroner summed up and told how the accused had already been arrested. As a result the jury were limited merely to decide on the cause of death. Who had committed the crime would be decided before another jury. He said going by the evidence the jury could come to no other verdict than the deceased was murdered. The jury found a verdict in accordance with the evidence that had already been given.

On the 13th of November there was a special sitting at the courthouse in Midleton to hear the case before resident magistrate Horne. The accused was brought from Cork jail by train to Midleton. In court he was said to not have looked too bothered about being charged.

A fellow worker at Bennett's Cornelius Shea who also lived in Bailick was sworn in. He had passed by the Heffernan's house about eleven on Friday the 30th of October. He was walking home when he saw a neighbour Mrs Molloy at Heffernan's window. They both listened and heard unusual noises inside like someone was trying to get up from the floor. Cornelius who knew Eugene well went around to the door but it was bolted. There was no light from inside the house at the time and both left in opposite directions.

He explained how he passed again going to work at five in the morning. He stopped at the house upon seeing light inside, he heard a groaning noise that he knew was Bridget Heffernan. Footsteps were also heard from inside and he recognised the voice of Eugene but could not hear what he said. Several more times that Saturday he passed but never once saw Bridget outside the house. He thought it was unusual that Eugene had not gone to work on Saturday.

At seven on Sunday morning he met Eugene at Bennett's yard, Eugene was crying and said to him "your friend is gone". Cornelius knew the old woman had died but Eugene said she fell out of the bed Friday night and broke her arm. He had asked the doctor to see her but the doctor didn't until it was too late.

Cornelius was aware that Bridget had not been well and in the past often asked Eugene how his mother was. Several times Eugene said he was nearly out of his mind with the way his mother was. On one occasion she had tossed up every thing in the house.

Dr Patrick O'Brien gave similar evidence to that heard at the inquest but said the injuries were inflicted 2 days before death.

Another local man James Kirby related how he also passed by the house on Bailick road on the 30th October. He heard voices inside, someone seemed to fall over and the light inside suddenly went out. James told the court how he thought it was suspicious and went off to get the police. On the way there he changed his mind thinking there was a reasonable explanation and the occupants were probably just drunk. Kirby went on to say a few weeks before he passed by the same way and heard Eugene hitting his mother with something. He recognised her voice when she cried out "Genie don't kill me".

Another local Andrew Wall told the court how he too passed Bailick road on the 30th October. He heard a woman's voice call out "Genie Genie" but couldn't tell where it came from.

The next witness was Julia Buckley who ran a public house in Ballinacurra. On the morning of the 1st November Eugene Heffernan came to her looking for half a pint of whiskey saying his mother had died. Julia however told him the only place to get it was at his Aunt Norah Cox's public house. Eugene replied that he wouldn't go there as he wasn't talking to them.

Mrs Mehigan was called next to give evidence; she lived with her sister who ran a public house in Ballinacurra. She told how Eugene Heffernan was drinking there about seven on the evening of the 30th. She noticed he was trembling and drank several pints quickly. She refused to give him another pint, giving him a half pint instead. He seemed to be drunk and said "they done me". She knew what he meant as there was talk about the village of money trouble with his cousins the Cox's. Eugene disclosed "I'll bury my mother with my father in Ballinacurra and I'll leave them to god".

Several more witnesses who all lived in the area gave similar evidence. On the second day in court in Midleton the judge returned the case to trial before a jury at the next Assizes.

As the weeks went on it began to emerge that things hadn't been quite so good between mother and son for some time. Eugene had complained to several people that his mother was unable to keep the house and he often went without breakfast. He seemed bitter that his mother was no longer able to care for him as much as she had in the past. There were other troubles between them regarding money. Bridget he said had received a legacy of £50 in the past and Eugene accused her of giving it to her sister's family the Cox's living in Ballincurra.

The case was heard at the Munster Winter Assizes in Cork Courthouse on December the 7th. The judge presiding over the case was Lord Chief Justice Peter O'Brien. A solicitor Mr O'Mahony represented the accused while Attorney General Mr John Atkinson headed up the crown prosecution. A jury of twelve men were selected from a much larger panel and sworn in. It was just over a month since the murder had taken place and would not normally have been in court so soon. The judge explained to all present how he thought the case was straight forward.

Eugene Heffernan was now charged with the deliberate murder of his mother on the 30th of October not on the 1st of November as previously thought. The Attorney General before hearing the witness statements described the case at length.

He told the jury how Eugene had put his mother into hospital a few months before where it was alleged she had suffered from neglect. It transpired Bridget had only spent 2 weeks in hospital before her son brought her home again. Much of the first day was spent with the prosecution detailing all the facts of the case. He explained how if Eugene had sought help earlier the sentence could have been reduced to manslaughter. It was claimed also that he knew exactly what he was doing and on the Saturday evening went for a doctor. The impression he gave the doctor was there was no hurry and put him off attending until Sunday. The prosecution also mentioned how Heffernan was an ex-policeman and knew well how evidence would be used against him. He stated how the case was peculiar in that all the witnesses were either, friends, relations or neighbours of the accused. The facts of the case were presented in such a way that it seemed an obvious conclusion that he had killed his mother.

One of the key witnesses in the case was Mrs Molloy who lived only 100 yards from the murder scene. She had not given evidence before despite hearing what had gone on that night. Mrs Molloy said after hearing a scream on the Friday night she tried to look into the window of Heffernan's house but the shutter was closed. She heard Eugene drunk ask his mother "where was the bottle of whiskey" he said "that is your share, take that and go down to bed". The next words heard spoken from inside the tiny house were "I don't care if you die tonight, I won't go to work tomorrow". Mrs Molloy stayed listening at the gable of the house and heard something being struck twice. Less than a minute later a loud crash of furniture and pots also fell inside. Mrs Molloy told how she returned later about 10:30 with a neighbour Mrs Froyne. They knocked on the window but got no answer. The women heard footsteps from inside the house and thought it was the old woman. Snoring was also heard and they assumed this was Eugene. Despite having given very damning evidence when questioned by the defence she backtracked saying how she had always been friends with the Heffernan's. She told the court how the strokes she heard were soft and the sound could have been the old woman falling and hitting her head.

Another local man Michael Collins was called to give evidence. He recalled one night the July before when Bridget Heffernan came running to his house about midnight. She was terrified and when Eugene arrived to bring her home she wouldn't go with him. Eventually she did go but screamed out on the road when going back with him. This he said happened on several occasions and once she had a black eye. Collins when cross examined said "he was very affectionate with her".

Dr P. J O'Brien again gave medical evidence regarding the cause of death; he was questioned at length by both the prosecution and defence. He made it clear that she could not have sustained the injuries by falling especially not on a clay floor. He also said the wrist would be broken differently if she had fallen.

The court was adjourned until the following morning. The next morning several more witnesses were called all of whom had already given evidence before the judge in Midleton.

When the defence was given the opportunity to present its case solicitor O'Mahony called two witnesses. One was a porter in the workhouse while Bridget was there. He told the court how Eugene visited his mother several times a week and was very good to her. Every time he brought jam, biscuits and sweets according to the porter.

The other witness of the defence was first cousin of the accused John Wool who worked at Bennett's as a ganger. He told the jury how at four one morning Bridget passed the malt house where he worked. When he asked her where she was going she didn't make any sense and was confused. He said the old woman had no money and nobody would benefit from her death. In his opinion Eugene was always very good to his mother.

Mr O Mahony addressed the jury making the case for the accused. He said the crown's case was simply that there was no other obvious conclusion. O'Mahony was still confident the jury would acquit his client.

The judge summing up said how he had been very keen to hear the doctor's evidence and asked could wounds on different parts of the head have been accidental.

He asked the jury "as reasonable men do you think the wounds were accidental?"

He asked them to consider the number of wounds and the words heard at the window. However he now said that if the jury considered the accused to be drunk that night or he had quarrelled with his mother it would suggest a verdict of manslaughter

The jury retired from court to come to a decision at shortly before five. Over an hour later the foreman returned to clarify a point of when the doctor had examined the body. It was nearly half six before the foreman again returned saying the jury had agreed. He read out that they found him guilty of manslaughter but not of murder and recommended mercy.

Hearing the verdict the judge addressed Eugene Heffernan saying:

"You have been found guilty and I am satisfied as I am sitting here that yours was the hand that took your mother's life, of that I have not one shadow of doubt. The jury have taken a most lenient view of your case. Never was a fuller and a fairer trial and never in my opinion was there a verdict so characterised by mercy and were it not for their recommendation of the jury I should sentence you to penal servitude for life, but owing to their recommendation my sentence is that you will be sentenced to penal servitude for fifteen years".

He was taken from the dock and removed from the court. While leaving he called out "I am innocent, I am innocent of it"

Eugene served some of his sentence but was released after several years and we assume came home again. Eugene died in October of 1913 aged just 47, he was still a bachelor.

After a day at the fair
Cloyne 1859

On the evening of the 10th October at about six thirty a party from Cloyne left the fair in Midleton to return. Amongst them was Daniel Clayton a shoemaker from Cloyne with a young woman Anna Courtney. John Sullivan, David Moloney, his brother Michael and his father were also with them. Some of the party had been drinking all day during the fair.

On the way home they stopped off at Leahy's public house in Ballinacurra for about an hour and a half. Coming out of the pub Clayton was seen fighting with a boy presumed to be a local lad. Michael Moloney intervened, broke up the fight and tried to bring Clayton along the road towards Cloyne.

Outside the pub David Moloney's father was looking for him to get him to head towards home. David was with a young woman Margaret Ryan. Clayton intervened and caught hold of Moloney Senior asking him what he was doing calling after his son. Moloney Senior knew to walk away and headed up Ballinacurra hill with his other son Michael. Both Clayton and David Moloney stayed behind on the road with Margaret Ryan.

Later John Sullivan and Clayton headed towards Cloyne and caught up with Michael Moloney and his father at the top of the hill. Clayton was angry and began to insult Moloney Senior saying neither him nor any of his sons would be able for him in a fight. The father hearing this threw him down on the road and everyone went on leaving Clayton behind.

They went into John Sullivan' mother's house in Cloyne and Clayton arrived in not long after them. The conversation quickly changed to birdlime, a sticky substance used for trapping birds. Clayton tried to steal some from Michael Moloney's pocket but Moloney would not let him. An argument took place between Michael Moloney and Clayton. They began to fight but Moloney struck Clayton and knocked him down with the first punch. This time it was one of the Sullivan's called Patsy that separated the fighters. Michael Moloney having come out the better of the fight seemed to have had enough and went over to sit by the fire. Daniel Clayton finding himself cut and bleeding wanted further satisfaction. He again went over to Michael Moloney and challenged him. He struck Moloney and again one of the Sullivan's intervened and this time Daniel Clayton was put out of the house.

Outside Clayton struck up a conversation with a boy called Paddy McCarthy. Paddy asked him why he didn't go back into the house and fight like a man. To which the aggrieved replied "don't worry I will have my satisfaction before the night is over". Daniel Clayton left and went home to his own house. Michael Moloney exited through the back door as he didn't want another fight to take place. However before long Clayton returned to the house where the fight had occurred and called Michael Moloney out onto the road. The occupants of the house replied that he had gone home. At this stage Clayton was angry and called anyone inside out to fight.

He was also annoyed with the Sullivan's and felt that they had taken Moloney's side.

None of the family was drawn out of the safety of the house and as everyone else had gone home they proceeded to have their supper.

After his supper about ten minutes later, John Sullivan went over to the door to see what was going on. Outside David Moloney had arrived and was talking to two boys Patrick Higgins and James Bride. He was the worse for wear after the day and was staggering about the road. David went with the boys towards Clayton's house; Patsy Sullivan went after them and let them know what had happened. He told David his brother Michael had been fighting with Daniel Clayton but had come out the best of it.

As they went on down Church Street they came upon none other than Daniel Clayton. He was alone sitting on a wall crying, a short distance away from his father in laws house. David went up to him and asked whether he had struck his brother, to which he replied he had not. He asked again saying that John Twomey had told him that his brother had been hit. Twomey ran across the street and threatened Clayton "if you speak my name any more I will kick you about the road". Twomey announced that Mick had come out of the fight better. He told Clayton it would be better for him if he went off home for himself. It was obvious they weren't afraid of Clayton and this must have aggravated him further. David Moloney and Clayton's row escalated to shouting and they began name calling. Daniel Keeffe, Clayton's father-in-law heard the shouting as they lived nearby.

Clayton had been married to his daughter with only nine months. Keeffe caught his son-in-law and began to drag him towards home.

It was now about half ten at night and many people hearing the loud voices on the street came out to see what was going on. David in the midst of the row said to Clayton "for god's sake go home boy, I have nothing to say to you". This didn't help matters and the row continued as bad as ever with David Moloney eventually giving in and saying "come now as you have irritated me so much try yourself". Clayton replied that he was going to "burst the blood out of his ears and nose". Moloney moved towards Clayton who was still being held by his father-in-law. Clayton struggled to be let go and said for gods sake let me go. He was released and took off his coat as did Moloney. A ring was formed around them and the fight began. Mary Sullivan had been listening from her mother's house where the earlier fight took place now rushed forward. She asked the others to help diffuse the row saying "shame boys won't any of you separate them". She rushed forward trying to get into the ring in an attempt to separate them herself but was pushed back by Clayton's father-in-law. The father-in-law said "let them fight it out, leave it to themselves, let no one interfere".

The struggle only went on for about two minutes, at which point they stopped. The two started at each other again but David Moloney became weak and was no longer able to fight. Clayton was seen throwing something away and the sound of metal was heard on the road. While Moloney's hands were hanging down by his side, Clayton managed to trip him. In the struggle both ended up on the road with Clayton on top. James Brien went and pulled Clayton off and picked David up but blood gushed out of him. Daniel Clayton realising what he had done ran for home as did his father-in-law. They locked the door worried that there might be revenge for what had happened. At this point one would imagine the police would have been on the scene by now but they were all said to have been at the fair in Midleton.

Clayton left his house and hid out in the commons during the night. When eventually the police did arrive they searched through the night for him. In the morning he returned home and was duly arrested. By now the people of the town all knew what had occurred the previous night and had all turned against Clayton. The police arrested Clayton and had great difficulty protecting him from the locals who wanted to get their hands on him. The police took the alleged murderer to Midleton barracks until the inquest could be held. Meanwhile Daniel Keeffe had been arrested during the night in a house five miles away near Churchtown South.

On the following Tuesday an inquest was held in the court house in Cloyne. Some of those present at the inquest were Henry Barry coroner of the district, John Litton of Ardnavilling and John Litchfield of Ballymaloe house and the local Dr Fowke. Having viewed the body the inquest jury heard evidence from Michael Moloney, James Bride, Patrick Higgins and Mary Sullivan. Dr Fowke also gave evidence saying that when he was called on the night, David Moloney was already dead. He went on to say that death was caused by huge wounds to the throat. The following morning he carried out a post mortem on the deceased. He found that all the large blood vessels of the neck had been severed.

Despite this Daniel Clayton was said to have maintained a level of coolness throughout the inquest and even cross examined some of the witness's. The jury of the inquest returned a verdict of wilful murder against Daniel Clayton and the case was sent to trial.

The Spring Assizes were held in Cork county court in late March 1860. The case had already been postponed for some time and Clayton was held in custody during this time. The Cloyne murder case attracted much interest and many of the other cases were quite trivial in comparison. A jury of twelve were sworn in from a large panel before the judge Justice Christian. Five lawyers prosecuted the case on behalf of the crown, whilst lawyer Mr Coffey was assigned to defend the case.

After an outline of the case was given, the counsel began to describe the distinction between murder and manslaughter. It was stated that where both parties entered into a quarrel on equal terms and one was killed this would be manslaughter. However if there was *malice aforethought* it would prove to be murder.

One of the first witnesses called was John Sullivan. He stated how he had been in Ballinacurra that day and in his mother's house when the row began. He was also there when the last fight took place and said in court that after a few blows he heard a noise like glass or steel on the road. He saw David Moloney fall on the street and Clayton fell on him. Daniel Keeffe pulled his son-in-law off Moloney who was bleeding and saw both men fleeing the scene.

The next witness Mary Sullivan detailed what had happened earlier in the night in her mother's house. She gave evidence of what she saw happen out on the road and of her attempt to stop it. She also saw Clayton throw something after Moloney fell to the ground. She said "if you stabbed a cow in the neck it would not bleed more". After the fight she searched near Ned Stafford's house in the direction where Clayton had thrown something and found the handle of a cut throat razor.

The third witness sworn in was James Brien. He stated that he was there when the row had broken out on the road. He corroborated what the others had said about the events leading up to the fight. He said that when Moloney fell on the road, it was he who picked him up but blood was spouting out of his throat as fast as it could. To him Moloney appeared dead as his head hung down. When cross examined Brien was asked if Clayton was drunk that evening or knew what he was doing. The witness replied that he wasn't that drunk and knew well enough to flee the scene after what he had done.

Mary Keeffe, Clayton's mother-in-law was sworn in and said she was in bed at that time on the night of the murder. She had heard Clayton return home and make some noise in the kitchen before leaving again. This we assume was when Clayton acquired the cut throat razor. She didn't know what he was doing but when he returned again after the crime had been committed, she turned him out of the house. Her husband she said ran off like a mad man afterwards.

Dr William Fouke next gave evidence of how he was called on that evening and how he saw the man bleeding on the road. At this point he said that the man was already dead. His evidence detailed the injuries inflicted and said it was impossible to be done with one blow. As there were three distinct wounds found on the left side of the neck. He went on to say how he examined the body the morning after and that any one of the three wounds would have been enough to cause death. The head was nearly severed so much from the body on the left side that the doctor could touch the spine with his fingers.

In the courtroom one of the jurors suddenly felt very ill upon hearing the details of the injuries inflicted. The Doctor had to cease his evidence and attend to them. After much deliberation, the court case was adjourned for two hours to enable the juror to recover. Otherwise it would be necessary to discharge the jury and swear in another jury at a later date.

When the case resumed again, it was nearing the end of the witness statements. Edmund Walsh said he found the blade on the ground near Stafford's house. Constable James Walsh stated that he received the blade from Edmund Walsh on the night and the razor blade was produced in court. The case was adjourned for the day.

On the 21st of March Mr Coffey gave a final speech in defence of Daniel Clayton. The judge summed up the case at length. Eventually the jury retired to consider the case and half an hour later returned to the court room. They returned with a verdict of not guilty of murder but guilty of manslaughter. The court was adjourned for the day and sentencing was deferred.

On the Thursday of the same week the court sat again for sentencing of outstanding cases. Clayton was sentenced to 8 years penal servitude for manslaughter.

Throughout the day of the murder Clayton had fought with 3 of the Moloney men, first the father, then Michael but it was David that suffered the final blow. A day that started out with fun at the fair ended disastrously for the Moloney family.

A quieter scene in Cloyne from 1856 three years before

Why did you kill my son?
Cooladurragh, Conna 1861

In the small townland of Cooladurragh just north of the village of Conna a labourer named Andrew Doyle rented a cottage from local farmer, James Gallagher. Doyle was not married and lived there with his elderly mother Mary.

James Gallagher lived only 200yards away from his tenant. He was a small farmer and his land was let from the landlord the Duke of Devonshire. He was married with three young children and also had a servant living with them called Michael McCarthy.

Andrew Doyle had given Gallagher a deposit of £11, which would be given back if he vacated the property. The farmer wanted his tenant out for some time and was said to be prepared to give back the money. However Doyle refused to give up the house and the two were in dispute since. There were several altercations between them with Doyle using very insulting language to his landlord. Andrew Doyle would sometimes go to Gallagher's door shouting abuse and calling names. Once he approached the family when they were going to mass and shouted abuse at them shocking other mass goers. Several of Gallagher's chickens were found maimed nearby. All these altercations resulted in both men appearing before the magistrates at the local petty sessions on several occasions.

On the evening of the 1st of May 1861 Andrew left his mother alone in the house and walked towards Gallagher's home. About the same time James Gallagher left his own house taking a shovel with him. His wife Bess asked "Where are you going? Won't you wait for your supper?" but he paid no attention to her and kept going. Not long after she also gave up on supper and followed him. This left the servant Michael McCarthy alone sitting by the fire, probably thinking when would he get his supper? A few minutes later Michael heard Bess outside say in a loud alarmed voice "What ails you Jim?" Due to her tone Michael went out thinking something had happened to his employer.

When he went out the door to see what was amiss all thoughts of supper quickly vanished with the sight before him. His employer stood there with a handle of a pike in his hands about to hit a man lying on the road. Bess was now worried and asking her husband why he had done it. Michael went and took the implement from Gallagher's hands without saying a word not knowing what to do next. McCarthy realised that it was Andrew Doyle who was lying there bleeding. He asked Bess what should be done and she suggested sending for Doyle's mother and that is what he did.

When Doyle's mother arrived at the scene she held her almost lifeless son in her arms and frantically asked what had happened to him. He could only reply "the shovel, the shovel". She turned on Gallagher and asked him why he had done this to her son. The farmers reply was "Why did he say last night that Bess took a false oath?"

The old woman managed to get her son home and took care of him as best she could. A priest and a doctor were called but he died at nine the following morning.

James Gallagher was said to have fled to a nearby friend's house but was arrested later that evening and held in Fermoy gaol. The *Cork Constitution* not knowing the full story reported "this is another instance of the fatal effects of drink turning a quiet man into a very demon of destruction".

On the 23rd of July the case was heard at the Cork Assizes before a jury and Lord Chief Justice Monahan. James Gallagher was charged with having wilfully caused the death of Andrew Doyle on May 1st. The accused was represented by solicitor Mr Coffey while the crown prosecution had a police sergeant and several solicitors including the renowned Sir Colman O'Loughlan.

Local constable James Devitt was questioned about the ongoing dispute between the parties. He recalled how Gallagher brought Doyle before the petty sessions for breaking the windows of the house but the case was dropped for lack of evidence. On another occasion he summoned Doyle and his mother before court for using abusive language. While being cross examined by the defence the constable said "the deceased Doyle appeared to me to be half-witted". But he went on to say Doyle was not

The spot on the road today near where Gallagher's house once stood

a violent man. He told that Doyle and his mother had disagreed over the deposit given to the farmer. She had threatened to go the law to recover the money. At one point Gallagher had given the money to a priest to settle the dispute. When the priest was unable to sort it he handed the money back to the farmer and the feud went on.

Dr. Nason examined the body of Andrew Doyle on the morning of the 2nd. He found on the right side over the ear two incised wounds, one of which went through the skull. These wounds could have been caused by a sharp instrument such as a shovel. On the other side of the head were enormous bruises under which the skull had been fractured. These he believed could have been done with a heavy stick. The doctor was of the opinion that any one of the wounds would have resulted in death. The defence solicitor cross examined and tried to claim the injuries could have been caused with a stone.

The key witness to the case was Michael McCarthy who was one of the first on the scene. He recalled that Jim Gallagher had been away on the day in question and when he returned home had drink taken. McCarthy said his employer was in the habit of going on the road in the evening with a shovel. He would scrape the road adding the manure to his heap in the yard. This is what he saw Jim Gallagher doing that evening and thought nothing unusual in it until he heard raised voices. When he went out to the road he heard the wife ask her husband why he had done it. McCarthy said he heard the reply "if he had let me pass, then I would have let him pass". He identified the shovel and pike produced in court.

The elderly mother of the deceased took the stand and became very agitated when she was asked to point out James Gallagher in the court room. She went on to explain her account of events that evening saying her son was gone about thirty minutes when she was sent for. She recalled speaking to her son and also asked Gallagher why he had done it. She said "I asked them for a drink of water for him thinking it would revive my son, but they wouldn't give it." She next described taking her son home alone while he staggered on the road from weakness.

Another witness that had come forward with useful information was William Mulcahy. He was a servant to a nearby farmer and passed by the road that evening bringing horses to water. William told the court how as he passed he saw Andrew Doyle stretched on the road lying on his face and hands. At the time he saw Gallagher scraping the road with a shovel. Mulcahy remarked "Who is that on the road?" but got no reply from James.

Gallagher's wife was also nearby and said "they were tearing each other inside the yard." The defence declined to cross examine this witness knowing it could not possibly benefit their case.

Another witness was Hannah Walsh who on the same evening was having tea at Bridepark Cottage with her neighbour Mrs McBeth. Hannah explained to the court that upon hearing a noise she came out onto the road to see what was going on. At that time Andrew Doyle was on the road and Gallagher was holding what she described as a weapon of some description.

Several constables were called and gave evidence on the weapons owned and used by Gallagher. Also produced was the blood stained shirt he was wearing at the time. Dr Blyth from Queens University Cork (UCC) told how he had analysed the pike handle, shovel and shirt. His testimony proved that the stains were indeed human blood but back then it was not possible to prove from whom. He also described finding actual human tissue on the pike handle. The prosecution now had no more witnesses to call and concluded their case.

The defence also had no witnesses to call. Mr Coffey spoke for his client and was said to have made a good speech addressing the jury. He referred to his client's good character up to recently and had several signed statements from local clergy and magistrates. He claimed the prosecution had failed to prove malice in the case against his client.

When the jury returned they gave their verdict guilty of manslaughter and sentencing was deferred until a later date.

A few days later several cases that had been heard during Assizes were all brought to court together for sentencing by the judge. Within an hour the judge had sentenced all the cases with every one receiving a jail term which included hard labour. One man was given eighteen months for the charge of bigamy. James Gallagher received four years penal servitude on the charge of manslaughter.

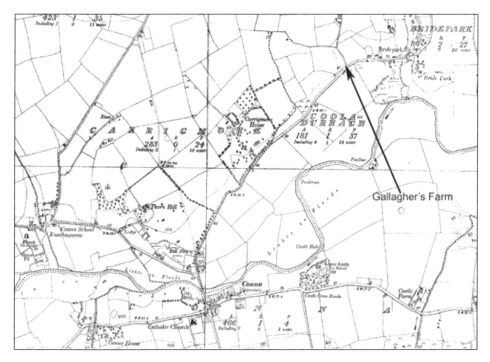

Map from the period showing Gallagher's farm in relation to Conna

A life sentence
Watergrasshill 1964

One Friday night, late in the month of April a man hid outside a farmhouse. He was watching and trying to listen to those inside waiting for his chance. He had arrived about four in the afternoon and still had hours to wait before it would be dark about nine. He had not been at this house for quite some time but he knew exactly where he was and had a fair idea of the movements of the occupants. He would later claim that his intentions were just to steal money he could easily get his hands on in the house. One of the farmer's son's went out to a dance with another man who worked there. As it was a Friday night the intruder assumed they would stay out late. That left only three inside the farm house and he waited until the lights were out and everyone had gone to bed.

When it seemed the coast was clear and everyone was asleep, he grabbed his chance. He found an iron bar and a screw driver in the yard and approached the house. He tried to force the kitchen window. Failing to easily open the kitchen window he went to the sitting room window and found a pane of glass already broken. The glass was quickly removed without much bother and he climbed in the window without rousing the occupants. He tiptoed around looking for what he could get his hands on. In the kitchen he forced open a desk drawer and found a wallet. Being so familiar with where he was going he took off his shoes knowing footsteps would raise the alarm. He crept up the carpeted stairs in his stockings without making a sound.

Upstairs he entered a bedroom and was opening a press when he heard a shout from behind "Who is there?" The owner of the house and his wife had been alarmed but in the darkness maybe didn't recognize the intruder. In a moment of sheer madness he lashed out with the iron bar and beat the man on the head. His wife also received several blows to the head in the midst of the struggle. The iron bar was abandoned in the room and the intruder turned to escape. Having left his shoes downstairs he now put on a pair of shoes found in the bedroom and fled. At the bottom of the stairs he took an over coat before running out to the yard. His own jacket had been left on a gate and was disposed of nearby. He removed ten pound in pound notes from the wallet and threw it into a ditch along the way.

With the couple left for dead in the bedroom the intruder made his way back to Cork city. At this point nobody realized what had occurred. In the farm house their son had slept and did not hear anything amiss. About 5am the other son returned from the dance with a labourer. They found the gate to the farm open and a light on upstairs. This they found unusual but didn't notice anything else out of place in the house. Both went straight to bed after being at an all night dance.

One of the sons woke in the morning at quarter to nine to the sound of another farm worker driving the cows into the yard. Their mother was always up before them and would normally call them to get up at half seven. When she didn't that morning they must have immediately suspected something was amiss. Both went to their parent's bedroom and found the worst possible scene. George Applebe lay dead in bed in a pool of blood from the head injuries he had sustained. Their mother, Anne, was lying nearby on the floor semi conscious but in a very serious state. She managed a few words but was not aware of what had happened. Also in the room lay the murder weapon in a pool of blood, an iron bar about eighteen inches long. A doctor was immediately sent for and the local Garda barracks were also notified. A Garda was on the scene from nearby Watergrasshill very quickly and not long later Dr John Healy arrived from Carrignavar. He immediately arranged for Mrs. Applebe to be taken to hospital in Cork where it would be some time before her condition improved.

Throughout the day Gardaí were enlisted into the investigation from stations all over Cork led by Superintendents from Cobh, Blarney and Fermoy. Men from the Special Branch in Cork also arrived on the scene and later the murder squad came from Dublin.

A post-mortem was carried out on the body by state pathologist Dr Maurice Hickey but no date was set for the inquest.

It was 6:45am on Saturday morning the 25th of April when the murderer turned up at his lodgings looking for his breakfast. George and Anne Applebe had not been found at this point. The previous evening he had taken a room in Parnell Place in the city but not stayed there. The landlord was well aware he had not slept in his bed that night but not in their wildest imagination did they know what he was actually up to. Later he checked out and got lodgings on Glanmire Road nearer to the train station.

Early on Sunday morning he caught a train to Dublin. He bought a newspaper in which he read about himself. The Gardaí had started a manhunt and had a clear idea of who he was and even knew that he would go back to Dublin. The headline of the newspaper read "manhunt after Cork farmer is slain, scar faced man sought in Dublin". The article covered most of the front page and gave details of the man Garda were looking for. A man aged 32 five foot three in height and had worked at the farm in Watergrasshill several years before. He was originally from Kildare but had only recently been released from prison.

So what was he to do now? The whole of the country was out looking for him.

Jimmy Ennis then walked into Store Street Garda station and gave himself up. He said to the Garda on duty "I have seen the papers, they want to see me, here I am".

Despite handing himself in, he began by fabricating a story of where he had been on Friday night. Ennis claimed he had met a young woman and walked out to Blackpool with her and spent the night in an unoccupied house. In the morning he walked back to the city and had breakfast in his lodgings and slept for the day, that part was true.

After a tea break he suddenly changed his mind and began to tell the truth saying "tear up that last statement, it is not the truth. I am going to make a true confession."

It was then that Ennis began to confess to what he had actually done the Friday night before. It wasn't the first time he had walked into a Garda station to make a confession. Ennis had worked as a farm labourer for the Applebe's in Watergrasshill for about two and a half years until some time in 1959. He left after two years for six months but returned again to work there for another six months. After returning back to the Applebe's several people reckoned he had changed, having become odd and moody.

Then he went back to his home county of Kildare and worked again as a farm labourer in the Naas area. In December of 1960 Jimmy Ennis, broke into a house near Clane and attacked a woman with a large agricultural knife known as a Beet Crowner. Ennis had asked the woman to boil some water for him and she went and did it. When he went back to the house he turned on her and demanded money but she refused .The brutal attack that followed left the woman fighting for her life after being hit almost fifty times.

In the midst of the attack the knife handle broke but he continued hitting her with a hatchet that was at hand. He made off with £5, left the woman for dead with serious injuries and fled the area. This time around he caught a train to Cork and then a bus to Waterford. On the bus he told the conductor he had committed a crime in Co Kildare and needed to get to a Garda Barracks to make a confession. The first stop the bus made was in Carrigtwohill and he got off. Within minutes he went straight to the Garda and handed himself in. The Gardaí who he gave the statement to didn't see the vicious violent side to him at all. He now freely admitted the terrible crime he had carried out probably not knowing whether the woman had survived or not. Later detectives arrived from Naas and Jimmy Ennis was escorted back to Kildare.

Two months later he pleaded guilty on the charges of robbery and intent to cause grievous bodily harm but not guilty to attempted murder. The attempted murder charges were dropped and he got four years in prison for the other charges. The judge said he could have given a much longer sentence but didn't as he had handed himself in and made a full confession.

Ennis had only left Portlaoise prison on Thursday the 23rd of April 1964 after serving three years of his four year sentence. Before being discharged Ennis seemed to know where he was going to go and had requested a one way train ticket from Portlaoise to Cork. Whether he intended to go back to his former employers in Watergrasshill is not clear. Many believe his intentions were not theft at all, but that he had an axe to grind with his former employer.

After being arrested and charged in Store Street Garda station Ennis was held in custody. The following Tuesday an identity parade was held by the Gardaí at the Bridewell in Dublin. Several witnesses that had been in contact with the accused travelled up from Cork and Portlaoise.

Ennis made several appearances before the courts in Cork in May, but there was never any question of him being released. The Gardaí meanwhile carried out a large scale investigation and began to prepare for the court hearing later in the month. Detective Tom Connolly in his book *Detective: A life upholding the Law* tells how he met Ennis in 1961. After Jimmy Ennis was arrested in 1961 Detective Connolly lent him a pair of his own shoes. Now three years later those same shoes were found at the foot of the stairs in Applebe's farmhouse. Connolly was able to prove that they were indeed the same shoes with help from his shoe mender. Dozens of witnesses were questioned from local ticket sellers at the train station to boarding house landlords where Ennis had stayed.

Jimmy Ennis was born near Kilmeague Co Kildare in 1932 but his father died when he was only two years old. His mother later remarried and Ennis was sent to Artane Industrial School when he was four years old. He was in his late teens when he left the school and never settled back in his birthplace. Instead he worked as a labourer but didn't seem to stay anywhere for too long. One reason for this may have been the fact that he was getting into trouble for petty crimes. Four times he was caught for such crimes until 1954 when he got six months for the theft of a bicycle. Ennis was then aged only twenty two and after the term in prison he seemed to go straight for the next few years.

On Saturday the 16th of May the case was heard at Carrigaline before Justice Buckley. State Solicitor Mr. Dempsey was responsible for the prosecution case. He said the evidence that would be heard was from three distinct groups. The occupants of the farmhouse, boarding house landlords and ticket sellers showing the accused movements and the evidence the Gardaí had discovered in their investigations.

There was plenty evidence against the accused discovered by the Gardaí in their investigation. Shoes, hat and a coat taken from the farmhouse had been found in a suitcase belonging to the accused. His own coat was also identified and had been found in a ditch near the house.

The land lady of the boarding house on Parnell Place recalled that Saturday morning in April clearly. At quarter to seven when the doorbell rang, it was Jimmy Ennis. When she answered the door she recalled him saying "I am back again, I stayed on Thursday night and I want my breakfast". Several other witnesses recalled meeting the accused on the road late that Friday night between Watergrasshill and Cork.

After several days of hearing evidence from a total of 34 witnesses the case came to a conclusion. The prosecution applied to have the case returned for trial at the Central Criminal Court before a jury. The solicitor for the accused made no application and Ennis when asked merely said "nothing to say, Justice". The judge agreed with the prosecutions application and the accused was sent back to prison to await another trial before a jury.

The trial began on the 3rd of November 1964 in the Central Criminal Court. Justice McLoughlin started by telling the jury they could go home in the evening but were only permitted to talk about the case amongst themselves. The accused again pleaded not guilty to the charge of murder. Opening the case for the prosecution Mr Wellwood addressed the jury. He said if his motives were theft he could have left the farmhouse after getting money from the desk.

On the second day of the trial State Pathologist Dr Maurice Hickey gave medical evidence. He was sure that the iron bar had been the weapon used to kill. It was obvious several blows had been struck but was impossible to determine exactly how many. The pathologist concluded that death was as a result of the terrible head injuries but found no other injuries on the body. The doctor also told how he had examined clothes belonging to the accused and found droplets of blood on them.

Three days into the trial the prosecution case concluded and the defence began. Opening the case for the defence Solicitor Meagher told how he would reply to the evidence of the accused and especially the medical evidence. He asked the jury to come to a conclusion that whatever his client had done was as a result of a psychological condition and claimed it had been unintentional. Meagher claimed what happened was due to sudden impulse and complete loss of self control.

A doctor from Mountjoy, Dr Thomas Murphy was called by the defence and described Ennis as a belligerent psychopath. He said that Ennis was highly unpredictable under stress but when asked was the accused insane he simply replied "no".

The statement Ennis had given in Store Street Garda Station was read out to the court. In it he had detailed his movements that night and had admitted to everything. It was read out before the jury how Ennis told of opening the press in Mr. Applebe's bedroom when he was caught red handed. He struck out several times with the iron bar at George Applebe. Ennis claimed for a few moments he didn't know what had happened but must have also struck Mrs. Applebe several times. The statement then detailed how he made his escape and returned to the city centre during the night. In it he also claimed he had not been aware George Applebe had died until reading it in the Sunday papers after arriving in Dublin.

The accused was also called to give evidence before the jury. The farm labourer described having a good relationship with his former employer for the years he worked there. When questioned he said there was never any kind of trouble between them. He now regretted his actions saying he only broke in "to get a few pounds". Ennis told how he broke into the farmhouse that night and said he knew entering when the bedroom who was there. He was opening the wardrobe when the occupants became alarmed. According to himself he heard someone say "who is there what are you doing". He claimed hearing someone get out of bed as he ran for the door. Ennis now claimed that he was caught hold of and a scuffle took place. He said "I was knocked down and struck a few blows on the shoulder, I think it was a fire screen that struck me". His story was that it was only now that he took out the iron bar from his jacket and shoved Mr. Applebe back on the bed and struck out several times. When cross examining Mr. Wellwood asked the accused why did you bring the iron bar up stairs? But he could only reply "I don't know". His statement didn't entirely make sense and was at odds with what the doctor had found. Dr Healy had found the body in bed and partly under the bedclothes.

After several days of hearing evidence the trial was coming to a conclusion on the 9th of November. The prosecution had conceded that there was no clear evidence of premeditation of murder. Justice McLoughlin spoke for three hours summing up before the jury would decide. He weighed up all the evidence that had been heard but made it clear the jury must decide between manslaughter and murder. The jury was also reminded that if it was murder, the case was a non-capital murder.

The jury was allowed leave the court room to decide their verdict. Despite the judge's long speech, the jury it seems were still in some doubt over their decision and returned to the court room with a question. Justice McLoughlin was asked "if a person with intent to commit a felony was discovered in the act, uses an implement to effect his escape and causes the death of an individual, would that be murder or manslaughter, if this person was classified as an aggressive psychopath?"

Obviously the judge couldn't answer the question that directly or he would have been deciding for the jury. But he replied they had to examine his state of mind based on his actions that night. He said "if he had not the intent to kill or cause serious injury then he was not guilty of murder".

It was well over another hour before the jury returned to the court room after a total of nearly three hours deliberating. They read out their verdict of guilty of murder and the judge agreed with their finding. The judge remarked that he would normally have no hesitation in handing down a death sentence for such a crime. But said with regret that due to the recent Criminal Justice Act 1964 the death sentence was now restricted. Justice McLoughlin was very critical of the new law saying "I doubt the wisdom of this legislation". He handed down the maximum sentence he could which was penal servitude for life. Only those who had murdered a member of Gardaí or other such capital crimes would now face the death penalty.

The defence made an application for leave to appeal on the grounds the sentence was too severe but the application was refused. For some time after the trial Ennis was held in the Central Criminal Asylum in Dundrum. Later he was transferred back to Portlaoise having only been released from there days before the murder.

It would be a year later in April of 1965 before an appeal was heard at the court of Criminal appeal in Dublin before another judge. The defence legal team made several grounds for appeal saying the correct charge was manslaughter and not murder. It was also revealed that Ennis had attacked a prison warden in Portlaoise. The warden was said to have been lucky to have survived the attack. It was with this that the defence claimed their client should be treated in a mental hospital and not in prison.

The appeal judge Justice Haugh upheld the conviction saying the trial had been carried out correctly. He went on the say "the trial judge made it quite clear that even if the Act allowed him impose a sentence less than penal servitude for life he would still impose the maximum sentence". Another application to have the sentence of life reduced was also refused.

And so it was after the appeal aged only 33 Ennis had the rest of his life to face behind bars. Up to this point between Artane and prison he had only been free for a couple of years.

He was eligible for release on parole in 1982 but didn't apply for it. It was claimed he was happy in prison and "not pushed" about getting out. Since then several Ministers for Justice have supposedly told him he is free to go. He must have become institutionalised over the years and most likely fears the world outside. In an interview with the Cork Examiner in 1997 Ennis admitted knowing Martin Cahill well but denied being institutionalised. Ennis has spent the last number of years in Shelton Abbey, a low security open prison near Arklow in Co Wicklow. He is released during the day to work as a gardener in the Arklow area.

Ennis has for some time been the longest serving prisoner in Ireland being there for 53 years straight. Newspapers have written several articles about him over the years often claiming he is to be released but it hasn't happened yet. One article even remarked that Ennis is there so long he even has his own key for the prison. Even though Ennis has never had much responsibility for himself or his actions, he costs the state over €100,000 a year.

A sing song gone wrong
1st November 1860 Saleen

The 1st of November is traditionally know as All Saints Day or All Hallows Day and celebrated as a religious feast day. It might explain why on that day in 1860, a Thursday, a public house in Saleen was very busy.

Amongst the crowd a sing song started and two groups began to better each other. A group of men from Scariff competed against a group from Rathcoursey. Each party tried their best to sing louder than the other until eventually a row broke out. The landlord must have had enough at this stage and turned them all out on to the road.

The row persisted on the road and quickly turned into a fight. The son of a boatman, John Card struck first hitting Maurice Neale. Maurice quickly returned a blow in defence. John Card's father also called John then entered the fight to take the side of his son. He swung for Neale and dealt him a blow. Maurice it was said in self defence returned a punch but landed a very heavy blow to the side of John Card senior's face. After being hit the elder John Card was thrown to the ground and never got up again.

Meanwhile John Card junior picked another fight with a John Gleeson while his father was fighting Maurice Neale for him. Young John managed to hit Gleeson once but wasn't prepared for what was to come. Gleeson grabbed him by the hair and gave him an all merciful kick in the stomach. This seems to end the whole affair with father lying dead and son in a serious condition.

We don't know if Maurice Neale was arrested at the time as nothing was heard of the case again until March of the next year. At ten o'clock on the morning of the 19th March 1861 the case came before the Cork Assizes. Presiding over the case was Chief Baron David Richard Pigot who was one of the leading judges of the time. Maurice Neal was charged with the lesser crime of manslaughter as the Crown Prosecution knew a charge of murder was too severe.

After hearing the details of the case medical evidence was given by Doctor Travers. The doctor had carried out an examination and gave his opinion saying death was as a result of shock to the nervous system due to the blow received.

Maurice Neale was acquitted on the charges of manslaughter and another case was called. The next case was that of John Gleeson charged with having assaulted John Card junior on the same date. Again Dr Travers was called as he had examined John Card after the assault. The doctor said Card's life had been in danger for some time as a result of the kick in the stomach.

As it was young Card who had provoked Gleeson it was hard to see how Gleeson could be found guilty especially since Maurice Neale had got off. But the jury found John Gleeson guilty of not only assault but also of intent to do grievous bodily harm.

It was a few days later when all convicted at the assizes were called before the judge for sentencing. The judge made a long speech to those convicted making reference to the rise in violent crime. He said the recent violence was mostly a result of drunkenness and often sudden quarrels, followed by revenge. John Gleeson was sentenced to nine months hard labour. This seems severe for assault when others guilty of manslaughter only received 12 months.

Map showing the area of Rathcoursey, Saleen and Scariff

New Year's Day squabble
Cork road Fermoy New Year's day 1915

David, Ned and Tom Ryan were 3 brothers who lived together in their family home in Cork road, Fermoy. All worked as cattle dealers as had their father before them. David was the eldest aged 40, Ned was 38 and Tom was aged 36. Their parents had died several years before.

On New Year's Day 1915 David and Tom went to a fair in Mallow. The brothers were well accustomed to being up early in the mornings to set off for fairs, where much of the cattle dealing was done in those times. When the fair was over the brothers returned home separately, Tom on the 3 o'clock train and David two hours later.

In the evening the brothers had a squabble in their neighbour's house, the Tobin's. It abated after the pair shoved each other around and they went home.

After nine that evening they sat down to have supper which Tom had made. While having supper together the trouble between David and Tom sparked off again. The brothers who all had drink taken were joking with each other and the situation quickly escalated. The row was heard by the neighbours. It wasn't anything out of the ordinary and the neighbours were used to hearing them arguing when drunk, which seems to have been quite often. This time though the row turned into a brawl and all three brothers ended up on top of each other outside the house.

Despite having heard the brothers arguing many times before their neighbour James Murphy, an eleven year old boy was drawn by the commotion. As the boy approached the source of the noise he saw all three of the brothers fighting. He observed Tom strike David on his right hand side and David fell to the ground calling out "I am done".

Young Murphy then cleared in the direction of his house and Tom followed him. The boy didn't go straight home but Tom got there before him and met Mrs Murphy who was coming out of her house. He told her to get her son in off the street and punish him for not minding his own business. Tom went back towards his own house but it is not clear whether he knew of his brother injuries or not.

Meanwhile David Ryan managed after a while to get himself up off the ground and get away. He was heard to say "I am done" again before limping off to Murphy's house for his safety. It didn't take him long to arrive at their door. They knew something was wrong and let him in. He made for a bed and threw himself down. Mrs Murphy who by now had a good idea what had occurred to Ryan ran for a doctor.

A doctor arrived at the house and later in the night David was taken to the nearby Fermoy hospital

On the 4th of January, Tom was arrested and charged with wounding his brother. In hospital David seemed to be doing alright after his operation. However on Monday night he took a turn for the worse and the doctors realised there wasn't much hope for him. At four on Tuesday morning David passed away in hospital. His brother Tom was rearrested soon after and now charged with wilful murder.

In the Council chamber of the Town Hall the inquest was held on the 6th of January before coroner Rice. There was a huge interest in the case in the town and the chamber was packed full of people eager to hear the statements. After a jury was sworn in, district inspector Villiers representing the police spoke. He explained how Tom had first been arrested for wounding his brother. Now he said he was charged with the capital offence of wilful murder. This meant if found guilty before trial jury he could face the death penalty. A solicitor Dr Baylor represented the accused that was not present at the inquest.

Ned Ryan was the first to give evidence despite the coroner telling him he didn't need to if he wished. He said all three were drunk that night and confirmed there was a row between his brothers. He claimed though that all three fell together and there was no weapon used. He said David got up without saying a word and walked out of the house. When questioned he claimed not knowing of the injuries until the following morning but then he contradicted himself entirely. Admitting he was there when his brother went to hospital in a covered car about ten. The district Inspector asked what he did when he learned his brother had gone to hospital. Ned's reply was that he went home, told his bother Tom and both men went to bed.

Dr Michael O'Brien was called as he had attended to David on New Year's night. He found David Ryan lying on the floor in Murphy's house. He found a stab wound in the abdomen with a mass of fat protruding from it but no major bleeding. The doctor told how he had not asked what had occurred but dressed the wound. Then a note was sent to the hospital for an ambulance. He concluded his evidence saying the cause of death was the puncture wound which caused congestion of the lungs.

Dr Baylor solicitor for the accused intervened and claimed that the cause of death was the operation which David Ryan had undergone in hospital.

Dr Magnier medical officer of Fermoy hospital argued that the treatment given was right and carried out properly. Dr Baylor's closing argument was that the evidence pointed towards an accident. The coroner had the last word and he thought Ned Ryan's evidence was deplorable and inconsistent. The inquest found that David Ryan died as a result of an incised wound caused by a sharp instrument.

The same day as the inquest Tom Ryan was called before a judge and charged.

The head Constable Collins applied to remand the accused to custody for eight days in order to gather evidence. Collins told how when he arrested the accused he said "I am innocent of stabbing".

The accused was asked if he had any questions. He merely replied in reference to the statement Collins had given saying "that is the statement I gave."

He was back in court again in Fermoy on the 13th of January. The prosecution called several witnesses but none had actually seen exactly what had happened. When all the evidence had been heard Tom Ryan was asked if he had anything to say. His reply was simply -"I have nothing to say but I am not guilty". Despite this the judge returned the case for trial before a jury at the next assizes.

On Saturday 20th March 1915 the Cork spring Assizes sat in the city courthouse. When the Fermoy case was eventually called Tom Ryan pleaded not guilty to the charge of killing his brother.

Many of the witnesses called gave the same evidence as what they had already given at the inquest and court hearings. Young James Murphy was again the key witness and recalled seeing David struck by his brother.

Dr O'Brien was back giving the same medical evidence again. His opinion was David Ryan would certainly have died from peritonitis sooner if the operation was not performed. He told that not only was the instrument used sharp but it was carried out with force considering all the layer of clothes Ryan was wearing. Simply falling on glass would not have gone through his waist coat and several other layers of clothes.

District inspector Villier was called as he had spoken to David Ryan in hospital. He recalled one remark David made particularly, he had said he got a cut in the stomach after falling on some corrugated iron in their yard. He never made an allegation against his brother at all. However the inspector searched the yard and could not find any corrugated iron.

When the case for the crown prosecution closed defence solicitor called Ned Ryan brother of both the accused and deceased. He said he had lived with his two brothers in perfect harmony except for their drunken squabbles. He admitted being drunk himself that evening and was joking with David who also had drink taken. Edmund said all three fell together during the row. He told how the yard had broken bottles; tins and such things at the time eluding to the fact it may have caused the injury. He explained how as cattle dealers they were in the habit of carrying about a scissors to mark the cattle bought at fairs. However Edmund said he couldn't recall seeing anything in Tom's hand during the squabble. Finally he said Tom ran to neighbours after the struggle implying he was getting away from his brother David.

Another witness called by the defence was a neighbour John Power. His version of events was somewhat different to what had been heard before. He recalled the events of New Years day witnessing an argument. He said at nine that evening he saw Ned and Tom Ryan arguing. Next he claimed David came out of the house and made a blow at Tom. According to Power Tom ran away and David went after him, saying there was nothing wrong with him at that time. Fifteen minutes later David Ryan approached Power telling him he was injured in the stomach. John told the court how he had seen the wound saying "it was crusted and not bleeding fresh". Cross examined Power claimed again the wound was crusted as if it had happened an hour before.

Solicitor Coughlan eventually got his chance to make his case for the accused. He admitted his client was often drunk but reasoned this went with his occupation. Getting up early in the morning and fasting all day at fairs led them to drink. He argued the primary cause of death was David Ryan falling in his own backyard. The secondary cause he claimed was the operation performed at the hospital.

The judge however felt that the hospital did all it could to save his life. He told the jury if there was any doubt to find a verdict of manslaughter and leave the sentencing to him. That is exactly what the jury did. They found Thomas Ryan guilty of manslaughter but gave a strong recommendation for mercy. Their reason was the belief was that the whole thing was nothing more than a drunken brawl.

Just trying to keep what was his
Kilmacahill, Cloyne 1849

On the 29th September 1849 Bailiff Richard White went with the landlord's agent to the townland of Kilmacahill. Wigmore, the agent, possessed a warrant to seize the goods of Charles McCarthy from that townland, which was about one mile south of Ballymaloe. McCarthy was married and had eight young children living with him on the farm. The Tithe Applotment records from the 1830's show McCarthy holding a farm of 19 acres. These however are based on the *Irish Measure* which is equal to 1.62 statute acres which are used today.

They searched the farm for valuable goods and found only a horse and cart. When the pair returned to the cart, McCarthy was in the process of trying to remove it before they did. Wigmore questioned him about what he was doing and as one would expect an argument broke out between them. The farmer was trying to protect what he considered his and a struggle broke out between the two men. Eventually the agent was thrown down onto the shafts of the cart.

A few days later on the first of October, Wigmore took further action and tried to take possession of the land. He placed William Higgins on the farm as a sort of caretaker but McCarthy remained and didn't give up possession. The very next day Richard White went before the local magistrate Longfield in Cloyne. The magistrate signed a warrant for the arrest of Charles McCarthy for assault. Longfield was also the landlord of the lands at Kilmacahill.

It was later in the afternoon before two constables Michael Foley and Samuel Robinson set out from Cloyne with the warrant. It was after 6 and nearly dusk when they arrived at Kilmacahill. Once they were sure which house McCarthy lived in Constable Robinson went around to the back door while Foley approached the front. Several times he knocked on the door but he didn't stop as he heard voices inside. McCarthy eventually enquired who was there and Constable Foley said he had a warrant for his arrest. The farmer refused to open the door to them or let them in. Before they had time to think what they would do next the front door burst open and McCarthy ran out with the blade of a scythe in his hand. Constable Foley told him to surrender and come to Cloyne for he would be bailed again in the morning. Country people had a distrust of the authorities so it is no surprise the farmer didn't give himself up. He made a go at Foley with the blade but he easily fended him off with his rifle. Robinson at the rear of the house heard the commotion and ran round the front to his colleague's aid. Constable Foley told him to load his gun and defend him.

While Robinson loaded his gun McCarthy saw his opportunity and fled into a nearby field. The two constables now with their guns loaded followed him into the field. With it getting dark McCarthy could have made his escape but probably feared being shot whilst running away. Instead he turned in the field and faced his pursuers with the scythe in his hand. He was adamant he wouldn't be taken and told them so. A boy came wielding a poker to the defence of his master McCarthy and two women also arrived on the scene shouting. Constable Robinson tried to fend off the boy leaving his colleague free to make the arrest. Foley suddenly rushed forward at McCarthy to arrest him and end the standoff. Again he defended himself using the scythe and the clash of it hitting the gun could be heard in the darkness. Charles McCarthy made in the direction of Robinson who thought he was going to be struck. He called out to his partner to protect him. A shot was fired by Robinson but the consequences of it were not realised in the dark. In the struggle Foley managed to get hold of McCarthy and called for the handcuffs. Before he could be arrested he fell down in the field and died shortly afterwards from a gunshot wound.

On Friday the 5th of October an inquest was held at Cloyne into the death of Charles McCarthy by coroner Mr Geran. Magistrates Adams and Hickson were also present, as was County Inspector Fox representing the police. The jury of twelve men were from the locality some of the names are still recognisable, Nicholas Mulloney and Christopher Upton junior both farmers from the Commons Cloyne, James Wall of Knockacrump , Timothy Brophy, Edward Burke, John Mackey, David Lane, Michael Kiely, John Kennefick, Thomas Ellis, John Sheehan and Henry Baker.

First there was some discussion as to the admissibility of Constable Foley's evidence but his testimony was eventually allowed. He told the jury how he was the senior of the two that day and received the warrant in Cloyne from Constable Browne. Once the standoff took place Foley said that several times he warned McCarthy to "keep quiet and come to Cloyne with me". He detailed the events saying from the time they entered the yard till McCarthy was shot was only fifteen minutes. When Foley was questioned he admitted that when they were in the yard Robinson asked would he fire a shot. However he ordered him not to fire nor do anything to raise the alarm.

William Higgins also told how he was on the farm that night and had been put there as the sort of keeper of the land. He witnessed the two policemen trying to close in on McCarthy with their bayonets fixed on their rifles. He informed the inquest that it had got dark and he didn't see what happened in the field but heard the single gunshot.

James McCarthy also from Kilmacahill explained how he was in the house that night when the police came knocking. He heard how Charles had replied to the police saying "come back tomorrow". Not long after Charles ran out James heard Constable Robinson outside saying "I'll fire on him". A few minutes after he went out and witnessed the police charge on Charles in the field. Next he saw Charles strike Foley and the other constable Robinson fired at him. This contradicted Foley's evidence who had said Robinson fired thinking it was he who was going to be struck.

Many more witnesses were called and the inquest went on till late that evening. Eventually the evidence came to an end and the coroner addressed the jury. He said the case was an obvious one, Charles McCarthy died from a shot inflicted by the police. The question now for the jury was whether they would find it justifiable homicide or manslaughter. He explained the difference between the two conclusions. The coroner read out the law specific to the case "an officer may repel force by force, when his authority to arrest or imprison is resisted and will be justified in doing so if death should be the consequence". The jury took and hour to consider their verdict before returning to the room.

The verdict was read out; they found Constable Samuel Robinson guilty of manslaughter by inflicting a gunshot wound on Charles McCarthy of Kilmacahill which caused his death on the 2nd of October 1849.

There are no records to show what happened after the verdict was announced, this would probably indicate that no action was taken against Constable Robinson.

Mystery of the Soldier
and the Young Lass
Fermoy 1895

By the 1890s Fermoy had been a garrison town for nearly one hundred years. Decades earlier in the 1830's it had the largest military presence in Ireland. Later when the military numbers reduced the town commissioners complained as it had affected the trade. The businesses of the town had over the years become dependant on the military. The army needed huge supplies which the town provided in addition to the money the soldiers spent in the town. By night the town was busy with uniformed men from various regiments who frequented the pubs and mixed with the local girls.

Mary Ellen Bailey who lived with her father on College Road was one such young girl aged only seventeen years old. She had been seeing a soldier until she suddenly went missing on Monday 1st July 1895. Mary was last seen late on the Monday night with a soldier Timothy Donovan aged 21. He was a driver in the 67th Battery of the Artillery at Fermoy Barracks. His regiment was due to leave for Glenbeigh the next day for gunnery practice. That night would have been the last the young couple spent together for some time. Nobody knew what had happened to Mary but it was well known in the regiment that she was seeing Donovan. He was known to be short tempered so many suspected he had done something to her.

Rumours were that they had just run off together to marry and Donovan had deserted his post. Mary Bailey's family were very concerned and grew even more worried by the day.

Their worst fears were realised when Mary's body was noticed floating in the river Blackwater outside Byrnes on Artillery quay (now O'Neill Crowley Quay) on Saturday the 6th July. Rumours around the town were that Donovan and Mary had a disagreement and he had killed her. His guilt seemed obvious as why else would he have deserted. Another rumour got around the town that Donovan had been arrested by the military police in Glenbeigh and was being brought back to Fermoy. Crowds gathered at the train station for his arrival ready to lynch him but he never arrived. It turned out he had failed to return to his barracks for roll call on Monday night. Neither had he turned up before the regiment marched to Glenbeigh on Tuesday morning.

Early on the Sunday morning things took another dramatic turn when Timothy Donovan's body was also found floating in the river. Immediately the rumours changed to that it was either a double suicide or that Donovan killed her and then took his own life. Now that he was found in the river it seemed the obvious conclusion, what else could have happened to them.

The inquest was reopened by Coroner Rice on the afternoon of Monday 8th at the Fermoy Courthouse. A jury of fourteen locals were sworn in and District Inspector Ball who had been in charge of the investigation represented the police. The Coroner told how the inquest had originally been opened on Saturday when Mary Ellen's body was found and was later adjourned because Donovan was found on Sunday. Many rumours were going around as to what had happened so it was now up to the inquest to prove or disprove these rumours.

The first witness was the father of the young girl, George Bailey, an army pensioner. He told the inquest that he was the last to see his daughter alive on the evening of 1st July. He met her alone on Bridewell Hill (now called Kevin Barry Hill) and nothing seemed to be the matter with her. He told how his young daughter was meeting Donovan against his wishes. When she didn't return home on that Monday night he assumed she had eloped with him. He had gone to bed at quarter past ten that night, his daughter normally returned home between ten and eleven. The next morning he went to work and didn't notice any thing was amiss until returning from work on Tuesday evening. When questioned he admitted his daughter had told him that Donovan had hit her for meeting another soldier.

Next to give evidence was George Bailey Junior who also said it was Tuesday evening before he realised his sister was missing. Mary sometimes didn't return home at all and spent the night with friends on Barrack Hill. However this time he thought she had gone to Cork with Donovan suspecting Donovan was going to desert from his regiment. He told the inquest that the family objected to his sister's relationship as they were both too young to marry. He revealed that Donovan had hit his sister

Artillery Quay in Fermoy where Mary Bailey's body was found
Image Courtesy of National Library of Ireland

several times as he was jealous when she had met another soldier. He informed the inquest that the other man was called Robinson who was a bandsman with the Essex Regiment.

Another brother William Bailey also gave similar evidence of not noticing his sister missing until Tuesday night. He said when she stayed out all night she was at Mrs Dillon's on Barrack hill but was always back to make her brothers breakfast in the morning. William told how his father went to the Provost Sergeant on the Tuesday evening and learned that Donovan was also missing since Monday night. Mary Ellen had told William that Donovan's regiment was leaving Fermoy Tuesday morning and she was going to see him off. He said he was bemused by who would have killed his sister.

At first he thought Donovan had killed his sister but now that Donovan was found he presumed they had jumped in together. Nobody had any ill feelings against her but she had fallen out with Donovan's sister who had come to town.

After this the foreman of the jury asked to hear the medical evidence but District Inspector Ball objected. He called for an adjournment of a week so the complicated case could be further investigated. The coroner asked the doctor if the medical evidence could show was it a double suicide but the doctor replied that there were marks of violence on both bodies. The inquest was then adjourned for a week.

The police were active in the town trying to investigate what had happened. Rumours around the town changed regularly and people were now inclined to think it was a double murder. If it was a double murder nobody seemed to have the least idea who had done it nor was there a clear motive. People had heard screams by the river on the night of the 1st July but didn't take any notice of them at the time.

The inquest resumed at Fermoy Courthouse on Monday the 15th of July. The interest in the case around the town had grown and people were keen to know more. Crowds packed into the courthouse to hear the proceedings as it was a week since the inquest was adjourned. The coroner explained that he had asked the doctor last week about the medical evidence in an attempt to compel more people to come forward with information.

Barnane Walk Fermoy where Mary often walked with Donovan

District Inspector Ball said some progress had been made in the investigation but he was still not in a position to prove what had happened. He said that the rumours about the town were that Donovan's sister was also in the river as she was nowhere to be found. He had inquired and found she had left Fermoy before her brother disappeared and was now in the Convent of the Good Shepherd in Cork. Several people said they had seen Donovan's sister in Fermoy on Monday 1st, but D.I Ball said he was sure they were mistaken. The inspector said he first wished to re-examine the brothers of Mary Bailey then they would hear the medical evidence. He told the court that the inquest could not be concluded today as only four men from Donovan's regiment were in town the remainder were still away in Glenbeigh.

Mary Ellen's brothers William and George Bailey were then called to be re-examined by D.I Ball. First he asked George several questions about where he was on the night of the 1st July. He was next asked had he walked along Barnane that night, he replied that he often did but not that night nor since. His brother William Bailey was called next and he corrected a statement he made the week before. He said he must have been mistaken on seeing his sister on the bridge that night. He went to see a play and had a drink at Gardiner's at the interval. When questioned further by the Coroner he said he drank by himself, returned to the play and then walked home alone. Bailey was asked had he done anything to stop Donovan hitting his sister, he said he had informed the police but left it to them. The line of questioning seemed to be implying that one of the Bailey brothers had confronted Donovan about his conduct towards their sister, William denied this. He even admitted his sister came home with a black eye complaining about Donovan but he claimed to have done nothing about it. He told how he was aware his sister often walked along Barnane with Donovan. He also knew that Donovan was leaving town the next day. Being a military man himself he knew soldiers were known to take advantage in such situations but he took no steps to prevent his sister seeing him that night. William finally remarked that he believed it was someone of the military who had killed his sister not a civilian.

After this the district Inspector said medical evidence would be heard that day but no more after that as he still felt revealing more information would affect the investigation.

Local Doctor Timothy Dilworth gave details of the post mortem he had carried out on Mary Bailey. He found a frothy mixture in her lungs which led him to believe that she tried to breathe after entering the water. There were bruises on her face and he was of the opinion she had received a blow. When stunned from being struck she was thrown into the river. Donovan however didn't breathe after being thrown into the river. He was most likely unconscious before hitting the water. His injuries were much more serious but could have survived them if he didn't end up in the river. District Inspector Ball questioned the doctor further. He was asking the Doctor had Mary Bailey been raped or had she had sex with Donovan without being so direct. This must have caused quite a sensation in the room. Dilworth replied that he could not tell but there were no signs of a struggle. She had no scratches on her body or tears to her clothes.

This ended the inquest for the day, District Inspector Ball said he had more facts but didn't want to disclose them yet. He applied for another adjournment until the 30th July to again allow him time to have the military witnesses in town.

When the inquest sat again on the 30th of July some of the Artillery men had been recalled to the town for the inquest. Captain Gubbins from Donovan's regiment was representing the military and had permission to question the soldiers. First called to give evidence was Dr Dilworth to clear up a question by the district inspector. He replied saying "the appearance of the examination of the girl Bailey would be consistent with an attempt to violate, with her consent, which was not completed". What he was trying to say was the young couple were having sex along the river bank but were interrupted possibly by those who killed them.

Dr Williams who had also carried out the post-mortem concurred entirely with his colleague's statement. He told the jury that the evidence showed the pair had been brutally murdered. Numerous severe fractures were found on Donovan's head and bad cuts on his face. He said these cuts could have been caused by being kicked by boots with spurs such as the military wore. He explained to the jury that Donovan was unconscious before being thrown into the river. The body had been found dressed in the usual Royal Artillery uniform wearing an overcoat, tunic trousers and boots with spurs on them. He also believed that death was not caused by drowning but by concussion on the brain. He was of the opinion that Donovan's injuries were sufficient to cause his death. The picture the doctor painted leads one to believe that Donovan lay on the river bank and was kicked repeatedly by several people before being thrown into the Blackwater.

One of the army barracks in Fermoy at that time

Dr Timothy Dilworth concurred with his colleague's evidence but said the wounds could not have been caused by one person more likely two or three. He also believed Donovan had been knocked down then kicked before being thrown into the river. He differed from the other doctor as he thought Donovan could have survived his injuries if he hadn't been thrown into the river. Dilworth said that it could have been a half an hour before being thrown into the river that Mary had sex.

Corporal of the 67th Artillery William Hall told how he checked the roll on the night of the 1st July. He explained how when a soldier got leave he was issued a pass. A counterfoil was kept at the barracks until the pass expired when the soldier returned. According to the counterfoil Donovan was the only one who was absent that night.

Corporal Hall didn't hear of Donovan again until he read about it in the papers while garrisoned in Glenbeigh. Driver Kilcoyne told the inquest he was in the same sub division as Donovan. He described Donovan as a quarrelsome man when drunk and also at mealtimes. He generally started trouble every other day and generated laughter in the room when he said "there was not much give and take about him. He was bad at the taking". Several times Donovan had been sent to the cells for causing trouble. He told how it was rumoured in the regiment that Donovan was going to desert and well known that he was going out with Mary Bailey.

District Inspector Ball said the case would have to be concluded that day as the regiment was again leaving town but he had selected which facts of the case were to be heard that day. The coroner reprimanded him saying he was assuming the role of the jury and that the regiment would have to remain if the jury desired.

A gunner Ratcliffe who was in the same subdivision as Donovan was called. He was with Donovan on the night of the 1st when he met Mary. He told how he thought Donovan was depressed and had been drinking for several days since his sister had come to town.

The district inspector read out letters that Donovan had sent to his mother in June of the same year. In them he asked his mother to write to the major and ask for permission for him to leave the army. It was obvious he had written several times to his mother and she had not done as he asked of her. He begged her to do it saying "do what I asked you for god's sake and get me out of this misery".

The next witness called before the inquest was a young local girl Agnes Cook. She had seen the pair walking along the river bank on the night of the first. Shortly afterwards four artillery men passed her crossing the bridge heading in the direction the pair had gone. One of the soldiers addressed her on the bridge saying "good night Polly".

She heard one of the men say "we'll do for him tonight" or something to that effect. Moments later walking away Agnes told how she heard the screams of a woman. Bombardier Sharpe recalled crossing the bridge that night at about nine with Driver Williams. He said "good night Polly" to a young girl he now recognised in the room.

Local man Thomas Shea who lived on the quay told how at eleven on the night of the 1st of July he heard the loud piercing scream of a woman. He was at home at the time in his bedroom and looked out the window. Minutes later he saw four artillery men coming from the direction he had heard the scream. He was sure they were artillery men as they wore round caps, Shea even recalled hearing the clinking of their spurs as they walked along.

With the conclusion of the evidence the Coroner addressed the jury summing up the case. He said the case was appalling and Fermoy was normally a quiet and respectable town. The Coroner told how the case was presented to them as a double murder and the jury could come to no other verdict.

After a short deliberation the jury returned an open verdict of wilful murder. The jury told how the deceased had been murdered on the night of 1st July at Barnane Walk Fermoy by some person or persons unknown. They had been beaten and then thrown into the river.

The jury commended District Inspector Ball for taking charge of the investigation of the complicated case. They expressed their dissatisfaction with the majority of the military witnesses. District Inspector Ball said the constabulary were continuing to investigate the case and he wished more people would come forward to give information.

There is no record of anybody being arrested or being brought before the courts after the inquest. It is possible that if it were soldiers that carried out the brutal murder it may have been covered up within the military. Interest in the mysterious case died away over time and Fermoy went on being a garrison town. Suddenly in February 1898 the Waterford News publishes a short story on the murder claiming a man had made a confession. The man was alleged to have been an ex convict who claimed he had been helped by a local man. When it was investigated it turned out the man who confessed could not have done it as he was serving a term in prison at the time. The only reason he confessed was to get some one else into trouble.

It was another 40 years before there would be any more light shed on the case. Some time in 1935 it was reported that a brother of Mary Bailey confessed on his death bed to having killed his sister and Donovan.

Gortroe Tithe Massacre
Ballinakilla near Bartlemy 1834

In penal times in Ireland, Catholics were seriously restricted and treated like second class citizens. During this time Catholics could not own land, vote in any election or even practice their own religion. Daniel O'Connell started a campaign for Catholic Emancipation in the 1820's. He was elected for County Clare in 1828, but couldn't take his seat in the House of Commons. By the following year the Catholic Emancipation act was passed and it reduced some of the restrictions.

What really outraged the Irish farmers was that they were still required to pay a tithe which was ten percent of farm produce. Anyone who worked over one acre was liable to pay a tithe. The records of these payments still exist. What was most insulting was the tithe was paid to the clergy of the Protestant Church of Ireland. The fact that the protestant clergymen who benefited from the tithes often didn't even live in the area caused even more resentment. In the early 1830's the situation led to the Tithe war where many Irish farmers started a passive campaign of resistance to the paying of tithes. With more and more refusing to pay the tithe some protestant clergymen found themselves deprived of the income they had got for nothing. Those that refused to pay knew there would be consequences and some were prepared to lose everything. Lists of defaulters were drawn up and orders issued to confiscate goods and property.

In 1834 the tithe owner for the parish of Gortroe, Archdeacon Collis died. It was thought Collis hadn't made much effort to collect the outstanding tithes with some time, due to his ill health. He was replaced in May of 1834 by Archdeacon William Ryder who was the complete opposite. Ryder was known locally as Black Billy, due it was said to his dark complexion but it may also have been reference to his character. He got the post as he was already a well known champion of the tithe system. A few years before in 1832 with his brother Rev Joshua Ryder, he had seized cattle in Castlelyons for outstanding tithes. In the parish there were about 2,900 Catholics and the tithes were annually worth £1,500. On the other hand there was said to be only 29 Protestants in the parish, 13 of whom were related to Ryder.

The tithes fell due on the 1st of November and within a short time he was trying to collect them. Ryder was only entitled to collect the tithes since May of that year when he took over. On the 15th of November Ryder's bailiff was out serving notices on those outstanding. When in the townland of Desert near Bartlemy the bailiff was set upon by a large group of locals. They managed to get the notices he had yet to serve from him. The crowd then forced him to go back to those he had served notices to and take them back.

Archdeacon Ryder didn't give up but was intending instead to deal with the locals using more force. On Monday 15th of December Ryder had two regiments of soldiers with some cavalry in Rathcormac. Armed with the soldiers they managed to break the resistance of the country people. That day several cows and sheep were confiscated in the Rathcormac & Castlelyons area. Outnumbered the locals tried in any way they could to impede the military. Some even attempted to grab the bridles of the officer's horses. Those that did were severely wounded, cut by the officer's swords; one even had his hand cut off. By the time the soldiers came to McGrath's farm, a huge crowd of well over a hundred had gathered. The gate was locked and the crowd assembled inside the yard. Several suffered bayonet wounds trying to prevent the soldiers coming in over the gate. The soldiers tried to break the lock with the butts of their muskets. Eventually Ryder quite literally took the law into his own hands. He took a huge stone and broke the lock with just a few blows. The soldiers marched into the yard and took a few heifers for the tithe. Despite their determination the locals were seriously overpowered and eventually had to relent. The following day the forces were out seizing goods in the area without much resistance.

Wednesday 17th of December 1834, Ryder along with armed soldiers went to the townland of Ballynoe south of Bartlemy to collect outstanding tithes. When he approached the farmhouse the haggard gate was locked and the haggard was filled with men. The men must have learned he was coming and were there to resist his attempts of collecting. This completely caught Archdeacon Ryder by surprise and some trouble broke out. It is said the landlord happened to pass that way and he returned to the farm.

The landlord a General Barry himself paid the outstanding tithe to save trouble breaking out.

Some of the troops camped on the green in Rathcormac for the night.

Early the next morning Thursday the 18th Archdeacon Ryder set out again to collect more tithes. He led the forces himself to the Bartlemy area. There were about one hundred infantry men from the 29th regiment under Major Walter. A small party cavalry from the 4th Dragoon Guards were led by Lieut Tait and there was also a small number of police. When they arrived at Bartlemy they met a large number of locals while passing through the village. The locals shouted abuse at the military and threw stones but no other trouble broke out.

Archdeacon Ryder was accompanied by Captain Collis and Captain Bagley who were also local magistrates. Collis also had another reason to be there, he was next of kin to the late Archdeacon Collis. This made Captain Collis entitled to collect the tithes due before May of that year. The large group of armed forces had been to several houses in the area and met no resistance. Nobody had paid the tithe but Ryder made some swear they would pay and the soldiers left.

They then went to the nearby townland of Ballinakilla where a widow named Ryan owed forty shilling in tithes. The soldiers marched down a boreen four deep until they came to her farm. They found the gate to the haggard blocked with a cart, logs and anything that could have been got. There were a large number of locals gathered on the ditches and inside Ryan's yard calling out "no tithes, no parson, no church". Captain Bagley read out the riot act but the crowd didn't disperse. Fighting broke out between the soldiers and the country people, who were only armed with spades and sticks. Some of the soldiers tried to get into the cart and the haggard but were driven back with sticks. The soldiers then tried to push the cart back but again, when they did the crowd inside resisted. Officers encouraged their men to use the bayonets and drive into the crowd to push them back. This was tried several times but they could make no way into the crowd. The widow Ryan was called by the military to come out and pay the tithe to end the trouble. The infantry then fired blank volleys in the air to frighten the crowd but it had the opposite effect. The crowd in fact got more courage in the belief that the infantry would not load their muskets and fire on them.

After about three quarters of an hour the riot act had been read out three times to no avail. Orders were given to load their weapons and fire upon the crowd. Captain Collis was then heard to say "fire away to the devil fire" and that is what the first four in line did. Men at the front of the crowd were hit and fell to the ground.   As they did their place was taken by more who then fell when the next volley was fired.

The crowd started to disperse and some of those running away were shot from behind. Eventually after the crowd cleared, a bugle to signal the end of firing was heard. Once the smoke began to clear in the yard it became obvious it was a massacre. Over twenty men lay on the ground. Nine were killed instantly and the remainder seriously wounded. The soldiers could now force their way into the haggard with the crowd inside scrambling for their lives. Once in the haggard Captain Collis tried to regroup his men and be ready to fire again if the crowd attacked. Major Walter had a better sense of the situation and didn't prepare his men as it would have led to more bloodshed.

When he got his chance Ryder rode into the yard and demanded his money.

The widow Ryan must have been shocked and told him she would pay. Ryder however acted with no remorse at all saying "pay me instantly, for I will not leave the place until you pay me". Maybe she felt guilty that she should have paid it sooner to prevent the bloodshed but it is believed that the widow then paid the outstanding money. What kind of man was Ryder to accept the forty shilling in the midst of the carnage he had created? He was said to have stood there and counted the money while the widow's son lay dead nearby. He seems to have had the attitude that he had a God given right to this money at any cost. Then you would expect Ryder would gather the military and clear from the area but no. He gave orders to Major Walter to round up his men and then they went on to more farms looking for more tithe money. At one farm the farmer wasn't there, maybe he lay dead in Ryan's haggard but Ryder still seized nine cows.

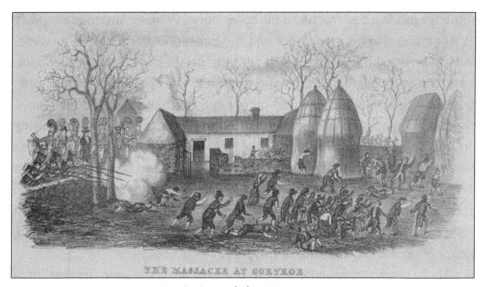

Depiction of the Massacre
Image courtesy of National Library of Ireland

It would be a long time before doctors arrived to tend to the wounded. Word was sent to Rathcormac and Dr Barry set out for the dreadful scene. Dr Downey from Fermoy was also informed and went to the scene. The bodies of the dead were taken to the nearby chapel and the bell rung continuously. People from all over the area came to see for themselves what had occurred. Three of those wounded later died bringing the death count up to twelve.

Those killed instantly were William Cashman from the Fermoy Road and Michael Barry from Watergrasshill. Brothers Michael and John Collins from Skehana also near Watergrasshill. John saw his brother being shot and then fall to the ground. He went to help him up but was also shot and killed. Richard Ryan was the widow's eldest son. The remainder of those who died was William Twomey a local thatcher, Michael Lane, Patrick Curtin, John Cotter and John Daly. The other three died later from their injuries, John Cotter, William Ambrose and William Ivis. Of the twelve who were killed, eleven left families who had been dependant on them.

There were many more wounded who were lucky to survive but would never fully recover from their injuries. Daniel Daly was shot in the neck but the ball was extracted from his shoulder. David Keeffe was hit in the shoulder but the ball fractured his collar bone. William Amarous was very lucky he was also hit in the neck and the ball hit his spine but he survived. Mick Ryan was hit in the stomach with the ball passing right through him. John Cotter received a shot in the thigh but the ball didn't hit his bone. Andrew Thinwick was hit in the elbow and the ball shattered his elbow. The ball then passed through his arm exiting through his hand destroying his middle finger. John Ivis must have been one of those running away as he was shot in the shoulder from behind. The ball was so deep that it was extracted from the other side. Daniel Hegarty had been hit in the abdomen and with the primitive medicine at the time there was no hope of him surviving. He does however survive as his name isn't listed as having died. Those injured were all taken to hospital

There seems to have been no more trouble in the area despite some of the military coming back to the scene of the killings.

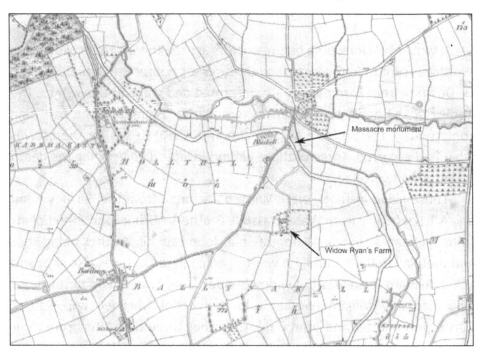

Period map showing the location of Ryan's farm
in relation to Bartlemy village

Only two days later on the 20th an inquest was opened at Rathcormac courthouse to investigate. On the first day of the inquest there was much debate about the manner with which the jury had been selected. Stephen Barry representing the local people who had been killed, accused the coroner of letting everyone know his intentions. By the end of the day two extra coroners had to be sent for from Cork and also some Members of Parliament arrived.

In the evening the jury was drawn at random and they finished up with a large jury of twenty three. One of the Members of Parliament Fergus O'Connor, a barrister volunteered to also represent the locals. Due to the huge amount of witnesses needed to be called it was obvious it would take several days. On the second day of the inquest William Ryder's brother Joshua arrived escorted by a troop of cavalry soldiers.

On the 23rd December several doctors gave evidence of having examined the bodies of those who had died. One doctor told how he had examined the wound of Michael Lane. He had been shot in the head, the ball entered near the ear passed down and exited near his spine. A juror asked how many of those killed received frontal wounds, the doctor replied four. This shows that the other 8 were shot when running away.

The next man questioned was William McAuliffe a farmer also in Ballinakilla. He said that before going to the widow Ryan's, the tithe collectors visited his farm. William Ryder he said took out a prayer book and got him to swear an oath on it that he would pay his tithes by 23rd of December.

Again on Christmas Eve the inquest sat and listened to more evidence. The archdeacon William Ryder made his first appearance and Captain Bagley also arrived.

A farmer Michael Haly from nearby townland of Ballinure was called before the inquest.

He remembered that day well he saw Ryder on horseback ride forcefully towards the cavalry. He then ordered them to load and they put their swords away to load their pistols. He then ordered them to fire. When they did Haly saw Michael Barry fall from the ditch he was standing on. Haly told that he couldn't recall when he last paid tithes, goods of his were seized over a year ago but he still didn't pay. Ryder had previously made him an offer of reducing the debt by a fifth but he still didn't pay. He told the coroner how he didn't want to be the first one around to "break the law of the country" and pay.

The inquest sat again in December after a short break for Christmas. Michael Connell of the nearby townland of Ballinwillin, told how he was standing on the straw in Ryan's haggard. He heard Bagley giving the order to fire and he was only standing about six feet away from him at the time. Before that he said there was not much trouble at all except for a stick that was thrown which hit a soldier's cap. When questioned further he told that their purpose in the yard was to keep the soldiers out but by peaceful means. He didn't see anyone hitting the soldiers before they fired except for that one stick. The soldiers then advanced and drove them off the ditches with their bayonets.

The next witness was Denis Connell a farmer from the nearby townland of Ballyda. He recalled that day saying he was standing behind the haggard ditch in an orchard. Ever before the firing occurred he met a man called Hegarty, who had been stabbed in the chest with a bayonet. Hearing the shooting he immediately ran and while running was shot through the collar of his coat. He also saw Daly run away, get hit and fall to the ground.

The widow Johanna Ryan gave her testimony at the inquest; she told how that morning she locked up her house and stables. The gate to the haggard was also locked and blocked with a cart. All this was done to avoid paying the tithe; she had always paid her tithe until recently when everyone else stopped paying it. She told the jury "I would have paid if others paid". This she said was the first time Ryder came looking for his tithe to be paid. When the haggard was cleared Ryder rode in and said to the widow "pay me my tithe". He then said "I will not leave until you pay me". The widow told how Ryder must have seen her son's body and others nearby but still demanded his payment.

While the inquest was going on Daniel O Connell wrote publicly his legal opinion of the dreadful affair; he had wanted a peaceful tithe campaign. As the first Catholic Member of Parliament in Ireland and a barrister, his opinion may have affected the outcome of the inquest. He stated that the military were first guilty of trespass of Ryan's haggard. Mrs Ryan was entitled to resist that trespass and the shooting was clearly murder.

On the 3rd of January Major Walter who was in charge of the 29th regiment was called to give his account of what had happened. He had been given orders to take his troops to Rathcormac and take directions from Archdeacon Ryder and Captain Collis. He understood they were

Much quieter scene of Bartlemy village in recent times

to protect the bailiffs while they removed corn from a haggard. Passing through Bartlemy the crowd shouted out "No Tithes, No Tithes" and Captain Bagley ordered bayonets to be fixed. Once near the widow Ryan's yard his men tried to force their way in but were repelled by the crowd. He told that it was Captain Bagley who gave the orders to fire. Major Walter told how of his 100 men only 41 had fired a total of 66 shots. Twenty men fired one shot, nine fired two shots and eight fired three shots. The major said that including all the men – infantry, cavalry and the police there were one hundred and twenty one men armed that day. Once in the haggard after the shooting Ryder came up to him and said "Major you may withdraw your men the tithe is paid".

The inquest was on its twelfth day on Monday 5th January and still hearing evidence from the military. Captain Sheppard gave a long account of where he was on the day. He had heard the last witness Major Walter address the crowd. The Major said "my men are loaded for god's sake go home or I shall fire, I have been ordered to fire". Sheppard then asked Bagley what should he do and was told "try the bayonet first, you must force a passage even if you have to fire for it". H then told at one point he got into the cart blocking the haggard but was beaten back by the crowd using sticks. He didn't get the order to fire but heard another party firing. He then asked Major Walter who told him to fire also. More soldiers were called giving similar evidence of the events that day.

The inquest sat again on the Tuesday hearing more evidence. More soldiers told their sequence of events that day. Captain Bagley said he had written to Captain Collis to attend the inquest. However Collis replied that it was not right for him to be examined and declined to come.

By Wednesday the 7th of January the inquest had reached its 14th day but with a verdict likely there was again great interest from the locals. Coroner Foot addressed the jury and tried to sum up the case reasonably briefly. He read out the relevant law about riots and also read the riot act to the jury. The coroner asked the jury to acquit the military as he said they only followed the orders of the magistrates. If they didn't the officers would lose their commissions in the army. The coroner finished and the jury retired to consider their verdict. Over six hours later at nearly seven in the evening the jury returned with their verdict. Thirteen of the jury returned wilful murder, two thought it was manslaughter and eight of the jury said justifiable homicide. At first it seems the coroners are unclear what exact course they should take with the case. Sometime later the coroners issued warrants for the arrest of Captain Bagley, Collis and Archdeacon Ryder.

The warrants don't seem to have been executed as Collis was seen in Dublin and it was alleged his fellow Fermoy magistrates had refused to act. Ryder was also seen at large in Dublin, his brother who was also a magistrate was thought to have been responsible for getting him off.

Ryder lived in Ballinterry House close to Rathcormac which had come into his possession through his wife's family. Now he feared the whole countryside had turned against him which was quite justified. He no longer felt safe and was said to have fitted steel shutters on his windows fearing revenge from the locals.

By March 1835 the case was to be called before the upcoming Spring Assizes in Cork. Captain Collis had given himself up and was subsequently imprisoned in Cork awaiting the trial. When the Assizes did sit an application was made to postpone the case. The judge agreed with the application and decided to postpone. The others must also have been in custody at this stage and they allowed them bail on a security of £1000 each.

It was August of 1835 when the case was finally looked at by the Grand Jury.

The jury was unanimous in its decision to scrap the charges against the three men.

It was claimed that because the Grand Jury came from all over the county their verdict would be unprejudiced. However the Grand Jury was made up of the landlords who would never take the side of the country people.

After the killings the Government stopped the automatic use of the military for the collection of tithes. Because of this the tithe system failed completely as nobody was prepared to pay. In 1838 the tithe payment was combined into the tenant rent payment and passed on by the landlords. This increased the rent payable by the tenants.

Rev William Ryder continued living at Ballinterry House despite the ill feeling in the area. Both his sons died young before they were married so his family name died out. His reputation as a cruel man was never going to be forgotten but one of his daughters was popular with the locals. She helped the poor during the famine and was even said to return goods that her father had confiscated for tithes.

The tomb where William Ryder is believed to be buried in Gortroe Cemetery

Monument at Bluebell cross erected in 1984

Farmyard Shooting
Carberytown, Glounthaune 1935

At barely over fifteen years of age Mary Hickey from Caherlag near Glanmire was sent out to work at a nearby farm Carberytown belonging to Thomas Cahill. Mary helped milk the cows as well as domestic duties. Every Wednesday and Sunday evenings Mary went home to visit her parents almost a mile away in the townland of Rowgarrane. She was the youngest of what would now be considered a large family, with five older brothers and an older sister Margaret. Her father John Hickey, was employed as a farm labourer in the locality.

Also living on the Carberytown farm was Thomas Cahill's younger siblings Anne Cahill and Jim Cahill better known as *Balty*. Thomas had inherited the farm from his mother some years ago despite not being the eldest son. Thomas was aged 36 and one year older than Jim. The Cahill's family was certainly a large one with fourteen in total but only the three remained on the farm. In addition to Mary working there, her brother William was also employed by Thomas Cahill. An uncle of theirs Patrick O'Brien had worked there for fifteen years. He lived in an outhouse that opened into the inner yard.

On Sunday the 28th of July there was great excitement in Cahill's farm as the Mayfield Harriers Club held their annual hunt fixture. The hunt started at Carberytown house before going on to the nearby townland Lackenroe. Mary served the dinner at Carberytown house and afterwards visited her parents who lived nearby. She stayed with her parent's and siblings for a few hours before going back to Carberytown. Before she left that night she was her usual self laughing and joking with her mother and father. Mary left her home at about ten that night and returned back to her place of work with her sister Margaret and a friend called Robert Jeffers.

Nearing Cahill's farm the group stopped at the gate and chatted for a while before parting company. While they were chatting, Jim Cahill brother of Mary's employer came into the farmyard. Mary parted with her sister and went through the gate towards the inner yard. Margaret and her companion had scarcely turned for home when they heard the sound of a shotgun being discharged in the farm yard Mary had just walked into.

The pair for some reason suspected that Mary had been involved and went back a little to see. Looking around the corner of the avenue Margaret saw her sister lying on the ground of the outer yard but daren't go any further. In dread the pair turned and ran, one could imagine they were hoping not to be seen thinking they could be next. On the long avenue that led to the farm near the main road they met Anne Cahill. She was going the other way and she too had heard the shot from further away. They must have told her what they had caught a glimpse of before running on. It was nearly a mile to Margaret's parent's house but wasn't long before they were there and told her father.

Meanwhile back at the farmyard Patrick O'Brien an uncle of Mary's who also worked on the farm heard the shot being fired. He was in bed at the time but was woken by the sound of the shot and knew the shot was fired very close to the inner yard. He went out to the yard to see but saw nothing and didn't think anything of it at first. When he Jim Cahill emerged from outside the yard and asked him what he had done. At first Jim replied he would do the same to him, it was then O'Brien realised how serious the situation was. He had earlier been out for a drink and they had drunk two pints together.

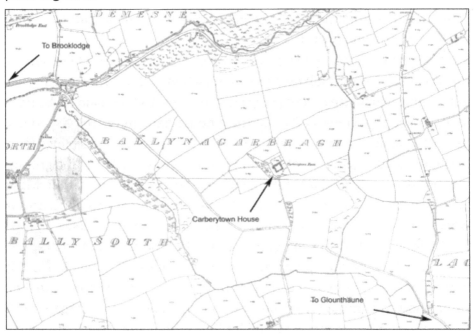

Map showing location of Carberytown house

Things were now very different with Jim and in a moment of rage Jim struck O'Brien and he went out through the gate. It must have come as a shock to see his niece lying on the ground and a scuffle broke out between them. Anne who had rushed up the avenue saw poor Mary Hickey lying on the ground. When she arrived her brother was scuffling with Patrick O'Brien who was still asking what he had done. Soon after Jim must have fled the scene knowing his actions had dire consequences.

A few minutes later Thomas Cahill came on the scene and found Mary lying on the ground with a shotgun nearby. Close to her were a newspaper and an empty milk can she had been carrying under her arm. Thomas realised she was dead seeing the large gaping wound to her forehead and the pool of blood.

Once Margaret Hickey reached home she told her father who was in bed. Although he could scarcely believe what he was told, he got up and threw on some clothes with haste. He rushed to Cahill's farm as quickly as he could, accompanied by one of his sons William. On the way there they met Thomas Cahill who told them the devastating news that Margaret's worst fears were true. Thomas Cahill had to tell Hickey that his youngest daughter had been shot dead.

Mary's brother William ran off to get the local priest and returned a while later with Fr Callanan from Glounthaune. Also at the scene of the crime were the Gardaí who were desperate to get to the bottom of what had happened. It wasn't going to be a case that needed too much investigation as the murderer couldn't live with what he had done. Fleeing the scene Jim Cahill walked to the barracks in Glanmire arriving there at about eleven thirty. He gave himself up to Sergeant Cotter who was on duty there that night. Jim Cahill told them "I have shot a girl stone dead tonight. I am placing myself in your charge sergeant. She is above in the yard at Carberytown. It was passion and nerves that got me". He was taken into custody but wasn't charged until the details could be confirmed.

Sergeant Cotter quickly proceeded to the scene of the crime to confirm what Cahill had said. Superintendent Fionan O'Driscoll from Cobh arrived on the scene at one in the morning and afterwards went to Glanmire barracks to interview the chief suspect. When Sergeant Cotter returned to the Barracks in Glanmire he entered the room where Cahill was held.

Cahill immediately asked him "is Mary dead?" Cotter informed her that she was dead.

The body couldn't be moved until a forensic photographer arrived to gather evidence. All night Mr Hickey stood vigil over the body of his youngest daughter despite his grief. Several times the guards pleaded with him to go and get sleep but he remained throughout the night.

After dawn the photographer arrived and did what he needed to do. Only then the body was removed to Carberytown farmhouse for the post mortem to be carried out.

The guards took statements from many people of the locality who may have seen anything leading up to the shooting.

Location where Mary Hickey was found,
with thanks to Irish Newspaper Archives and Cork Examiner

Jim Cahill was charged with the murder at Cork court house before District Justice P O'Sullivan. The hearing was only general evidence of the arrest from the Superintendent and Sergeant Cotter. The Superintendent applied for the remand of Jim Cahill for a further fourteen days to carry out his investigation. Solicitor of the accused made an application to have the prisoner medically examined while in custody in Cork jail. There were no objections made by either side to the applications.

The funeral took place on the 30th July at three in the afternoon at Glounthaune Church to burial at Caherlag graveyard.

At four that same afternoon the inquest was held in Riverstown by Coroner Rice from Fermoy. Supt Fionan O'Driscoll who was in charge of investigating the case represented Gardaí while Solicitor Buckley appeared for Jim Cahill. Dr. Patrick Cagney from Whitescross told the jury how he had done the post-mortem the previous day. He found the body to be about eighteen hours dead and she was a normal well nourished girl. Dr Cagney described in details the injuries he found. The skull was broken in two places. There was a larger gaping wound near the left eye and her eyes and face were destroyed. The cheekbone was smashed and left jaw bone also broken in more than one place by the blast. He also found the base of the skull to be fractured and resulted in bleeding. When questioned, the doctor said it was quite possible she was walking at the time of being hit but towards the source. To further questioning he replied "the impact of the shot must have been so great that it flung her right down to the ground with a crash". The cause of death he said was shock and haemorrhage of blood from a gunshot wound to the head. Dr Michael Dunlea from Riverstown who assisted with the post mortem corroborated the medical evidence heard before. William Hickey gave evidence of identification but Supt O'Driscoll called no further witnesses. Jim Cahill was held in jail in Cork until the prosecution were ready for a court hearing.

On Saturday the 17th of August there was a special sitting of the Cork District Court before Justice Sullivan. Jim Cahill was charged that on the 28th July 1935 he did unlawfully wilfully and of malice aforethought kill and murder on Mary Hickey.

The prosecution was led by Supt Fionan O'Driscoll and state solicitor Maurice O'Connor. Mr T.A Buckley represented the case for the accused.

The girl, Mary Hickey, aged 17 years, who was shot dead.

**Picture of Mary Hickey, with thanks to
Irish Newspaper Archives and Cork Examiner**

CORK SHOOTING TRAGEDY.—Our representative interviewing Mr. Hickey, father of the deceased girl, outside his home at Caherlag, Glanmire, Co. Cork. ("Examiner" Photo).

**Mary Hickey's father outside his house after the murder,
with thanks to Irish Newspaper Archives and Cork Examiner**

After the hearing the accused was remanded in custody for a further week until another hearing on the 24th August when it was thought the case would be completed.

William Hickey brother of the deceased said before the court that he also worked at Cahill's farm. He told how Mary Hickey and Jim Cahill were not speaking for a few weeks before. William couldn't say much as he had been off sick for a month before that. However he was there on the farm on the 28th of July when he, Jim Cahill and his sister Mary milked the cows together. William spoke to Jim during milking but his sister didn't speak at all. After milking the cows William left the farm leaving only Mary and Jim in the farmhouse. He said he later saw his sister near their parent's house about seven. William told how he had known Jim Cahill since his childhood.

One of the key witnesses was Margaret Hickey, as she was one of the last to see her sister alive. Margaret explained what had happened that night, as they walked up the avenue before the shooting a man walked ahead of them. He had entered the avenue through a gap in the hedge and went towards the yard before them. She said in court that this man was Jim Cahill and it's safe to assume he saw them too. After chatting for a while she said she had barely turned around when the shot was fired. Going back to see what happened she said "I saw accused coming from the direction of the wooden gate and go towards the spot where my sister was lying". After some objections to a question Margaret answered that she had known Jim Cahill with many years. She always found him to be a normal ordinary man.

Again like the inquest both Dr Cagney & Dunlea repeated the medical evidence. Doctor Cagney told the court she was standing only three or four yards from the gun as the spread of shot was five or six inches.

**The crowds attending the funeral, with thanks to
Irish Newspaper Archives and Cork Examiner**

Anne Cahill sister of the prisoner, told the court how she had been out on the night but arrived home at 10:40. She heard the shot from some distance away and met Maggie Hickey and a young man running down the avenue. She said "on entering the yard I saw the body of the dead girl lying there". Her brother Jimmy and Paddy O'Brien were fighting and she heard O'Brien ask "what did you do to her?" She asked her brother herself and he said "I shot Mary Hickey, she is all right I said an act of contrition in her ear". Anne told the court how she was surprised that her brother Jim was back on the farm that night. He normally stayed out much later than her on a Sunday night.

Another key witness called was Patrick O'Brien and he recalled dinner being served by Mary Hickey in Cahill's farmhouse that evening. Afterwards Patrick went to O'Leary's public house with his brother John and Jim Cahill with whom he had always been friendly. They parted company and he walked home with his brother John. He hadn't seen Jim Cahill again until he was awoken by the shot. When questioned in court O'Brien said that he always found Jim to be an ordinary sensible man. He went on to say he was not drunk that night and was perfectly sober in fact. He was asked about what he thought caused the terrible shooting. O'Brien told how they milked the cows together in mornings and for the past weeks Mary and Jim hadn't spoken. Neither of them told him the reason and he didn't ask. In the mornings after the cows were in they would go in for a cup of tea. He recalled seeing Jim staring at Mary Hickey and continued his stare as she walked around the kitchen.

Thomas Cahill told in court how he had employed Mary Hickey in March 1934 and she had always been a trustworthy employee. The Cahill's mother had died in January the same year. In their mother's will she had left the farm to Thomas but Jim was to have a right of residence provided he continued to work on the farm. Thomas also told the court how he had not spoken to his brother for three years. This made things very difficult on the farm and any instructions were conveyed through one of the employees. Mary sometimes told Jim what Thomas wanted done on the farm. Thomas said he was aware that for a few weeks before the shooting Mary and Jim were not speaking. He had noticed the trouble between them and at least once he had given Mary instructions for his brother. Mary however refused to pass the instructions on to Jim but said no more on the matter. Thomas had arrived home that night at quarter past eleven and saw Mary lying in the yard. He immediately recognised his shotgun which he normally kept in a cupboard in the kitchen. He picked up the gun and found a discharged cartridge in one barrel but the other was empty. Thomas said he had a box of cartridges over the door in the pantry away from the gun. He told the court that never before had his brother Jim used the shotgun. Before finishing Thomas again said that Mary was a good and trusted employee. When his sister Anne was away Mary would take entire charge of all the domestic duties of the house. The solicitor for the accused didn't cross examine the witness.

Gardaí Patrick Nash recalled in court the night Jim Cahill came into the barracks and handed himself over to them. Nash was on duty as the barrack orderly when there was a knock on the door at about half eleven. Cahill was in an extremely distressed state, he immediately told that he had shot Mary Hickey. Sergeant Cotter then left to go to the scene and Cahill was put into the dayroom of the barracks. He continued talking to Garda Nash and told him "I will hang for this in Mountjoy, I was a foolish man to shoot her dead. The devil got the better of me". When asked did Mary Hickey say something to him after he shot her he said, "I don't think she could, as I shot her at very close range".

Avenue leading up to Carberytown farm as it is now

Superintendent Fionan O'Driscoll was called to give evidence. He interviewed Jim Cahill at the Glanmire barracks at 3:10 am the morning of the killing. That night Jim Cahill told the super he was not feeling up to making a statement. O'Driscoll returned the usual that he didn't have to make a statement but anything he did say would be written down and recorded. Cahill began hover and told him "I am very sorry for the girl and her people". When asked more about whom he had shot Jim Cahill replied "I would be better off if I never did it. I shot her on the spur of the moment through passion and nerves. I had no intention of doing it. She was very obliging to me, but she often gave me impudence. She was a green country girl. I cannot go any further with you tonight". When asked that night the reason for shooting her he replied "I could give you an explanation but that would get other people in trouble".

After three Saturdays in court by the 31ˢᵗ of August the evidence for the state was concluded. Mr Buckley for the defence said he did not intend to call any evidence at this stage and reserved his defence. The charge was read out to Jim Cahill and he was asked if he had a statement to make. He simply replied in a very low voice before the court and said no. The judge returned the accused on the capital charge for trial at the next sitting of the Central Criminal Court.

Later in the year the Central Criminal Court sat in December before Justice Meredith. Before the court Jim Cahill was found to be insane and he was to be kept in custody under orders from the Attorney General.

Jim Cahill later died while in custody and his body was buried in Templeisque cemetery near Sarsfield Court. Balty never told the reason why he killed Mary who was eighteen years younger than him. It's easy to assume it was love that drove him to it but that doesn't seem to be the case. Certainly Jim and Thomas were on very bad terms for several years maybe since their mother died and Thomas inherited the farm. Some say Jim was stealing eggs from the farm and Mary knew. At some point Jim was blaming Mary for the missing eggs and trying to get her into trouble. Eventually Mary told her employer that Jim was doing the stealing and it caused even more trouble. Thomas alluded to it in court saying Mary was an honest employee. So it would seem Mary was just an innocent party who was caught up in a family feud.

A case of mistaken identity
Mondaniel, Rathcormac 1874

In the summer of 1874 there was a level of unrest amongst the people of North Cork as a brutal murder had recently taken place near Mitchelstown. No one had been arrested for the murder of an old couple who were beaten to death. Their cottage was afterwards turned over by the murderer looking for valuables. On Friday 31st of July another similar brutal murder was discovered near Tallow. A feeble old woman was broken into and beaten to death for whatever money she had. It was presumed that the same person had carried out both murders and remained at large in the area.

Rathcormac lying almost halfway between the two places was no different than any other and who would have thought they would be next.

On Saturday 1st August, Johanna Cotter, a farmers wife living in the townland of Mondaniel north of the village of Rathcormac went to Fermoy to sell some butter. She returned home to her farmhouse with the proceeds of her sales. It was summer and she was sitting at her spinning wheel with the door open. A strange man approached and asked for a drink of water which she gave him before he left again.

While she fetched his drink the man had done his reconnaissance of who was in the house. Not a quarter of an hour later the man returned again now familiar with the surroundings. This time he asked where her husband was and she replied that he had gone to Rathcormac. A young daughter who was in another room saw the man strike her mother with a pitchfork. When she fell to the ground he struck her on the head several more times.

The young girl screamed and the noise disturbed a sow that had a litter of banbhs in the house. The sow went for the intruder and the man struck the sow before he pursued the young girl. She climbed onto a table and dragged her self through an open window but a string of her pinafore became entangled in the window. The man reached for it and had her caught by the string. She managed to frantically break away and ran to raise the alarm. Her elder fourteen year old sister was working in a nearby potato field. She came to the cottage to find the man rifling through boxes, looking for any thing of value. He again made a go for her with the pitchfork but didn't succeed. The intruder turned and fled the scene running off down the road.

The local barracks was informed of the murder and a huge search of the area helped by the local farmers was initiated. Every horse and labourer in the area was given up by farmers in the search for the man on the run. Any gun owners loaded them and set out to find the murderer. Many more joined in on the search armed with sticks and stones. He was reported to be heading for the woods near Cairn Thierna but being clever he doubled back to the village of Rathcormac by a long route. He was noticed in the village and headed south towards Cork until he came to a place called Kilshannig. There again he doubled back to throw his pursuers off and took a road heading east towards Tallow. Sub inspector Fleming from Fermoy, helped by a local farmer named Hannon, who was said to have great judgement led pursuit. Fleming and Hannon took the right road and came in sight of the man by Leary's cross near the village of Bridebridge. Fleming was in plain clothes and so decided to approach the dangerous man and surprise him. Leaving Hannon out of sight he rode on, passed the man out then jumped off his horse and pulled out his revolver. The man was caught completely off guard and wasn't in a position to resist arrest.

Such was the intensity of the search in the area he was lucky to have met one of the police. If it was the locals with their sticks he would have most likely have been lynched on the spot. After being arrested he refused to tell the police his name and was taken to the local barracks in Rathcormac. He was described as being twenty six years old, five foot six tall and of powerful build. The man only said he was not from the area and had recently returned from America.

On Sunday morning after mass, four of the local congregation were used for an identity line up. The daughter of the deceased Mary Cotter was brought to the barracks and unhesitatingly identified the prisoner as the man she had seen in her house the day before. Two local farmers were also called and identified the same man. A similar amount of money that Mrs Cotter received for her butter in Fermoy was found in the man's

**Leary's Cross near Bridebridge close to where
the murderer was arrested**

procession. She had also purchased in the town that morning new bootlaces, she had given them to her children but kept two for herself. The two new bootlaces were found on the man after he was searched. Later two policemen from Midleton also identified him as being arrested in Midleton two weeks before in connection with a robbery.

Wasting no time, an inquest was held the Monday after the murder at Rathcormac Courthouse. There was no coroner available so magistrate Dennehy presided over the inquest. The unnamed man was brought into the courthouse through a large crowd that had gathered outside. The crowd shouted abuse at the prisoner which he was said to have faced defiantly. When the inquest sat the prisoner who was accused of murder was placed standing beside James Cotter, husband of the deceased. Cotter became quite agitated and had to be restrained when he tried to get his hands on the man who murdered his wife. The pair had to be separated before the case proceeded. Mr T Rice crown solicitor prosecuted and the accused seemed to have no legal representation. He commended the people of the locality and the police for hunting down the man who stood accused.

James Cotter, husband of the murdered woman told the inquest where he was that day. He was at a nearby farm that morning and when he returned his wife had gone to Fermoy. His work brought him to Ballinterry over two miles away driving two pigs in a crib. Later he returned and met his eight year old son on the road. His mother had sent him for bran that she had forgotten to get in Fermoy earlier. The pair went back to Rathcormac and bought the bran in Mrs Barry's shop. They were delayed in Mrs Barry's for some time as she was telling him about the terrible murder which had taken place in Tallow the night before. Little did he know what he would face when he returned home. He drove quietly home until close by his house when neighbours informed him that his wife was dead. He went to his house and found his wife lying on the floor in a pool of blood. Cotter thought he recognised the man accused of murdering his wife but couldn't be sure. He recalled how he may have seen him before in Tallow or Midleton but it would have been a few years ago.

The prisoner having no legal representation, was asked did he have any questions to ask the witness but replied he didn't. He was asked to declare his name but refused saying "I told you often enough, I would not before".

Eleven year old Mary Cotter was described as a bright and very interesting looking girl as she took the stand. She related being at home with her mother when the man came back to the house that day. Her mother told her to get a chair for him while she was busy spinning wool. She heard the man asking her mother several times where her husband was. Then he took hold of a two pronged fork and proceeded to kill Mrs Cotter. She fled out on to the road while the murderer ran up a boreen to make his getaway.

The prisoner having no solicitor got a chance to question the witness. Strangely he asked "were you not standing at the gate with two little ones when I passed down?" Her answer is irrelevant because the prisoner by asking that question then placed himself there. The accused went further and asked the girl "did you see me enter the house" and she replied she didn't. The girl was then recalled to clarify her answer; she was asked if she saw him approach the house which she confirmed she did.

Dr Sisk and Dr Nason gave evidence, having already carried out the post mortem in the short time since the murder. They described the extensive fractures to the head of Mrs Cotter. The injuries were horrific and Dr Sisk concluded she died instantly after the first blow. A pitchfork was produced in court and the doctors said it was likely to have been used to inflict the injuries found.

The jury were confident that enough evidence had been found and briefly considered their verdict. They were unanimous in finding the man guilty of the wilful murder of Johanna Cotter.

What normally happens in cases such as these is they are adjourned to a further date. This time there was no such luck for the accused. Straight after the inquest a magisterial inquiry was held calling for further evidence to that of the inquest. Two local farmers were called and both recalled giving directions to the prisoner to Cotter's house on the day the murder took place.

A publican from Rathcormac Mrs Murphy told how she served the prisoner a pint of porter at about six in the evening only hours after the murder. While the man was drinking a messenger came in and read out the description of the man. The man who fitted this description was sitting at the bar and his face changed colour. Several other local young men challenged him and he made a fast exit. Mrs Murphy immediately alerted the police as to what had happened.

After hearing the further evidence the magistrates returned the prisoner for trial before the next assizes. The accused was afterwards transferred to the county gaol to await his trial. The same day the funeral of Johanna Cotter took place and a huge crowd follow the procession to Ballinaltig graveyard.

While in the county gaol the man was recognised by the wardens as William Tobin. He was the son of a small farmer and originally from Killeenagh near Tallow. They said he was a returned *ticket of leave* convict who had been sentenced to five years penal servitude in 1870 for the crime of sheep stealing amongst other offences. It turned out he had only been released from Spike Island jail the May before. After being released from jail he received a £5 payment and used this for his ticket to America. He returned after a short time in the States and had spent about a month in the area he was familiar with.

For some reason the Cork Winter assizes didn't sit in the month of December as was normally the case. It was months later before the case was heard at the Cork Spring Assizes in March of 1875. Justice Lawson addressed the Grand Jury commenting on how little cases appeared before the court. The most serious case he said was the charge of murder against William Tobin. The prisoner was called and pleaded not guilty in a firm voice and he agreed that he was ready for his trial. One of the prosecution solicitors told how Tobin had no money to pay an attorney. It was agreed that a Mr O'Connell and a Mr Lawrence would be appointed as counsel and informed to be ready when it was called next Friday morning.

The case was called on Friday the 19th of March. Colman O'Loghlan one of the several crown prosecution solicitors told the jury the prisoner faced the penalty of death if the murder could be proved. He described the case at length and went into the details. He said William Tobin was looking for a man called Cotter who lived nearer Tallow. This other Cotter was a collector of large sums of money for companies in the town. That morning Tobin believed he was at the money collector's house and not that of a farmer. He expected to get a much greater haul of money after killing the wife. O'Loghlan was quite confident there was evidence to convict Tobin for this terrible crime.

The same witnesses were called and again gave similar evidence to that of the inquest and inquiry. Margaret Cotter the fourteen year old was called and said how she was out digging potatoes when her sister raised the alarm. Margaret went to the house to find her mother stretched out on the ground near the sow in the kitchen. A man emerged suddenly from the bedroom and went for her with the handle of a pike. She ran and managed to get out onto the road but the man fled up the boreen. She was not able to identify the man in court as she hadn't seen him clearly that day.

The younger sister Mary Cotter told how she was in the house when the murder took place, as she had told at the inquest. She did say how that day Tobin asked several questions about where James Cotter was. He more than once said to her mother that James was in Tallow a few weeks ago but she said he was not. In a rage he struck her several times with the iron part of the pitchfork.

Bartholomew Foley told how he saw Tobin early on the morning of the 1st of August. Foley was on the road from Castleyons to Fermoy when he saw the prisoner emerge from a cock of hay in a nearby field. He assumed he had slept there as he then put on his coat. More witnesses were called including the doctors and the arresting inspector Fleming. After all witnesses had been heard solicitor Lawrence addressed the jury on behalf of the prisoner. His address was so long it must have gone on for hours. He asked the jury to give the prisoner the benefit of any doubt in the evidence. He proceeded to question every piece of evidence and sought to put doubt into the jury's minds. He even suggested that the cottage was so dimly lit on an August afternoon that Mary Cotter could have mistook the man. However given the evidence in the case his long speech was completely in vain.

The judge before he charged the jury spoke briefly about each of the witness's evidence. He said it was all circumstantial but that Mary Cotter's was direct evidence. Justice Lawson said during his vast experience he always found children the best witnesses. Their memory was more accurate and they described things vividly. He reminded them of the questions Tobin had asked the girl during the inquest which incriminated himself. After going through all the evidence he then told the jury they may find the prisoner was not in his right mind that day. However several people had conversed with him giving him directions and he appeared to be perfectly rational. Finishing up he told the jury they were bound to find him guilty.

The jury retired after three in the afternoon and returned to court two hours later having reached a verdict. The clerk addressed the prisoner "You have been indicted for murder, to that you have pleaded not guilty and put yourself upon your god and your country. That country has found you guilty. What have you to say why sentence of death and execution should not be passed upon you?" The prisoner made no reply and the judge addressed the prisoner. He told him "You have been found guilty of one of the most shocking murders that I think I ever remember. You took her life away and I have now to state to you your life is forfeited to the laws of your country". Continuing the judge told him he was to be hanged in the grounds of the Cork County Gaol on the 19th of April. Tobin who was said to have seemed indifferent during the trial was suddenly taken aback when the death sentence was passed. The prisoner was taken from the court back to the gaol through an angry mob who had gathered outside.

William Marwood the famous executioner

Ten years had passed since a prisoner had been executed there. In the meantime the law had changed and prisoners were no longer allowed to be executed in public. For the last public execution hundreds of people had gathered to watch. It would now be done privately on the grounds of the jail. Several other inmates of the prison were willing to carry out the hanging if professional executioner Marwood could not make it. William Marwood was the famous British executioner who had developed the long drop method of execution. The long drop method ensured that the person who die instantly having their neck broken at the bottom of the drop. Previously with a shorter drop the prisoner died a slow death by strangulation.

Tobin was up early on the morning of the 19th of April to attend mass. Afterwards he was restrained by the executioner before being led to the scaffold. Professional executioner Marwood wasn't available in the end and an American sailor who was an inmate of the gaol stepped in to carry it out. Tobin displayed no emotion nor did he give a confession but finally admitted that his sentence was just before he was hanged. It was expected at the last minute he would admit to having carried out the other murders in the area as it would now make no difference either way, but he didn't. Shortly after eight the black flag was raised up the flagpole to announce that William Tobin was dead and had atoned for his sins.

A matter of honour
Fermoy, May 1832

On Wednesday the 30th of May 1832 the 58th regiment marched into Fermoy from Limerick where they had been stationed. The officers knew some of the regiments in Fermoy from their time in Limerick. Later officers of the 58th were invited to dine at the mess of the 92nd regiment that evening.

During dinner a disagreement broke out between two officers in the mess. Captain Markham of the 58th regiment was said to have made some comment that his men were superior to those of the 92nd. The Colonel of the 92nd who had been in command of his men for several years took offence to the comments.

Early the next morning the alarm was raised, an officer was found lying dead on the race course not a half mile from the barrack. The race course was also used as a ground for army exercise; it was located in the area north of where Blackwater Motors is today. The body was identified as being the young Captain Robert Markham who had only arrived in town the day before. The town was awash with rumours of what had occurred and who had been there. Several other officers were said to have been present when Markham was shot but they were reluctant to come forward. Nor were there any witnesses willing to say who they saw that morning in the area.

Within hours word reached Cork of what had occurred and a coroner Richard Foot set out for Fermoy to hold an inquest. He arrived in Fermoy about seven in the evening and wasted no time at all. A jury of twelve local men were sworn in that same evening and as required they viewed the body of Captain Markham. That night the inquest proceeded to hear evidence from two witnesses.

The first witness John Sergeant also a Captain in the 58th regiment merely gave evidence that he knew Markham and he was healthy the evening before. It was six in the morning when Sergeant was told of the shooting. He ran to the place where Markham lay and found a gun shot in the right chest of the body.

The town of Fermoy about the time of the duel by James R O'Flanagan

The doctor from the town, William Campbell described the examination he had carried out on the body. He had also found a shot wound in the right side of the chest. The ball had passed through the chest and lodged in the right arm pit. The doctor was in no doubt that this wound caused the death.

The next morning the inquest resumed, the first witness that morning was not from the military but local Michael Pigott who lived near the race course. He had been there at five on the morning in question. Pigott told how he saw five men in the distance and shortly after heard two shots fired that morning in very quick succession. He headed in their direction but it took several minutes before he reached them. There were five men in blue officer's clothes standing and one man in black lying dead on his back in the field. The five men looked at him then turned and walked away at a quick pace. He immediately went and reported what he had seen to the guard on duty at the barracks who in turn notified the Sergeant.

Typical scene of a pistol duel

The next witness was Alexander Achmutie who was the waiter of the 92nd regiment officer's mess. He had seen Markham dine with three officers from the 58th regiment the evening before his death. Alexander however claimed he heard nothing untoward happen in the mess that evening. He said Markham had left at about eleven when called out of the mess by Mr Lockhart. Alexander went on to say Lockhart returned to the mess minutes later but the next time he saw Markham he was dead.

Private Thomas Ward also of the 92nd regiment was called next and sworn in as he was on guard duty at the Military hospital the morning before. The Military hospital was not far from the race course, (approximately 500m and located where the Lidl store now is). Thomas explained how he was on duty at four that morning and had met the Paymaster of the 92nd regiment Mr Meiklejohn just before that. The paymaster was looking for the doctor of the 5th regiment and Ward showed Meiklejohn to his apartment. Next he saw the doctor and the paymaster going out together and several minutes later heard shots fired. Ward did not leave his post but the news arrived that an officer had been shot nearby. Some time later Ward saw five men return and pass by him. He recognised the Paymaster and Colonel of his own regiment and the doctor of the 5th but didn't know the two others. When questioned was Lockhart there he claimed he had not seen him but identified the Colonel as being John McDonald.

The inquest went on with its line of inquiry despite most people in the area knowing full well what had happened. There had been no shortage of rumours and stories circulating as to who was present when the officer was shot. The coroner it seems was keen to come to a verdict and quickly.

James Levans who was the local police sergeant in Fermoy was called to the stand. He had been employed by the coroner to serve summons on several men to attend the inquest. Levans explained how he tried to serve Meiklejohn but failed as the paymaster was not to be found. Also he attempted to serve the doctor of the 5th regiment but learned he had gone to Limerick shortly before.

After this the jury retired and returned not long after with their verdict. It read as follows "that the deceased Capt Robert Markham was killed by a bullet discharged from a gun or pistol but by whom discharged no evidence has been produced to enable us to ascertain; and we find that the deceased was found dead yesterday morning, at a place called the Race Course in the barony of Condons and Clongibbons in the County of Cork aforesaid."

It seems obvious now that the inquest had no intention of really trying to find out who had fired the gun or why. Before long the rumours around the town had found some foundation and appeared in the newspapers for all to read. It turned out Captain Markham had been involved in a duel with Colonel MacDonald resulting from a difference of opinion the night before. It was also clear Paymaster Meiklejohn and Lieutenant Lockhart were involved in the affair probably one acting as a second making the arrangements. The role of seconds was to act as go betweens for the offended parties and find a peaceful resolution.

It was rumoured that Captain Markham was alone at the duel with no second but this goes against all rules of duelling. It is most likely that a Captain Pack, Paymaster of the 58th regiment, acted as Markham's second. Also reported as being present was James Ferguson the doctor of the 5th regiment, a doctor was required by the duelling rules.

The very minimum that could have been present that morning was five, the principals (those duelling), their seconds and the doctor.

Colonel MacDonald had years before been shot in his right arm in the line of duty. This disadvantaged him having to fire the pistol with his left but still his shot found its target. His opponent Captain Markham was the son of the Archdeacon of York

After the inquest the police don't seem to make any more inquiries into the shooting, maybe because those involved were in the military. It was several months later before the military held an inquiry into the circumstances. In October the Major General Edward Blakeney and the Judge Advocate arrived in Fermoy to hold a military court. They sat for about two days where Colonel MacDonald and Lieutenant Lockhart were present. The military findings were never made public but everyone was sure that no further action was going to be taken as it was properly conducted.

Duelling seems to have been more common than one would have thought. At a meeting of the Assizes in Clonmel in 1777 rules for duels were drawn up. By then duelling with pistols had replaced sword fighting. These were known as the Irish Code Duello and became the standard rules in many countries. Daniel O'Connell was even involved in a duel in 1815 when offence was taken to a remark of his. He shot his opponent in the thigh, the offended party later died. It seems despite the rules, duelling was never actually illegal but one could be charged with crimes such as manslaughter. Duels were only carried out by gentlemen of a certain class and the judicial system seems not only turn a blind eye to but agreed with them until its demise a decade or so later. The Attorney General John Scott gained a reputation for his duelling skills after surviving four.

In Fermoy a duel didn't seem to be too rare an occurrence. Not weeks after Markham died another duel took place on the demesne of Castlehyde. It was the result of a priest being insulted during a mass. This time however it was held at five in the evening and attracted a crowd of spectators. The insulter was hit in the stomach by the first shot but the crowd turned on the man who fired. He fled by diving into the Blackwater and swimming while holding his pistol. This was said to be the last public duel in Ireland, duelling died out in the following decades.

If I can't have her, nobody else can!
Clondulane Fermoy 1957

One miserable wet Monday morning in January, John O'Brien went to wake his farm labourer also John O'Brien but he wasn't in his room. This was strange because the bed appeared to have been slept in and where would he have gone so early with the terrible weather outside.

While the farmer & his wife were having their breakfast, their employee burst into the house. The farmer remarked to his employee that it was a bad morning but got no reply. It is confusing that both men were named John O'Brien, but they were not related. John who was twenty five years old had worked at the farm for four years until 1954 but left and went to England. He returned and was back working for his namesake again over a year later. The farm was located in a townland called Curragh Upper about four miles east of Fermoy.

The farmer thought his employee was annoyed as the key had not been left out for him the night before. Sunday was the labourer's day off and he normally stayed out all day until midnight.

Despite not having got a reply from his employee, John O'Brien asked would he have a cup of tea. John his labourer said "it will be the last cup of tea I have in this house". The farmer thought surely he will not leave because he didn't let the key out for him. His employee was now leaning at the mantelpiece near the fire having been out in the rain. Next he walked over and threw something onto the washstand. After taking off his saturated overcoat his employer spotted blood on his hands and suddenly grew worried. Right away he asked his employee what's wrong John? Is there something wrong? The answer he got he could never have expected and was definitely going to shock.

John his labourer replied "I am after killing" but stunned by the answer he had to ask again. The farmer jumped up from the kitchen table and repeated the question hoping he had not heard it right. But asking again wasn't going to change the answer, the reply this time was "I'm after killing a Power". Both the farmer and his wife still could not believe what they had heard and both said "surely to god you would not do a thing like that"

Pointing to the washstand John said "look at that, there is proof of it". The couple were no longer in doubt seeing a bloodstained carving knife on the washstand. The farmer's wife Catherine said "John, I was looking for that knife yesterday" and all he said was "I took it".

The farmer said "well John if you are after doing a thing like that you had better go down to the barracks with me". The labourer said he thought of not telling anyone but knew he would be caught. He poured himself a cup of tea and seemed to calmly drink it before putting his coat on again. Without saying anymore he walked out of the house expecting his employer to come with him. Without too much ado both men got into the farmers car to go to the Garda barracks. On the way there they talked about what had occurred and how it all came about. He said "I am sorry now that I did not go to the river". The river Blackwater flowed about 500m of where he had left the body. Approaching the barracks John admitted to his employer how he had begun to fell weak.

Sergeant Dalton arrested O'Brien and charged him with the murder. O'Brien replied when arrested and said "I lost my temper when I done it".

The sergeant called a priest and went to the place O'Brien had described. Both he and the priest searched the gate lodge and found a girls body in an outhouse.

Her body was later taken to St Patrick's Hospital where a post-mortem would be carried out. Later at the barrack Dalton took a statement from the accused which could later be used against him in court as evidence. John O'Brien seemed to be aware of what he had done and repeatedly asked the Gardaí had he done the right thing turning himself in. He told them he had considered running but saw on a film how the police would track him down. Later that day there was a special sitting of Fermoy court where O'Brien was charged with murder and remanded on custody until a later date.

The day before the murder Sunday the 21st of January, John O'Brien had the day off from his farm labouring duties. As usual he went to mass on Sunday morning and afterwards went to the pub to drink a few pints of stout in the nearby village of Clondulane. He later called to a house and

Picture of the outbuilding where Margaret Power's body was found with thanks to Irish Newspaper Archives and Cork Examiner

here somebody noticed that a knife was sticking out of his pocket. When mentioned to O'Brien he remarked that it would be needed later on that evening. When he was leaving the house he told how he was going to meet Margaret Power at the gate lodge when she finished work about 2pm. He did meet her there and both were later seen outside Clondulane Stores. She went home and he went to Crotty's pub until about seven. Margaret Power went to Fermoy that evening with her brother and another friend. As the three cycled to the town they passed John O'Brien at Bellevue Cross but never spoke to him.

John was seen in Fermoy that night and seemed to be keeping an eye on Margaret and what she was doing. When she came out of the dance, to go home her bicycle wasn't where she left it and couldn't be found. Instead she got a lift home with her friend.

The next morning Margaret was up early and left home about half seven to go out looking for her bicycle. She managed to find it and was home again in time to leave for work. About quarter to nine she left home to cycle the mile and a half to Ellis's farm. Eighteen year old Margaret had been working for farmer George Ellis of Bawnaglough for about two years. This was the last time her family would see her alive.

The road now near to where the gate lodge once stood

The day after the murder with O'Brien held in the barracks, an inquest was opened but adjourned again until after the criminal proceedings. A post-mortem examination was carried out by state pathologist Dr Maurice Hickey and Fermoy doctor Dr J Magnier. After the post mortem had been carried out Margaret Power's body was removed to St Patrick's Church in the town. The next day on the 23rd the funeral was attended by a tremendous crowd despite a huge down pouring of rain.

During the month of February the accused was brought before the court at Mitchelstown, Fermoy and Youghal on several occasions. A date was fixed for 22nd of February to begin hearing the testimony of nearly 40 witnesses in all.

The case began as planned on the 22nd of February at the Fermoy courthouse before Justice Cahill. The defence applied to have the hearing held *in camera* meaning it would be private. Their grounds were to prevent prejudice of the accused by making the evidence public. The judge however refused the application saying the press were entitled to report on the proceedings.

Many witnesses were to be heard and the case would continue into March with many more special sittings of Fermoy court to hear them all. On one occasion when called before District Justice Cahill the accused replied in a firm voice "not guilty sir". In all thirty two witnesses were called to give evidence.

Sergeant Dalton related how he had found a bloodstained scarf at the murder scene. The accused had later identified that the scarf was his property.

Farmer John O'Brien told how his employee had seemed perfectly normal the day before the murder. He did say it was unusual that his labourer returned back briefly about midday on the Sunday as it was his day off. It was assumed that this was when he had taken the knife from the kitchen. The farmer's wife Catherine O'Brien told the court how at dinner on Sunday the knife was no where to be found. At the time she assumed it was simply mislaid and didn't see the same knife again until it was in the washstand bloodstained.

Another witness was John Devaney from nearby Clondulane. The Sunday night before the murder he walked to Fermoy with John O'Brien. Previous to that he had seen the accused bicycle left near Ellis's gate lodge. On the way to Fermoy that night he talked with O'Brien. One comment that the accused had made was most peculiar and stuck in his mind clearly, "it would be a great night to stab a person". Devaney thought at the time he was only joking and didn't make the connection then. When a friend of Margaret's Nina Healy passed on a bicycle, O'Brien said to him "when I see her again her feet wouldn't touch the ground". He explained it was Nina who had told Mrs Power he was seeing Margaret and remarked she couldn't mind her own business. However Nina Healy was called to give evidence and denied even knowing that the couple were seeing each other.

At the end of the hearing the judge returned the case to trial before a jury at the Central Criminal in Dublin on the charge of murder.

With the criminal trial looming, John O'Brien was granted legal aid. It was stated at the application that he earned £2 10s a week and couldn't afford to pay for a solicitor.

The judge assigned a solicitor Mr Bawlor, with Mr Fawsitt and Crosbie as his legal counsel. The trial was set to start on the 14th of May and expected to last for three days.

The case was heard at the Central Criminal Court before Justice Murnaghan and a jury. John O'Brien pleaded not guilty even though on the day of the murder he had given himself up. He sat in the dock that day with his head between his hands knowing his fate. The prosecution under James McGivern were quite confident in proving his guilt. McGivern said it was a clear case of deliberate and savage murder. He said it was not done on the spur of the moment but deliberately planned and premeditated. The solicitor claimed he had evidence to show that O'Brien would have done it the day before had the opportunity arisen.

The State Pathologist Dr Maurice Hickey described how he had examined the body and the stab wounds. He thought the knife was the murder weapon and the blood on it was the same blood group as the girl.

Sergeant Dalton was called to give evidence of the arrest of the accused and he also read a statement he had taken from him after arrest. O'Brien told him he had been keeping company with Margaret Power for the weeks previous. On the 18th of January he met her at Bellevue Cross. While there she told him her parents were against their relationship and that "it was all off". She however did arrange to meet him in Fermoy that Sunday evening unknown to her parents. He also said how he met her at the gate lodge on Sunday afternoon. But she left saying she was meeting a man at Bellevue cross at 3pm.

He said he then left and went to Crotty's public house; it was late when he returned home. When he did the door was locked so he climbed in a window and went to bed.

Early on the Monday morning he got up about half seven and left the house. He claimed it was then he took the knife from the house. O'Brien described waiting three quarters of an hour for Margaret to arrive at the gate lodge on the morning of the 21st. He knew she would be going to work about nine that morning. When she arrived on her bicycle, she got off to open the gate to the lodge.

He asked her to come inside the gate to talk but says she refused. Margaret accused him of taking her bike the night before in the town. He caught hold of her and forced her to come inside the gate with him. He asked her if it was finished and she said it was. She told him her mother had said she would rather see her daughter dead than to be with him.

Bellevue Cross where Margaret Power had told John "it was all off"

He held her in the outhouse and said he loved her but if he couldn't have her nobody else could. O'Brien said he tied a scarf around her mouth and stabbed her several times. Afterwards he went back to his employer's house and disclosed what he had done.

Sergeant Dalton was cross-examined by Mr Fawcitt for the defence. Dalton described how John O'Brien's father had died when he was young. The sergeant had once heard how his father had been suffering from a sleeping sickness. John O'Brien he said was in an industrial school until he was sixteen. It was also told in court how his parents were second cousins.

The next witness called was employer's wife Catherine O'Brien. On the morning of the 21st January she milked the cows alone, the accused normally helped her. She noticed going back into the kitchen afterwards that the alarm clock was back in its usual place on the wireless in the kitchen. The night before it was missing and she had assumed the accused had taken it to get up early. Not long after telling her husband, the accused came into the kitchen and shocked them all. The alarm clock doesn't seem very significant but it does show John O'Brien planned to be up early that morning.

A neighbour Mrs Elizabeth Roche related how the accused had called to her house on the Sunday afternoon before the murder. When he got up to leave her son noticed a knife in John's pocket. He remarked about it but John replied "never mind the knife" but said "I might need it before the evening is out". She left with him and they talked while cycling together. He asked her who had told her he was going with Margaret Power but she didn't say who had. O'Brien told her he had met Margaret on Tuesday night but her mother had found out and by Friday put a stop to it. Mrs Roche said she had known O'Brien for years and he didn't seem himself that day.

Wife of local publican Mrs Frances Murphy was called to give evidence. She told how on the Sunday O'Brien had come into the pub after mass. This was unusual he normally drank there four or five nights a week but not normally at 10:15 on Sunday. That day before leaving he made a comment which stuck in her mind as it was most unusual. Before leaving at ten minutes before one he asked for a packet of cigarettes. When she gave them to him he said "that is the last packet of cigarettes you will ever give me". She was quick and asked was he going to give them up and he hesitated. Frances was curious and asked him where he was going and he replied "a man in trouble doesn't know where he is going". The publican's wife asked what kind of trouble was he in, had he left his employer but all O'Brien said was "no worse than that". Cross examined Frances said O'Brien paced about the pub when alone and seemed very agitated that morning.

Medical evidence was given by Dr Dunne who was the chief medical Superintendent at Grangegorman Mental Hospital for the defence. He had examined the accused John O'Brien earlier in May in Mountjoy at the request of the defence solicitor. The accused had told the doctor that it was on his mind for several days before that if anything came between the couple he was going to kill her. He had told the doctor the thoughts were on his mind night and day when alone. The doctor said O'Brien was suffering from a number of abnormalities. He didn't register emotional feelings normal people did when terrible things occurred. He also believed O'Brien was incapable of knowing right from wrong. The judge intervened saying that was a question the jury would have to decide. Dunne however said O'Brien's actions led him to believe he was suffering from schizophrenia. Doctor Dunne's testimony concluded the evidence for the defence.

Two more doctors were called to give statements on O'Brien's mental state by the prosecution. One was from Mountjoy, the other Limerick Mental Hospital. Both these men came to the same conclusion that he was not suffering from any mental illness.

The defence solicitor applied to give the closing speech, on the grounds that they had not given any factual evidence. The judge however decided it was the prosecutions right to have the last word.

Summing up for the defence solicitor Fawsitt appealed to the jury to find his client was not in his right mind at the time. He claimed an ordinary man would not have advertised before hand what he intended to do. The accused he went on to say displayed no emotion after the crime where a normal person would have shown regret. The solicitor told how the accused had whistled the tune *The bonny bonny banks of Loch Lomond* in the Gardaí car on his way to jail. He asked the jury did they think this was something a sane made would do knowing he was facing jail and a murder trial.

The prosecution however made the case he knew what he was doing and it was clearly premeditated. The judge then asked the jury to give careful consideration of the evidence and approach it in a detached way. He said it had been up to the defence to prove that the accused was insane but now up to the jury. The judge said it was not as difficult as some murder cases. He felt one piece of evidence had been overlooked. When the accused had said it would be his last packet of cigarettes. He asked the jury did this imply O'Brien would not be back in the pub and knew the consequences of his intended actions. In all the judge spoke for almost an hour before the jury retired to deliberate.

The jury was out for three hours before returning to the court with a verdict. They found that O'Brien was guilty but insane. The judge then ordered that he be held in custody at the pleasure of the government, which practically meant for the remainder of his natural life.

The Price of Land
Templevally near Tallow 1828

In 1817 Michael O'Neill married Ellen Cody; the Cody's were farmers in the townland of Templevally, 2 miles from Tallow and close to County Waterford.

When the couple married, Ellen's father James Cody was a farmer and promised a dowry for her to the value of £300. Cody's land in Templevally on the estate of the Duke of Devonshire was held on lease at a rent of £76 per year and his interest in it was valued at several hundred pounds. He later agreed to pass the farm to his son-in-law O'Neill for £400, the majority of this the promised dowry. O'Neill only had to pay the remaining £100 for the farm.

The arrangement may not have suited everyone in the family as James Cody had several children who wanted part of the farm themselves. When Ellen had married, her brother James Junior was only six years old. Maybe James Cody thought at first he could manage the £300 dowry and keep the farm for his son. Later when he couldn't find the money he had to change the arrangement to include the farm. The young James Cody as a result grew up knowing he wasn't going to inherit his father's land.

However the farm still wasn't transferred to O'Neill by the time James Cody Senior died in 1827. Over the years it seems there had been some dispute over the land. By now O'Neill and his wife had four children and he made his move on the farm taking up residence there with his recently widowed mother-in-law. It was also likely when James Cody junior now aged just 16 instead of taking over the farm moved out against his will. He went to live with his sister Miriam who was married nearby to a respectable farmer John Uniacke in Knockrour Co Waterford. Miriam was only married with 4 years; it is hard to imagine that she got such a generous dowry with her sister's still unpaid. The Tithe Applotment records for 1825 show Uniacke had a farm of 93 acres of arable and pasture land for which he paid a tithe of £24 annually in addition to his annual rent. Despite having his own farm John Uniacke also asserted a claim on his father-in-law's farm and held procession of some portion of it.

This led to a dispute between the two men with O'Neill claiming he had a right to the farm by way of the dowry arrangement. Trouble continued between the two men but O'Neill was confident in his claim to the entire farm and had no intention in letting Uniacke have a portion of it. Sometime in early March of 1828 O'Neill had taken action against Uniacke who was now ordered to be evicted on the 25th of the month. Hearing this Uniacke became enraged and stormed around to O'Neill's with his wife and James Cody. They tried to enter the house using force but resorted to issuing threats against their relations inside. Over the course of the next few weeks several more altercations took place between the two sides. John Uniacke seemed adamant that he would not vacate the Cody land despite already having a significant farm of his own. At this point it is unclear with which daughter James Cody Senior's widow was on but it seems she was staying at Michael O'Neill's.

A few weeks later on Sunday evening the 16th March around dusk Michael O'Neill was at home with his family. They were all sitting around the fire he had one child in his arms and his wife another. A younger child was asleep in a cradle with the remaining child also nearby. Suddenly there was tremendous bang from outside and in the same instant a pane of glass was shattered. Michael fell from his chair and was spread across the floor in front of the fireplace; his wife knew a shot had been fired from outside the house. Quickly she grabbed a pillow from her child's cradle and propped up her husband's head. It was probably then that she realised that he had been shot in the chest.

She ran to the broken window but couldn't see anyone outside, she must have been sure another shot was not going to be fired or just didn't think about it. She ran to the door at the other side of the house and caught a glimpse of a man running away whom she recognised. Her attention suddenly turned back to her husband who still lay there with the children around him but in no time at all he was dead.

The inquest was held the day following the murder by local magistrates a Rev Edgar and a Mr Kirby. During the proceedings John Uniacke sent a message indicating he had something to relate about it. By the time the inquest concluded both Uniacke and James Cody were held in custody in Tallow.

John Uniacke offered to become the approver, meaning he admitted being an accomplice to the crime and was willing to give evidence against others. Around the same time Cody voluntarily gave a signed statement despite Edgar warning him about what he was doing. Uniacke had an alibi for where he was on Sunday evening but Cody's statement contradicted it entirely. After the inquest both men were called before a local magistrate and charged with murder. They were held in custody to await trial before a criminal court and jury.

On Thursday the 3rd of April not even three weeks after the murder took place the case was called before the chief Baron at the Cork Spring Assizes. Sergeant Gould addressed the jury and gave the background of the case, explaining how the men were in dispute about the farm. He explained how Uniacke had borrowed a pair of pistols from a Mr Parker two weeks before the murder. The reason he gave Parker for needing pistols was for protection going to a fair in Cloyne by night. Coincidentally Mr Parker sent his son to retrieve the pistols on the 16th of March. The boy returned with the pistols loaded but saw James Cody going in the direction of O'Neill's with another gun in his hand.

The main witness called to the stand was widow Ellen O'Neill. She was very distressed when called as she was giving evidence against her young brother and brother-in-law. She was first asked to identify the men accused but it took her some time to compose herself but eventually she did. When John Uniacke was pointed out by her he ignorantly laughed aloud for all to hear.

Ellen proceeded to explain the case from her point of view. She admitted that her husband had put her brother out of the house sometime before and that there was extremely ill feeling between the parties since. She spoke about the night her husband was shot and recalled looking out afterwards. She said "twas a bright night without wind or rain", and revealed when she looked out the door saw Uniacke running away but saw his face. Under cross examination Ellen told how her mother was also in the house that night. Several times she was asked did she swear it was John Uniacke she saw running away. Every time she answered that she was sure it was John Uniacke and saw his face when he turned. When asked did she hear them speak, Ellen said she heard her brother James

Cody say "he would bring in fresh lodgers in the morning". When asked to identify in court the man she saw running away Ellen replied "I do not wish to see him". It took some encouragement to get her to point out her brother-in-law.

Sergeant Gould spoke again and explained why Mrs Cody, Ellen's mother was not called to give evidence. He said it was clear that she had encouraged the act to take place and said she had also been put out of the house by her son-in-law.

Templevally Graveyard close to the scene of the crime and where Michael O'Neill is most likely buried

When it came to reading out James Cody's written statement his lawyer Mr Scannell tried his best to prevent it. The judge however overruled and allowed it to be used as evidence; the statement was then read out before the court. In it he admitted to having gone to O'Neill's house with Uniacke many times at night the weeks before. But every evening O'Neill was at the fire side and his children were too close by.

On the 16th of March Cody brought the gun and met Uniacke at the gate leading to O'Neill's. He told how he hid outside in briars while John Uniacke peered in the window. In his statement he says he ran when

Uniacke fired the shot. It was nine the next morning when he got word that Michael O'Neill was dead.

When the prosecution case concluded, the lawyer Mr O'Connell attempted to make a case for the defendant Uniacke. He stated that it was only on the words of Ellen Connell that his client was a murderer.

He called Johanna Lyons a servant of John Uniacke to give evidence.

She provided an alibi for her master saying he was at home on the night of Sunday the 16th. According to her Uniacke ate supper at home that evening and Cody only arrived there afterwards.

Another witness called was Johanna Uniacke, sister of the accused. She agreed with the servant saying her brother John was at home that evening. Her version was that he spent the evening reading to his two and three year old children. When questioned by Sergeant Gould, she claimed to not have heard of any dispute between her brother and O'Neill.

The judge spoke at length before the jury retired to find a verdict. Half an hour later they returned and wanted to question Ellen O'Neill further. She now explained how Uniacke was quite close to her that evening when she opened the door and stated that he faced towards her.

The judge again addressed the jury before they broke to reconsider the evidence. He said it was on the general points of the case they must look not the details. This time the jury returned to the room much quicker than the last and the foreman brought the verdict, guilty.

Now instead of laughing Uniacke turned pale and began to tremble before the court. While Cody on the other hand appeared unmoved as if he didn't comprehend and stared about the room.

That one word was all that the judge needed to hear and now he addressed the two prisoners with their sentence. He spoke about how it was normally difficult but the gravity of this case relieved him of some of that difficulty. He reminded them how they went to their relations house repeatedly but were disappointed not getting a clear shot at their target. However he went on to say how they persevered and achieved their goal in the end. He told the pair "whoever sheds mans blood, by man shall have his blood be shed". Finishing up he advised them "I shall detain you no longer; employ the time, the short time you have left in prayer and penitence". The judge ordered that they be executed within 48 hours, on Saturday and the bodies would afterwards be dissected before the public.

It was stipulated under the Murder Act 1751 that only those convicted of murder could be dissected for the study of anatomy. However the demand for corpses exceeded the number of murderers and the practice of grave digging became more common. A few years later the law was repealed and those convicted of murder were no longer dissected. In an attempt to prevent the illegal trade in corpses, unclaimed bodies were now allowed to be dissected.

They were not the only ones to be sentenced to death that day. Not long after three men from Ballyhooly were convicted of abducting a woman and would soon meet a similar fate.

At ten on the Saturday morning those that wished to see the convicted men for the last time were given their opportunity at the County Gaol. It is safe to assume there were also members of the family who didn't want to see them after what had transpired. John Uniacke's family were present, his mother, brother and sister. Also present his wife Miriam who was soon to be a widow. She had given birth to a baby who was five days old. This was probably the one and only chance for Uniacke to see his child. The baby was baptised there and then before the execution. When the ceremony was over Uniacke took the child into his arms, kissed it and said "when you are able to speak, your mother will teach you to pray for your unfortunate father".

The family members left leaving Uniacke and his wife alone. She spoke to him and contained her grief until she too had to leave.

The pair of convicted men got their chance to speak and make any final statement. John Uniacke didn't say much except that he forgave the world while Cody sorrowfully admitted that he was the cause of it all.

The men were led to the gallows outside the County Gaol, which Uniacke did so without hesitation. At the last minute the ropes were found to be too short, so they improvised by getting stools to increase the fall. As the caps were pulled over their faces Uniacke took hold of Cody's hand. A priest Rev O'Connor was present and he held Cody's other hand on the scaffold. The priest tried to leave and let the execution take place but Cody called him back. Cody now standing on the stool was shaking so much he was going to fall before the executioner done his deed. The priest stayed and held Cody's hand until he was quite dead. All of this took place before a huge crowd of spectators.

Afterwards the bodies were cut down and taken to the surgeon at the infirmary for dissection.

At the time of the execution John Uniacke was described as a respectable looking farmer aged 24. While his brother-in-law James Cody was said to be rather a stupid boy of 17.

It seems when all was said and done James Cody senior managed to get his daughters married to local respectable farmers. What more could a father want for his daughters in the 1800's but the trouble was that both were not happy with their own lot and wanted Cody's farm. James Cody junior, who in the normal course of things would have inherited his father's farm, if he was a few years older. Instead he seems to have been used like a pawn in a game of deadly high stakes where nearly all the adult men in the family lost their lives. In addition the remaining family lost the majority of the land they once possessed. Griffiths Valuation for the townland of Knockrour shows Uniacke's farm now in the possession of a Cornelius Hickey. In Temple Valley in 1830 Ellen O'Neill still had 27 acres and William Cody 29 acres nearby. However by the time of Griffith's valuation some years later there is no mention of O'Neill or Cody in the townland.

Hidden Weapon
Main Street, Midleton 1835

In May of 1835 in Midleton news was spreading that a man had been killed in the jail the Saturday evening before. Initial reports were that a row had broken out in the jail and the jail keeper was forced to intervene. In the midst to the trouble between a prisoner and some visitors, the prisoner was killed.

Those reports however turned out to be wrong. The trouble had occurred on the main street and not in the jail.

That Saturday night 18th May was a wet summers evening. Margaret Murphy had come from her home in Ballycotton to see her brother in jail. Her brother was charged with rape and wanted desperately to know would he be sent to the Cork Gaol. Knocking on the door of the Bridewell as it was then called, she was told by a young girl that her father the keeper was out. Margaret turned back and went down the main street and by chance saw the man she was looking for, the Bridewell keeper Samuel Henderson.

After coming all the way from Ballycotton Margaret had no intention of letting him get away without finding out what was to happen to her brother. She pursued him down the street and relentlessly questioned him. Strange as it may seem she asked him, was her brother to be married to the woman whom he was charged against. Henderson replied that he was to be married on Saturday but it didn't satisfy her. She kept asking the question as she had not believed his answer. Henderson tried his best to get away from her walking on. Annoyed and trying to shake her off, he blurted out "no, you may go to the devil".

Just as he did the confrontation took a drastic turn. A comment came from a young man standing in the doorway of Curtin's pub. Owen McCarthy and a woman had been sheltering there from the rain. Hearing what had been said Owen intervened "no she will not go to the devil nor any of her religion". Margaret didn't know who he was and before she had time to find out the row between the men intensified.

The men clearly were aware of each other and may have had some prior run in. Henderson was well known in the town but was not popular.

The reply was nothing short of fighting talk "so you are putting me there". Owen however wasn't backing down now and quickly went back to him with "tis there the best of quality of ye go". There was a very obvious divide back then and the hatred easily could spark off trouble. Hearing the trouble a few people gathered and one advised Henderson to let it drop and continue about his business. He however wanted satisfaction saying "no the ruffian, he insulted me".

A crowd quickly assembled to see what was about to happen and how would it end. It's hard to imagine anyone supporting Henderson except the police. However no one stepped in for Owen either as he was said to be a fine strong man of twenty who was well able for his opponent.

The jail keeper had a cane and threatened to ram it down his throat. He didn't quite go that far though but pointed the point of the cane within inches of Owen's face trying to intimidate him. This didn't have the effect the jail keeper thought it would have as Owen was still not in fear of him. Henderson lashed out and struck Owen twice with his stick. Owen responded by catching hold of his collar with both hands. He shoved Henderson off the pavement out onto the street.

It now broke into a brawl on the middle of the main street with many onlookers. Both the men struggled doing no more harm than knocking each others hats off. Henderson drew back and made a sudden dart at his opponent with his stick. He drove again at his opponent and this time struck him in the belly. The struggle was over as quick as it began, and both men got up off the street. Henderson told McCarthy he deserved what he got and Owen kicked his hat away from him.

Owen ran off away from the scene but only made it about 40 yards up the street before he fell to the ground. Several people rushed to help him and Henderson walked away. A doctor was called but within ten minutes Owen was dead.

Not long afterwards Henderson was arrested walking the street which in itself is surprising. On being arrested Henderson was told he had stabbed a man on the street but claimed he had not. Henderson was asked to produce his stick. He had to go get it as he had hidden it behind a press in the jail. The stick was found to have a spring loaded dagger about four inches long. The police were now sure that they also had their man and the murder weapon.

It turned out Owen McCarthy aged 20 had booked passage on a ship to America, a day or two later. He had only come to town to make some arrangements and say goodbye to his friends. In town he had purchased wood to make a chest for his journey. Now it was said the wood was being used for another purpose to make his coffin.

An inquest was held in Midleton on Wednesday 20th May and a huge crowd of townspeople had gathered to hear the proceedings. Several times the coroner Richard Jones threatened to clear the room if the crowd would not keep quiet. It was impossible to keep them in order and every time the mob heard something they liked they cheered.

Over an hour was spent picking the jury and even then there were too many potential jurors. Several were objected to on various grounds, one admitted to not liking the accused man, another had already written to a newspaper on the matter. Eventually the Coroner whittled it down to the twelve that were needed but with an equal number of Catholics and Protestants.

The first called before the inquest was Dr Barry who attended to Owen McCarthy the night he died. Barry said he arrived at the hospital to find Owen unconscious and dying. He passed away a few minutes afterwards and there was nothing he could do for him. Two days later on the 20th the doctor examined the body, finding one small wound in the left side of the belly a few inches above the groin. The wound he said was deep travelling inwards and upwards into Owens intestines. So deep was the wound he said that the intestines, spleen and spine had been wounded badly. The doctor's opinion was there was no doubt at all that death was a result of the stabbing and a huge accumulation of blood in the abdomen.

Patrick Kenna told the inquest how he had witnessed the struggle on the street that night. He saw Henderson strike Owen and clearly heard him say "I am very glad you received that, and that is what I would do to every man of your religion". The crowd in the room responded to this by booing and calling out. Patrick resumed his testimony saying Henderson struck his cane against the ground to retract the blade and walked away.

Many witnesses came forward for the inquest and told what they had seen on the street that night. Several of them saw Henderson strike Owen several times with his stick and heard Owen tell him to go about his business. They also told of seeing Henderson shake his stick and the dagger sprung out. He made for Owen's belly with the point of the dagger.

With so many witnesses to hear from, the inquest sat for the whole of Wednesday and reconvened the next morning for the verdict. "We find the deceased Owen McCarthy came by his death in the town of Midleton between the hours of seven and eight o'clock, on the evening of the 16th May, from a spring dagger wound given him in the left side of the belly by Samuel Henderson, late Bridewell keeper of Midleton without any justifiable provocation".

In August at the Cork summer Assizes the case was brought before judge and jury. It looked bad for Henderson as the case up before him was a theft of a priest's house in Bandon. Both men were found guilty of taking some silver and received a death sentence. Now the charges against Henderson had been reduced to manslaughter but still he had taken a man's life. It seems he was now no longer employed as the Bridewell Keeper of Midleton and had been in custody since May. The prosecution was led by lawyer Mr Bennett, while Henderson was represented by Sergeant Jackson MP.

The first witness sworn in was Margaret Murphy who was bound to have seen it all that night as she was present at the start of the argument. Margaret described how the row broke out. Before Owen was struck, Henderson said "leave off of me" but McCarthy refused. According to Margaret it was only then he struck with the stick for the first time. She saw him strike the stick on the ground and the dagger sprung out.

Under cross examination Margaret revealed that at some point she recalled McCarthy having a hold of Henderson by his head of hair.

Several more witnesses such as Johanna Kennedy and her brother Thomas gave evidence of having seen the trouble on the street that night. They did not however see Henderson caught by his hair at all.

Dr Barry again gave the same medical evidence he had given before the inquest. When asked this time though he told how he was aware of all the unrest in the town of the payment to tithes. He also knew as did the whole town that Henderson had become involved in the collecting of money for outstanding tithes and this made him despised by the country people especially.

Policeman James Rawley was sworn in as a witness for the defence. He knew Owen McCarthy and described his past working relationship with Henderson. Owen had at one point he said tried to break a friend of his from jail in Midleton. He also knew that Owen McCarthy had been in jail previously, when Henderson was the jail keeper.

Rev Richard Freeman told the court how he knew the accused with approximately six years and always thought he was quiet and peaceable. According to Freeman he was well liked in the town as Bridewell keeper but that changed when he became an auctioneer. Henderson auctioned off cattle to pay outstanding tithes. Freeman said "he became obnoxious". Several times he saw Henderson attacked on the street by angry mobs. Rev Freeman admitted to the court that it was him who had given Henderson the sprung dagger cane for his own protection.

John Smith Barry of Fota House was called to give a character reference for the accused. When he commanded the Barrymore Cavalry, Samuel Henderson had been a musician in the regiment. After the band was broken up Smith Barry appointed him as Bridewell keep in Midleton. Smith Barry finished by saying he always found the accused to be "a quiet, peaceable, honest, humane, civil and sober man". There were several more gentlemen organised to give similar statements for the accused, but after John Smith Barry's account the defence was happy they had enough and ended their case.

After hearing all the evidence the judge summed up the case before releasing the jury to come to their verdict. He was clear in his opinion that manslaughter was the correct charge in this case. He explained that manslaughter varied from almost justifiable homicide to nearly murder. This he said was not for the jury to decide but merely whether he was guilty of manslaughter or not. They didn't take long to decide at all and returned to court with the verdict of guilty. Sentencing was however deferred to a later date and the court went on with its business calling another case.

It was a few days later on Tuesday the 11th of August before Henderson was sentenced. The judge seemed to take his own view of the case and could decide how severe he felt the manslaughter was. Outlining how close to murder manslaughter could be in many cases but it was not in this case he said. A life was taken the judge didn't deny but said Henderson was assaulted first and had nobody on the street to assist him. According to the judge he was entitled to carry such a weapon in his line of work. He also felt that Henderson's life had been endangered that night and now the law was taking that into consideration. Finally he was sentenced to three months imprisonment starting from the first day he was taken into custody. So all he had to serve now was a couple of days as he had been arrested the night it occurred.

Did Henderson get a fair sentence? It does seem lenient even by today's standards when back then poor people got harsher treatment for stealing food to feed their families. There is no doubt at all that Owen McCarthy instigated the incident with a sarcastic throw away comment. He never thought for a second though that it would end up as it did with him lying dead on the street. What Owen didn't allow for was that Henderson's hatred would drive him so far to do what he did.

Murder, Witchcraft or Treason
Ballyvolane House, Castlelyons, Fermoy 1730.

Ballyvolane House was built near Castlelyons in 1728 by Sir Richard Pyne a retired Lord Chief Justice of Ireland. It was built to replace a medieval house on the site. This new house was a Georgian design and was three stories tall.

An elderly man Andrew St Leger rented the house with his wife Jane, they had no children. Andrew St Leger had been a Lieutenant Colonel, Jane's maiden name was also St Leger and the couple were first cousins. Amongst well to do families such as the St Leger's marrying your cousin was almost normal; after all it was in the royal family. The St Leger's grandparents were also first cousins when they married in the 1600's. The couple were well off but being from a junior branch of the Doneraile St Leger family do not seem to have inherited an estate. St Leger's could trace their line all the ways back to their arrival in England with William the Conquer in the 11th century.

Early in the morning of the 4th of November 1730 a shocking discovery was made in the master's bedroom. Andrew St Leger was found dead in his bed having been shot in the head by a pistol. His wife Jane was found nearby she had been stabbed several times and died at 7 that morning. At first the discovery by the servants indicated there had been intruders during the night. However it was suspicious that none of the servants had heard the gunshot that killed their master about 2am. The gardener was also found lying dead struck on the head by an axe and it appeared that he may have come upon the intruders. It caused quite a stir amongst the well to do gentry, for a couple to be killed like this in their own beds was shocking and totally unheard of.

These murders happened almost 300 years ago and in that time there has been plenty of time for the story to change and what exactly happened will never be known. Local legend says that it was not until the funeral that it became apparent who had carried out the crimes. The cortege left the house for Aghern with the servants of the house present. Along the way Jane St Leger's dog whined and could not be stopped. Two of the St

Leger's servants were noticed to be acting suspiciously, Timothy Croneen the butler better known as Tadgh and Joan Condon, a maid.

Condon became annoyed with the dog but it was Croneen who got down from the carriage and took the dog. He let the cortege go ahead and was said to have slit the dog's throat without being seen and hid the dog in a field. This crossroads is still known today as Spaniel's Cross on the road west of Aghern. Croneen managed to catch up with the slow funeral cortege thinking he had not been noticed. The other servants did however observe that the dog had disappeared and now watched Tadgh's every move as they felt he would crack. Local legend says as the cortege approached the graveyard the horses refused to cross a river. Some of the cortege whispered amongst themselves that witches would not cross water. At this stage people must have started to become suspicious of Joan and her involvement in the murders. Eventually the horses were forced to cross the river but not without strenuous efforts. The funeral went on and neither Tadgh nor Joan did anything to arouse further suspicion.

The night of the funeral Tadgh fled the house with Condon, the maid. To this day they are said to have buried the stolen treasure on the grounds but left in such a hurry that they never got a chance to dig it up again.

The pair knew their only hope was to get out of the country as everyone would be looking for them. They behaved predictably and made their was to the town of Cove as it was then called and booked passage on a ship bound for France. Getting on the ship they must have thought they were safe at last, if those on the ship didn't know about them by now they would never know. All they had to do now was get off the ship in France and make their getaway. A gale blew up before the ship left and despite several attempts the captain didn't manage to get out of Cork Harbour. They returned to Cove for the night and the captain informed everyone that he would try again tomorrow. In the age of sailing ships, a delay waiting for the right wind was quite normal. The pair of fugitives however couldn't wait, they now worried that word would arrive about them.

Spaniel's Cross today where Tadgh Croneen killed Jane St Leger's dog

They decided to risk returning to dry land rather than wait and get out of the country some other way. On the 14th of November in Dublin a proclamation was issued by the lord Justices of Ireland to apprehend Tadgh Croneen who was at large. It was posted all over Munster, with an extra £100 over the usual reward to whoever caught him, so as to deter others from committing such crimes. No mention was made in the proclamation of Joan Condon who was alleged to have been with him.

Leaving Cove the desperate pair seem to head back inland and made their way to Limerick, we can only suppose to get on another ship leaving the country. This time word had got out and £100 was quite a sum of money back then. When the pair arrived in Limerick a sharp Customs officer somehow recognized them boarding a ship bound for France and quickly made his move arresting them.

Croneen was charged with petty treason which was described as the betrayal or murder of a superior by a subordinate. The more well known crime of high treason was against the sovereign. This was covered under the Treason Act of 1351 which was enacted by Edward III. Also included in petty treason was a wife killing her husband. This shows how the law and society at the time saw the husband as the wife's superior. Where a husband kills his wife it was just a straightforward murder. The act also laid out the punishment that those convicted of petty treason would receive.

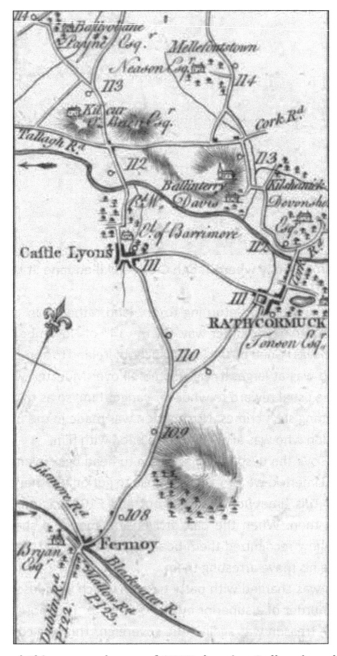

Taylor and Skinner road map of 1777 showing Ballyvolane house in relation to Castlelyons, Rathcormac and Fermoy

If the charge was just ordinary murder he would have been tried by an Assize Court but because it was petty treason he faced a special commission called Oyer and Terminer. On Monday 15th of January 1731 Croneen and Condon were called before the commission headed by an Assize Judge. Well known figures acted like a jury such as, James Barry the Earl of Barrymore, Henry Boyle Earl of Shannon, Robert Jocelyn the Attorney General, Anthony Jephson MP for Mallow, Redmond Barry MP for Tallow.

It did not take long for them to be found guilty of the charges against them and Croneen was taken immediately on a cart to Gallow's Green to face his punishment, Joan Condon would have to wait. Gallow's Green was located in Greenmount, near where Pouladuff Road meets Gould Street.

Croneen got his chance to make a statement, knowing his fate was sealed he admitted his part in the murders. He stated that "the devil was too great with me. I first resolved only to rob my master, but when I went into the room shot him in his bed and gave my mistress five stabs. The gardener consented to go with me and held the candle. I took £20 and the watch out of my master's pocket and rode off (having first killed the gardener) and given the maid a small share of the money".

This statement is different to that of the local folklore but comes directly from the Gentleman's Magazine written the very same month. It even suggests that Croneen killed the Gardener to save splitting the share of the money with him. Surely though the maid Joan Condon had played a more active role and Croneen was trying to save her, knowing his own fate. Croneen it seems shared a room with the gardener so it would have been difficult to do it without the gardener knowing.

Croneen faced his brutal punishment. He was hung using a short drop for two minutes until almost dead then cut down. His bowels were cut out and thrown into his face before the body was quartered before the crowd which would have gathered to see the brutality. This form of punishment is known as hung drawn and quartered; where drawn implied the bowels were drawn out. His head was then put on a spike and displayed for all to see as a warning.

The drive leading to Ballyvolane House as it is today

Joan Condon had to wait a few more days knowing full well what was coming. The punishment for a woman convicted of petty treason was to be burned at the stake. For a woman being hung drawn and quartered involved being nude, it seems allowable for a man but a woman being nude was not acceptable back then. Burning is how she most likely died the following Saturday at Gallow's Green. Often the executioner would strangle the woman with a cord before the fire got to them, so she would be at least unconscious before being burnt. Some local legends tell us she was burned closer to the scene of the crime at a place now called Hag's Cross. Other sources however claim that the origin of Hag's cross is an old woman was once found dead there.

There has always been a connection between burning and witchcraft and coincidently another Joan, Joan of Arc was also burned at the stake. In law however witchcraft was seen as a felony and in England at least punishable by hanging. It was on the continent and Scotland where suspected witches were burned to death. In Ireland a few decades later a new law, in 1790 banned burning at the stake for women convicted of treason, they would now be subject to the Murder Act 1751.

Ballyvolane House was remodelled in 1847 and modernised by removing the top storey and adding a Victorian Italianate façade. It remained in the ownership of the Pyne family until 1953 and was then sold on.

Today Ballyvolane House is described as a luxury country house/boutique hotel. It's a popular venue and any internet search words such as wedding, menu or glamping are the top search results but if you continue to look you will find the history of Ballyvolane House.

Highway robbery or not.
Kilworth, Fermoy 1819

When Alexander Hoskins found a coat in a field near Kilworth early one morning in June he thought it was most unusual. There was a pocket book in the coat and he didn't know what to make of it. Not a few paces away he found a body half buried in a ditch. Immediately he recognised the body as local man James Andrews. Hoskins knew the dead man's brother Richard and went for him without delay. He handed over the pocket book to the brother and they both hurried back to the crime scene led by Hoskins. Richard seemed shocked and speechless to see his brother's body thrown there half buried.

It was known in the locality that there was a summons out for the arrest of the dead man. People were aware it was because of a debt to his nephew for the large sum of £50. The dead man was from a respectable family and his brother Richard the owner of a large sized farm.

Initial reports said he had been set upon by thieves returning from a fair the night before but a considerable amount of money was found on him so it didn't entirely make sense.

On that Friday morning the 11th of June 1819 Richard Andrew's sent word to the police and the local magistrate of his brother's mysterious death. An inquest was held to establish the facts of the case but nobody came forward with information. A doctor examined the body and found the skull had brutally been smashed in by a blunt instrument with terrible force.

The following Sunday a local man by the name of Clancy was seen drunk with blood stains on his clothes. This aroused the suspicions of several people who notified the police. About 2 o'clock Clancy was arrested in Kilworth by local magistrate Captain Collis and taken to Fermoy. He had been found drunk with blood stains on his trousers and waistcoat so the police were confident they had their man. Clancy however completely denied having anything to do with the murder.

A while later though Clancy began to change his story and tell what he knew had happened to James Andrews. On Thursday the 10th Richard

Andrews asked Clancy to escort him and his brother to Mitchelstown about 8 miles away. Richard said there was a writ out against his brother and was worried he would be arrested. Clancy was to go with them to their sister's house and later James would flee to America. John Clancy admitted to agreeing to this and set out from Kilworth that evening. He met the brothers at the agreed spot and they commenced their journey until Richard suggested they take a short cut across some fields. Suddenly Richard pulled an iron bar and struck his brother several times on the head and he fell to the ground. He was not killed at first but was repeatedly hit on the head again by a stone. Clancy admitted to helping to drag the body across several fields in order to conceal it. Richard removed the coat from the body and searched it. Before parting they hurriedly threw the body into a hollow and partially covered it with earth. John Clancy said they both went their separate ways and he headed home.

The funeral was held on the Monday following the murder but at that stage Richard was nowhere to be found. The police were now searching for Richard and looking for information of his whereabouts. It was the next day before the police made any progress in their search. Late Tuesday night he was found in bed in his brother-in-laws house about 2 miles from Lismore. When caught by the magistrate and armed police Richard calmly got up and dressed himself. He didn't give any resistance at all and was arrested and taken into custody without any incident. Soon after his arrest Richard's motive became clear. It seems not only was it James who owed money but Richard was also indebted to his brother James. Richard had property and he would lose it if he had to repay his brother. Maybe he planned his brother's escape so that he didn't have to pay him back. However when it came to it maybe pressure drove him to a more permanent solution.

When the case was called before the Cork Summer Assizes on the 20th August, the accused Richard Andrews had already been held in custody for over two months. John Clancy had long since turned informer; now giving evidence for the prosecution in the hope he would not be charged as an accomplice.

Medical evidence was given by Doctor Edward Collet who had examined the body on the 11th of June. He arrived at the conclusion that the injuries could not have been sustained accidentally or by a fall. He described the many fractures on the skull which he said were inflicted by a heavy hard object.

John Clancy was called to the stand and sworn in as the key witness in the case. He described the events on that Thursday evening the 10th of June. Earlier in the evening Richard Andrews had taken him to a public house owned by Ignatius Young and bought him several pints of porter. While they drank together Andrews asked him to meet later outside the village to escort his brother. He explained how at this point he had no inkling at all of what was about to happen next. When the three met up later there was no argument between the brothers.

After walking for some time Richard suddenly struck his brother with an iron bar and he fell to the ground calling out "murder Dick". Clancy said at this point James was still alive but Richard got him on the ground and continued with deadly blows until he was dead. After Richard dragged the body away to a hollow they left the scene alone.

Under intense cross examination Clancy admitted that he should have given information the morning after the murder but obviously did not. When asked how he came to have blood on his clothes he replied it must have been when helping the body over a ditch. He denied taking payment for assisting in the murder and also denied having been involved in any such crime in the past saying he was never charged with it.

A juror asked again why he had not given information the following morning. This time Clancy replied he would have had if he had any wit but thought the situation was bad enough without making it worse. The reality was Clancy most likely was in fear of his life knowing he could hang for it, or was he in fear of Richard who may have threatened him.

Local man William Sinnott was called to the witness stand, he had passed the two brothers walking that night. He told how Richard was carrying something in his hand but he didn't know what it was as Richard tried his best to hide it.

Ignatius Young was next called to take the stand and give evidence as he was a publican in Kilworth and had served porter to Richard Andrews the night of the murder.

He told that when word first got out about the murder Captain Collis said all publicans were to be summoned as to James Andrews's movements.

The day after the murder Ignatius met Richard Andrews and told him this. Richard didn't seem to like this and said "you need not mention anything about my being at your house last night". The publican explained to the court that he took this at the time to mean Richard didn't want it to be known he was out so late and in bad company, he never suspected at the time he was anyway involved. Ignatius confirmed that Richard and John Clancy were indeed in his house drinking porter that night, they both left about eleven after Andrews had paid for what they had drunk.

The next witness was Robert Bible, brother-in-law of Andrews who lived about two miles from Lismore. Bible returned home Tuesday night after attending the funeral on Monday to find Richard Andrews in bed in his house. Andrews enquired of him of news from Kilworth, the funeral and the inquest. Robert told him how it was clear he had killed his brother with an iron bar and asked why he had done such a thing. Andrews merely replied "the devil and drunkenness". Bible said he had known Richard Andrews a long time but that night he was much different than usual, he seemed deranged and out of his senses.

Several more witnesses were called for the prosecution such as the magistrates that arrested both Clancy and Andrews; however their testimony was nothing new. The last witness called for the prosecution was attorney Mathias Hendley. He recalled clearly meeting with the accused while in custody who admitted carrying out the murder. He asked Richard "for god's sake Andrew's what motive had you for killing this unfortunate brother of yours, was it because you could not pay the amount of the receipt I gave him on you? Richard replied that it was the reason he couldn't pay his brother the money he owed and was under immense pressure because of it.

Mathias went on to explain that he was also present in a transaction between James Andrews and a nephew, Richard was also present on that occasion. When it was settled James owed his nephew £50 and a receipt was given to the nephew.

The case for the prosecution closed and gave the defence their opportunity to call any witness they had. Only one was called who gave a character reference for the accused having known him the last 25 years. The witness never recalled Richard Andrews in any trouble in the past; he described him as a man of property and competence.

The judge summed up the case for the jury before allowing them to leave the courtroom to decide a verdict. The jury had no trouble coming to their verdict and were back in the courtroom again within about three minutes of leaving. Their decision was the one that everyone was expecting and no one in the room could have been shocked except Richard Andrews when the verdict of guilty was read out.

The judge stated that murder was such a serious crime but one brother killing another was much worse. He said it was not done in the heat of the moment or sudden impulse but planned hours in advance. Addressing him directly the judge said "you hardened yourself with liquor for the occasion and deliberately prepared an associate for your diabolical scheme". The judge recalled how he might have easily got away but for a few drops of blood seen on Clancy's clothes. The convicted man was also reminded how all hope of mercy was now gone, in those days there was no such thing as an appeal for crimes like this. The judge announced the sentence of execution and told him to "make the best use of the short time left and repent for your offences".

The judge explained how Andrew's would normally be executed within 48 hours of conviction but in this case 48 hours later was a Sunday. Therefore he announced that Monday the 23rd he would be executed at Gallow's Green Cork.

Early on the Monday morning huge crowds gathered to see the execution more than usual due to the unusual facts of the case. It also caused great interest amongst the public to see a man of such a social class convicted of a terrible crime. When he got his chance Andrews spoke and openly admitted his guilt in murdering his brother. He also took the opportunity to clear John Clancy from any part in the crime. Richard however denied any involvement in the death of his father-in-law that he had been rumoured of murdering also. He further denied killing another brother of his, claiming he was alive and well in America. What he did admit to was being behind conspiracies to kill his nephew including poison on one occasion. In his final moments he seemed to be sorry for what he had done and used his last minutes to pray with. The execution was carried out without a hitch and he died instantly with no struggle. The body was then cut down and taken to the County Infirmary to be dissected for the study of human anatomy.

Richard Andrews had claimed he was driven to fratricide (killing of a brother or sister) because of the enormous financial pressure he was under. But the murder wasn't to just clear his own debt but was also to inherit his brother's share of the family property. But like so many other cases they lost everything including their lives. Innocent James Andrews trusted his brother and never suspected a conspiracy. Richard had trusted Clancy and was so driven by greed he never stopped to think he would be apprehended.

He should have just kept going
The Mall Cobh 1867

On Sunday night the 8th of September 1867, Patrick Horrigan spent a few hours in Buckley's pub on The Mall in the town of Cobh. Sometime about eleven he set off for home not very far away on Queens Street (now Connolly Street). He was after a few drinks during the evening but was in no way drunk. He lived with his father John who was a ships pilot in the harbour. John was one of the most experienced of the sixty pilots working the harbour at that time. He had piloted the largest ship in the world the *Great Eastern* in to the Harbour a few years earlier.

Patrick walked along the street alone and was only a short distance from home, when at a point on the street where the footpath was narrow, he encountered four foreign sailors. One of the sailors banged into Patrick and shoved him from the footpath but continued on their way. Despite being alone and way outnumbered Horrigan wasn't going to let them get away with it and called after them. He was heard to say "get away you foreigners". Maybe they didn't understand him but they understood his body language. One of the sailors hit Patrick but when he returned a punch, more joined in. The sailors set upon him and Patrick tried his best to defend himself. Not long into the fight Patrick was knocked down by one of them. When he got up he only made about two steps when another kicked him and he fell against a wall. Nobody saw what happened next but one of them pulled a knife, sailors were always in the habit of carrying one. Shortly after one of the sailors warned his shipmates to flee as he had used the knife and knew they were in trouble.

Despite it being a busy area of the town not many people were around at the time. In the midst of the attack a married woman by the name of Catherine Caulfield was said to have been the only one to intervene. She called out for help as she saw a night watchman down the street but he didn't come. Mrs Caulfield assisted Horrigan make a few steps but he fell on the street unable to stay on his feet. She realised how grave the situation was when she opened his vest, finding blood gushing from him. She left Patrick in the care of another woman while she ran for a priest and doctor.

In the meantime Patrick was removed from the street to a nearby house and several doctors arrived quickly. At that time Patrick was still conscious and able to describe what had happened but he deteriorated quickly. The doctors examined him and discovered three stab wounds, two in the back and one in the chest near his heart.

The police had learned of the incident and were on the scene within minutes. The constables split up to search for the four sailors. Based on information received one group of police headed east towards Cuskinny. They knew the sailors would make an attempt to get back to their ship. Nearby at the lifeboat slip clothes were discovered by the waters edge, along with a sailor's knife. The sailors must have taken to the water in order to swim to their ship.

Some of the locals also got involved with the manhunt and further along the shore were trying to apprehend one of them. He had taken to the water with his ship mates but realising he wouldn't make it he turned back. All attempts to catch him failed until the police arrived but there was still three more at large.

More splashing could be heard further from the shore so the police launched a boat from the beach to row after them. In their haste to catch the foreigners they had forgot to put the plug into the keel of the boat and not far from the shore it began to fill with water. Still in their eagerness to apprehend the remaining men they decided to chance it and continue on. By the time they reached the second man the small boat was half full with water and becoming unsafe. It didn't help at all that they now had to get the man from the water into the boat but somehow they did. The policemen rowed to the shore with the men they had apprehended.

The search continued throughout the night but the remaining two were not caught. Poor Patrick Horrigan's condition worsened and the doctors tried their best to save him. However sometime after midnight he died as a result of the stab wound close to his heart. The news quickly got out of what had happened and that two people were still on the run. This angered the people of the town and if the remaining two were not caught soon they would lynch them. The most painful fact was Patrick was to be married later that week.

Typical busy scene in Cobh from above the Mall
Image courtesy of National Library of Ireland

It took sometime for the police to find the last two sailors. During the night they searched several Italian vessels at anchor in the harbour. Aboard each one they asked the captain to account for his crew and were any crew still ashore on leave. Finally they came to the *Bachichino* anchored off the *Spit* lighthouse. Within seconds of landing on the deck the police spotted something suspicious. Two of the crew on deck were only in their shirts and showed sign of having recently being in the sea. It turned out one had made it to his ship, while the other made it to another ship and was transferred to his own. The two prisoners were brought back to the town and landed quietly in fear the locals would seek revenge. The clothes found at the shore were examined and blood was found on the knife.

An inquest was arranged to be held on Monday the 9th but the coroner could not attend for a few days so it was delayed.

The local magistrates wasted no time and on the Monday held an inquiry into the circumstances of the death. The court sat before local resident magistrate John Cronin. The four arrested men were bought before the court and identified as Antonio Eremittagio, Davide Marcellari,

Ermidio Fatzini and Baldassarre Maroni. All were Italian sailors from the same ship. Only Antoni could speak any English and an interpreter was sworn in to read the charges against them.

Dr Forde was first called as he attended to Horrigan until he died. The doctor told how he examined the dying man and told him there was no hope for him. Before he became too weak the dying man told the doctor what had happened. He swore that he wasn't drunk and had never met the Italian sailors before. Dr Forde also told how Patrick lost lots of blood from his chest wound and this must have been caused by a knife.

Street close to where Horrigan was found stabbed
Image courtesy of National Library of Ireland

A young boy called Edward Rundle was called to the stand and told that he was out on the street playing tig at eleven the previous night. He saw the fight and was able to identify one of them. In court he pointed to Baldassarre Maroni but couldn't identify the others as they had quickly run from the scene.

The key witness to what had happened was the woman who had intervened Mrs Caulfield. She told the court when retuning home the night before she came upon four men beating Horrigan. She called for help and witnessed Patrick fall on the street. When the sailors fled she helped him along the street.

Several more people were called and were able to identify the accused as having been in a public house on Queens Street the evening before. They all saw the four men leave just before eleven; this was just minutes before they set upon Patrick Horrigan. After hearing this evidence the inquiry was adjourned until the following Wednesday morning.

That Wednesday a large crowd gathered at the courthouse to observe the proceedings. A solicitor Mr Blake was there for the accused and an interpreter was also present to communicate with them. The crown prosecution was also represented by a Mr O'Connell. The only one missing was the magistrate John Cronin and suddenly news arrived he was unwell. He was on his way to court but feeling ill went to the RCYC clubhouse (now the Sirius Arts Centre). The doctors present in court left immediately to see if they could they do anything for him. Dr Power who was also a magistrate had to remain and take over the inquiry. Not much happened in court especially after someone came and said Mr Cronin was dead when in fact he was still alive.

Sometime later another messenger arrived and this time said Mr Cronin was in fact dead. The inquiry was adjourned until a later date, but Mr Blake said he could not attend for a week. The only progress made was the decision to release the Italian ship as they had received orders days before. It was also decided that the captain and mate of the ship were also free to go and not required at the inquiry.

Over the next few weeks every time the four accused were taken from the barrack to the courthouse crowds gathered. The locals followed along the streets booing and jeering at them.

After being adjourned several times, the court eventually sat on the 23rd of September to decide if there was a case against the men. The prosecution called the medical evidence first. The doctor in charge of the Military Hospital in the town Dr T Mathews was called to give medical evidence. He told how he had carried out the post-mortem with Dr Forde a few days after the incident. The doctor explained before the court about the stab wound to the chest. The instrument had punctured the lung and also the membrane surrounding the heart. This he said most certainly was the cause of death. Dr Forde also concluded on the cause of death.

Baldassarre Maroni who had been one of the accused now changed tact and was now witness giving evidence against his shipmates. Strange as it may seem to us now whenever Baldassarre Maroni referred to Patrick Horrigan he called him "the Englishman". This is how we were viewed by foreigners at the time.

When Baldassarre Maroni took the stand he recalled the night of the 8th when he walked down the street with his shipmates. It was Antonio Eremittagio who bumped into Patrick and a quarrel broke out. Baldassarre Maroni claimed to have tried to stop it but the pair started fighting. He said Horrigan was boxing when Antonio Eremittagio pulled out his knife. He witnessed his shipmate Antonio Eremittagio using the knife before saying "run away boys, I have given four or five stabs."

All four fled the scene knowing the locals would get them before the police. He said that Antonio Eremittagio could not swim and took to the water but soon after turned back to the shore. A knife was produced in court and the witness identified it as belonging to Antonio Eremittagio.

A local shoemaker Michael McCarthy was a witness and recalled seeing the fight that night. He said he kept a cautious distance from the fight but said it was five men in total.

During the fight one of the sailors fell but got up again , Patrick fell to the ground and all four sailors fled. McCarthy said he had been to court now several times and each time stared at the man he saw fighting. He identified the one he saw fighting but pointed to Davide Marcellari.

When cross examined his answers at first caused confusion in the court but eventually he clarified. He explained how Davide Marcellari was the second man to fight Horrigan but he couldn't identify the first man. He said when Horrigan knocked the first man to the ground Davide Marcellari began fighting. After the foreigners fled he heard Horrigan say he would have been able for them but they drew their knives.

The prosecution solicitor stated that despite having more witnesses he felt there was enough to prove a reasonable case against the accused.

Mr Blake for the defence said he couldn't object to that but asked for Ermidio Fatzini to be discharged as there was no evidence against him.

Evidence of a witness was read to the court telling how all four attacked and Blake's motion failed. He asked for bail for his clients but that was refused. The men were taken back into custody to await their trial.

Where the Italians fled and entered the water to make their escape

When it was first reported that Patrick Horrigan was stabbed it was claimed Cobh was normally a quiet town. With all the people passing through the town it's hard to believe. Another stabbing incident occurred on Harbour Row by the end of the month. This time it was sailors again but in a public house. It was reported the row broke out when they "were refused drink for women of improper character". Some soldiers also in the pub intervened and ended up getting stabbed in the stomach by one of the seamen. The soldier wasn't seriously injured and the sailor got two months in jail.

The Italians however must have been in custody for over six months before they were brought before a jury. The Cork spring Assizes sat at the Cork courthouse and the case was called on Monday the 16th March 1868 before Justice O'Hagan and a jury. First Davide Marcellari and Ermidio Fatzini were called and charged for the murder. Both men pleaded not guilty and the prosecution dropped the case for lack of evidence against them. The pair had also since given statements against their shipmate and were now discharged.

Of the four arrested Antonio Eremittagio was now the only one being prosecuted. He was charged but pleaded not guilty. Many of the same witnesses were called that had previously been heard before the magistrates.

Catherine Caulfield also gave evidence of being present there that night. When she saw Patrick was bleeding she fled to get a doctor and priest. One of the key witnesses was Margaret Leary who told how she came on the fight that night. She saw three men beating Horrigan. She witnessed one man turn and gave him a blow to the chest before he fell. Margaret claimed she heard one say "let us run away boys as fast as we can".

Immediately Mr Plunkett for the defence questioned her asking was she sure she heard someone say that. She however repeated that she heard one of the Italians say it in English. The solicitor asked why it would be in English a language they didn't understand very well. Margaret said it was Antonio Eremittagio who said this. All three Italians gave evidence in court saying that it was Antonio Eremittagio who had stabbed him.

A statement taken from Eremittagio was read out where he claimed somebody else had done it. He said he only ran from the scene after his three shipmates had already fled. The solicitor for the defence Mr Plunkett made his statement and said the jury could not come to a conclusion of murder under the circumstances. Bizarrely he also asked the jury to bear in mind that the accused was Italian and prone to "sudden and ungovernable rage than any other nation". He said after being knocked down "the fiery Italian blood" drove him to this sudden act. The solicitor referred to Horrigan as having contempt of foreigners. He also reasoned that three of the sailors were from Rome and clung together. While Antonio Eremittagio was from Naples and not one of the them.

He also pointed to the fact that the knife found actually belonged to Baldassarre Maroni. The knife was produced and he showed a faint initial of the letter G. This he said was for Giovanni, Baldassarre Maroni's middle name. His argument now was Baldassarre Maroni knowing his knife was found decided to give a statement to get himself out of trouble.

Mr Plunkett questioned the law on approvers, those that were once implicated but now turned witness. Their evidence he said could not be used as identification.

This left only Margaret Leahy who could identify Antonio Eremittagio. He questioned her evidence saying her story was fabricated. He again asked why they would speak in English when none of them understood it very well. It was claimed she did it because she knew Horrigan well and wanted to get revenge.

Afterwards the judge charged the jury and asked them to come to a verdict. It took less than half an hour and the jury returned to court with the verdict of not guilty. The crown prosecution asked the jury to find the accused guilty of manslaughter.

Antonio Eremittagio was however acquitted of the charges. Most likely the jury were in doubt about some of the evidence against him. Who actually did it was never to be known but one of the four must have done it, only the 4 Italian sailors knew the truth.

An example to all
Ballinrostig, 1800

John & Margaret McCarthy were said to be an industrious and hardworking couple who had built a house close to the church in Ballinrostig near Aghada. From this house they ran a shop and locally there was gossip that they had money hidden there.

On Monday the 17th of November 1800 the McCarthy's hosted stations in their home. Unfortunately that night was to be the last for the McCarthy's. During the night intruders broke into the house. John was struck in the jaw by a blunt instrument so severely that it broke his jaw. He got a blow to the crown of his head from a wooden club which fractured his skull. When he was found his brains were said to have been spattered against the wall and oozing still from his skull. His poor wife had fared no better, she was also found dead, strangled by a handkerchief. The house had been completely turned upside down.

There were no local witnesses to this terrible crime but a military officer's cane was said to have been found near the bodies. Also found was a sum of money in a pile of turf that the intruders had failed to find in the fading light.

Fort Carlisle was less than four miles from Ballinrostig and it was probably known to locals that soldiers were in the area that night. Colonel Fitzgerald stationed at Fort Carlisle investigated the cane and all men who were on leave from the fort that evening. The sentry on duty was able to identify who had passed him that evening with the cane. By the Friday of the same week a soldier either came forward or the information got out of him. He gave evidence against three of his comrades, a corporal and two soldiers. The three arrested were William Stacey, Thomas Hamilton and Joseph Cook all from the Cavan Militia which was at the time stationed at Fort Carlisle.

Ballinrostig

On the 22nd of November the case came before John Drury in Cove. Four men were now suspected, the fourth man was Scanlan. Evidence was produced against them and Drury returned the men to Cork Gaol for trial at the following Assizes.

One story tells how McCarthy often did business with the military in the area. It was known he didn't often travel to Cork to purchase new stock and would keep the money at home until he did. That very day he had been in Fort Carlisle and mentioned the fact that he was going to Cork any day now. This may have been what gave the idea to the militia men to break into his house and steal the money.

From their statements it was determined that McCarthy had been struck with the butt end of a gun and an oak bludgeon fractured his skull. They even admitted to trying to kill the wife by choking her with a knee on her chest. This however failed and the soldiers at first fled. Soon they returned again to the house and now choked the wife. They stabbed John in the neck with a bayonet, we suppose to be sure he was indeed dead.

The local priest who had held the stations that day reported that he had left his things in McCarthy's for safe keeping. The chalice he said had been found broken. The intruders had checked if it was silver with their teeth, finding to be of no value they threw it around the house. The priest's vestments had also been thrown in the fire by the intruders.

During the French revolutionary war due to growing unrest in Ireland Militias were formed from civilians to reinforce the regular army. Each county had its own responsibility to raise a militia hence the names like Cavan Militia. In England at the time men were got by ballot but in Ireland men volunteered. The militia's were excluded from serving overseas and could not serve in their home county to prevent them being familiar with the locals. This would explain why the 18th Cavan Militia were garrisoned in Fort Carlisle during this time. The Cavan's were raised in 1793 when there was a real treat of invasion from France. In 1796 they marched south west to repel the French forces attempting to land in Bantry. Two years later the Cavan Militia saw action during the 1798 rebellion at the battle of Arklow and also Vinegar Hill.

The 4 men were all held in Cork Gaol until their trial. On Monday the 1st of December the four militiamen were tried by court martial in Cork of the murders of the couple. By 1 o'clock three of the men had been found guilty, each had given their own confessions to the horrendous things they had done. Militia men were not legally treated as soldiers but civilians in the eyes of the law. However Ireland was at the time still under Martial Law since 1798 and this may be why the men faced a court martial instead of a trial by a jury.

In those times justice was swift and those found guilty of murder were to receive their punishment two days after sentencing unless it fell on a Sunday. The men would have been well aware of what lay ahead and how soon it would happen. They were clearly reminded of it when they were measured for the final part of their punishment. Early on the Wednesday morning the three men - Stacey, Hamilton and Cook were taken from their cells. From Cork Gaol they were brought back to the scene of their crimes. In a field close to where the crimes had taken place the three were seen by a Reverend Fortescue before they received their punishment. A temporary gallows had been setup to hang the three men. Hamilton broke the rope and fell to the ground before being killed. Another rope was got and he was quickly suspended again and received his final punishment.

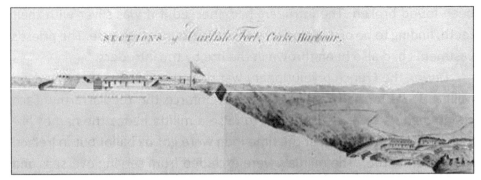

Carlisle Fort as it appeared at the time

Scanlan escaped execution; he may have been the one who initially came forward giving evidence against the others. It is also possible he was aware of what the others were up to but had not actually been directly involved.

Afterwards the bodies were taken down and brought back to Fort Carlisle where they would deter others from similar crimes. The Murder Act of 1751 prohibited the burial of those convicted of the crime saying "in no case whatsoever shall the body of any murderer be suffered to be buried". It prescribed dissection of the body or medieval practice of gibbeting or in some cases both.

Fort Carlisle at it is today, by Edward O'Shea

Depiction of a crowd gathered near a gibbet

The three bodies were placed in gibbets, each caged in iron hoops and again suspended from a gallows for all to see. Often the bodies were coated in pitch in order to preserve them from the elements. The iron frame around the body would keep it together so it would remain on display for much longer than just leaving it hanging. This practice was outlawed in 1834 but execution would continue for many years. As brutal as it sounds it was much worse in medieval times when murderers were often put in the gibbet alive for all to see. They suffered a much slower and tortuous death.

About three years later a traveller wrote an article about his experiences in Cork. He had sailed into Cork Harbour past Dognose Point and Fort Carlisle. The author remarked how the beauty of the area was not at all helped by the sight of the three bodies still hanging in the gibbets. The three men had obviously been hung in such a position that all ships entering the harbour would clearly see. Hamilton's body was said to have hung at the fort for four years but the other two lasted for eleven years.

The fort didn't undergo any major changes until 1861 when large modifications were planned. Hundreds of men were employed for several years to enlarge the fort. In August of 1862 some of the workmen uncovered the remains of human skeleton still encased in iron bands. Not long afterwards nearby the remaining two skeletons were also found in the same condition.

The tailor's wife.
Leamlara, 1826

On the morning of the 13th of April 1826 James Collins ran to a neighbour's house near Leamlara desperately looking for help for his wife. Collins who was the local tailor told his neighbours that she was in a bad way having fallen over a stile. When the neighbour got to the house Ellen Collins was propped up against a chair with injuries to her head. Her eldest son was present and trying his best to comfort her. James was in a state of panic and ran off to get the priest. The woman was clearly unconscious from injuries she had sustained.

Ellen died later that day, the following day an inquest was held to hear the circumstances of how exactly she had died. A medical examination had been carried out before the inquest by Dr J Barry and his evidence would change everything. He told how the cuts on her head could not have been caused by falling and was more likely the result of being struck by a sharp instrument. The skull was fractured more than once yet there was no injury to any other part of the body.

Her husband James Collins was arrested not long after and charged with the murder of his wife despite no actual evidence against him. He remained in custody for four months waiting for his trial before a criminal court.

It was August when the Cork Summer Assizes were held and the case came before Justice Baron Pennefather on Wednesday the 2nd. There was no actual witness that saw James kill his wife but he was charged that with killing his wife by striking her with a shovel on the head. Collins had something else on his side, two defence lawyer's one of which was Daniel O'Connell. He was said to be the best in the country, with nearly thirty years experience at this point and had gained a reputation of being fearless in court.

The first witness called was Denis McGrath who on being sworn in, laughed and claimed that he couldn't speak English. The judge insisted though that he couldn't give his evidence in Irish and McGrath had to give in and speak in a language foreign to him.

McGrath told how his nearest neighbour called him from his bed early on the morning of the 13ᵗʰ of April. That morning Collins told him his wife was coming over a stile with a basket of soil when she took a fall. Denis arrived at the house to find only their son present with Ellen. He removed her cap, took a look at the wounds on her head and even went so far as to feel the fractures to the skull. He sent Collins to fetch the priest which he did. He also recalled seeing the basket of earth near the very stile she was to have fallen on, saying how he thought she had fallen there. Denis described the stile for the court saying how it was narrow with three steps that led to the yard. He detailed what he knew of the relationship between the couple saying they were on bad terms.

When Daniel O'Connell got his first chance in court he wasted no time at all and questioned McGrath about several more details. He got the witness to admit that Ellen was lame and it was very likely she could have fallen at the stile. Also McGrath now admitted there were stones about the stile which in his opinion could have caused the cuts. Under cross examination the witness now recalled how upset Collins seemed that morning that his wife was injured. McGrath had known the witness since childhood and never known him in any trouble.

At last McGrath replied to questions from the jury and said when he got to the scene Ellen was still alive but he never heard her speak at all. Another juror asked a question and McGrath told that he saw blood on the stones near the stile.

The next witness sworn in was another neighbour who lived close by the Collin's house, David Mulcahy. He was also at the house on the morning Ellen died and recalled seeing the shovel near the stile. He explained to the court how the shovel was of interest to him as he owned it and had only lent it to Collins. He also knew how Collins was working with the shovel that morning, near to where his wife fell from the stile. The witness explained how he lived only 200m from Collins house. He was aware that the couple didn't get along and often rowed. Living so close David overheard the arguments between the couple and also was aware that it had at times come to blows. He said that Ellen Collins was always accusing her husband with "keeping company with another woman". On this occasion it seems O'Connell didn't cross examine the witness, or had heard enough of the troubles between the couple.

Key to the case for the prosecution was the medical evidence as no one saw Collins strike his wife. Dr J Barry described in detail the head wounds that Ellen Collins had died from. One wound on the head he said was four inches long and likely to have been done with a sharp instrument. The doctor also detailed a fracture of the skull which he concluded was also the result of a sharp object. He told how in his examination the wound had been compared to the shovel and was of the opinion the shovel had been used. The doctor apologised for using technical medical descriptions when describing the wound as semi lunar or crescent shaped. The shovel he found to be very sharp and that was the reason why it could make this shaped wound. He said even if the stile was four feet high a fall like this on stones could not produce such a wound.

Daniel O'Connell arguing a case in court

Daniel O'Connell now jumped at the chance to try to tear apart the doctor's evidence and even admitted to having some medical experience himself. O'Connell told how a brother of his had previously fallen from a horse and got a sharp wound from falling on stones. The pair exchanged words about stones and wounds. O'Connell remarked that a straight stone wound produce a straight wound and a semi lunar stone would produce a semi lunar shaped wound and laughed aloud in court. He tried to cast doubt amongst the jury saying doctors differed and the whole of the medical evidence was merely a matter of one man's opinion.

The last witness for the prosecution was 10 year old Dennis Collins who had to give evidence against his father. Before the trial Dennis had been questioned and found quite capable of appearing before the jury. Once he was sworn in Dennis told the court "I will tell the truth". The boy recollected the night before his mother died; she sat by the fire crying. His father did not come home at all and he slept with his mother that night. Dennis didn't understand why his parents fought and never witnessed them exchange blows.

The next morning Dennis said his mother was up before him and he got up when his father called him. He went out and helped his father bring his mother into the house and stayed at her side. The boy backed tracked revealing that two years before when they lived at another house his mother had indeed struck his father. He went on that it was mostly at night they fought and he would leave for the night. In these fights his mother often complained about a woman he knew called Johanna Leahy.

Daniel O'Connell had one last chance to question the young boy and try to save the boys father from a death sentence. He asked what awoke the boy that morning and learned that it was his father's cries from outside. When they brought her inside his father appeared very sorrowful and was crying. A juror asked the boy what his father was doing when he ran out of the house. Dennis said his father held his mother in his arms and was trying to get her into the house. He never heard his mother speak as they helped her.

The case for the prosecution closed and Daniel O'Connell remarked "I leave the case with your lordship". There were no witnesses for the defence nor did anyone give a character reference for the accused. With such little evidence against him and having O'Connell his chances of getting off looked good. Finally the other defence solicitor Mr Daltera who didn't say much up till now intervened. He wanted the stone from where Ellen Collins was found to be produced in court. He had to defer to O'Connell's superiority who said there was no need to produce the stone in court.

The doctor was recalled by the jury, he reconfirmed to them how the shovel and the wounds matched in size.

After the judge summed up the case the jury took very little time to decide on the verdict. In a very short time they returned to the courtroom with a verdict of guilty. Justice Pennefather wasted no time and entered into a tirade against Collins leaving no doubt at all how he felt about the case. Addressing Collins directly he said "you took away that life which you should have forfeited your own to preserve. You did so, as I must believe yielding to a wicked and sinful passion for another woman, whom you should not have associated with as freely. It is dreadful to consider that these take place and that such depravity exists". He mentioned the three children that would be left behind telling James Collins how they would now be orphans and disgraced for the rest of their lives.

The judge said that O'Connell would have produced the stone had it helped the defence, but now the judge was sure it would not have. He sentenced James Collins to be hung until dead in two days time on Friday the 5th of August.

Daniel O'Connell wrote to his wife at Derrynane not long after and mentioned the case. He was not pleased with the outcome of losing the case but privately he concluded that he thought Collins had indeed killed his wife. He also admitted that Collins seemed to deserve the fate that awaited him.

Two days later Collins was woken for breakfast hours before his execution. He didn't bother with food that morning and instead spent his last hours praying in an attempt to redeem himself. While being led out from the gaol to the scaffold at Gallow's Green Collins looked around him, as if he didn't understand what was about to occur.

In his final moments before climbing the scaffold he gave in and admitted to having killed his wife but said "I did not strike her with a shovel". He had already told the priest that the law wasn't justice enough for his terrible crime. At half past twelve he was on the scaffold and in an instant had met his fate. As was normal at the time his body was afterwards taken to the infirmary for medical dissection.

So how did an eminent solicitor such as Daniel O'Connell come to represent a country tailor in a murder trial? It could have been due to a local connection, O'Connell was said to have often stayed at Leamlara House, the Standish Barry family seat. Garret Standish Barry was the first Catholic Member of Parliament elected after the Catholic Emancipation Act of 1829.

He was only a bystander
Youghal 1887

On the Ponsonby estate in the region of Youghal, the tenants were struggling to pay their rent. Charles William Talbot was a retired naval officer and had inherited the estate from his uncle in 1866. He assumed the name Ponsonby and lived for a while in Park House near Youghal. Later he decided to move back to London becoming an absentee landlord leaving the estate in the hands of his agent.

The estate was just over 10,000 acres in the regions of Killeagh and Gortaroo; it had nearly 300 tenants averaging 30 acres each. The smaller plots were rack rented to such an extent that some tenants were up to three years in arrears. In 1885 after talks with the tenants the landlord allowed 20% reduction in the rents.

The wet summer of 1886 exacerbated the situation further when some couldn't manage to save their barley. Those that did manage to save some of their crop found the prices had fallen considerably. The landlord at first made no attempt to evict the outstanding tenants knowing that they couldn't pay. Only a handful of tenants with arrears of over three years were evicted.

A group of tenants got together and approached the landlord's agent Mr Blakney asking for a 35% reduction in rent. Several times the tenants and Fr Keller tried to reach an agreement with the landlord but it didn't happen. It was felt that an agreement could have been reached but Ponsonby had given over control to the Cork Defence Union. The union was setup as a landlords association to prevent boycotting and assist with evictions. By November of 1886 five of the biggest tenants on the estate were served with eviction notices.

Park House near Killeagh where Ponsonby lived for a while

The tenants responded the same month and organised themselves by coming together under the *Plan of Campaign* of the Irish National League. Once organised the tenants held the land forcibly and refused to pay rent to the landlord. The rent minus 35% was instead paid into a fund of which Fr Keller was said to have been the trustee. Members of the National League came from all over East Cork as far away as Cloyne. There was almost five hundred men present helping the tenants plough the grassland. One of the leaders of the National League William O'Brien came to visit the affected farms near Gortaroo.

On Monday the 7th of February a demonstration went through the streets of Youghal led by a donkey and a band. The donkey carried a stuffed figure supposed to represent Blakney who was Ponsonby's agent. The large crowd stopped outside the Green Park Hotel where they tried to set fire to the figure. The figure was damp and wouldn't light and the donkey bolted. The crowd carried on to the Imperial Hotel where some evicted tenants were staying but dispersed without any trouble. More tenants were served summons to attend the bankruptcy court in February, with several in the Killeagh area affected. The tenants did everything they could to hamper the messengers of the courts.

On Sunday 13th February Dr Tanner, MP for Cork and supporter of the Plan of Campaign arrived in Youghal for a meeting. The authorities were aware of his plans and fifty armed constables were on the streets. Several times they charged the people in order to clear the streets. Dr. Tanner gave a speech at the pier but again police carried out their orders and charged the crowds with their rifles.

By early March it was widely known that Judge Boyd of the Bankruptcy court in Dublin was trying to serve a summons on Fr Keller. Judge Boyd wrote to Fr Keller asking him to attend court in Dublin to act as witness against the evicted tenants. They were also trying to identify him as being involved in the tenants rent fund. Enclosed was the sum of £3 for travel expenses, the priest refused to go and instead gave the £3 to the National League as a donation.

The tension in the town increased daily and the people of the town did everything to protect their parish priest from appearing in court. Locals guarded the parochial house and the approach roads to Youghal were also watched continuously. If any suspicious looking person was seen, the chapel bells were rung. The people of Youghal would descend to the town quickly on hearing the bells and make it impossible for the bailiffs to serve the summons, so they retreated to the police barracks.

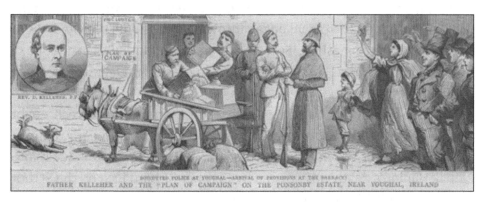

Shows police provisioning barracks

The situation intensified further on the 7th of March when the town was in a state of terrible confusion. Many of the shops shut and virtually no business was conducted in the town. The crowds were said to have been in control of the town and the police retreated to their barracks. Several of the prominent members gave speeches to the crowds on the streets and bands played throughout the town. The people vowed to protect Fr Keller and anyone else from arrest by resisting the authorities. The majority of the town stayed on the streets the whole night keeping vigil, prepared to resist the authorities.

Police reinforcements were brought into the town on the 8th of March. District Inspector Sommerville arrived from Cobh by train with 22 men. He marched his men through the town followed by a group of locals shouting abuse at them. As they reached the Devonshire Arms Hotel the group increased. Passing Windmill Lane the crowd became larger still and stones began to be thrown. Sommerville ordered his men to fix their bayonets and shouted to the crowd that he would charge if it persisted. It didn't stop instead the crowd corralled and grew closer to the armed police. At the Clock tower Sommerville regrouped his men and half of them turned to face the crowd but that did not deter the crowd.

The crowd retreated and some who ran down a lane were pursued by armed constables. In their mad dash to getaway down the lane someone was stabbed in the back by a bayonet.

It was Patrick Hanlon a thirty year old fisherman from Ballymacoda who had only come into the town to support the cause; he was certainly no ring leader. The stab wound pierced his left lung. With Hanlon lying dying on the street the crowd began throwing stones until the windows of the barracks were smashed. Several leaders of the National League spoke from the Imperial Hotel asking the crowd to cease throwing stones which they did eventually.

The day following Hanlon's death even more police were brought into the town. The people of the town wondered if they were there to arrest Fr Keller or to put down further demonstrations. The inquest into Patrick Hanlon's death was opened by Coroner Richard Rice on the 9th but adjourned until Friday after the funeral.

The County inspector Brownrigg, who was supposedly in control of the town, received a message. It told how Dublin castle intended to deal with the situation. It read "deal very summarily if any organised resistance to lawful authority. If necessary do not hesitate to shoot them". Luckily Fr Keller came to an arrangement with the police, no constables would be seen on the streets for the funeral and there would be no trouble.

THE POLICE CHARGING THE CROWD WITH FIXED BAYONETS AT YOUGHAL
In this Charge Hanlon was killed

Depiction of the police charge on the streets of Youghal

The state of the town hadn't settled at all by the following day, with crowds still out on the streets. The police having drafted in reinforcements now maintained a presence around the town. Such was the hatred for the police that a newsboy refused to sell a paper to a constable. The constable justified the feelings of the town in his response to not getting a paper. He beat the young boy in plain sight on the street but was afterwards summoned to appear in court for assault.

The body of young Hanlon was laid out in state in the Town Hall for a funeral at 10am on the Thursday. A huge number of people turned out from all over the area especially those on the Ponsonby estate. Despite the danger of being arrested Fr Keller was present and didn't appear like someone who could be arrested at any moment. At least the police in the town respected the funeral and didn't appear on the streets during it; Fr Keller's agreement with them had been upheld.

**Another view of the street close to where the riot took place
Image courtesy of the National Library of Ireland**

The funeral procession left the town at one o'clock, for the Hill Cemetery in nearby Ballymacoda nearly eight miles away. The funeral cortege was immense stretching along the road with nearly everyone from the district present. After the funeral several of the clergy spoke to the crowds. One commended the people for the great patience they had shown despite the great provocation from the so called authorities. Fr Keller spoke also asking the bands not to play on their way back and they would meet no police. He said the people had not yet come to terms with what had happened and the circumstances were too sad to take action. Justice would be done yet he said and their feelings would be justified before the world. The crowd did as they were advised and afterwards dispersed peacefully to their own homes. The day after the funeral the town went back to some kind of normality with the shops open again but very little business was done.

On Friday11[th] of March the inquest sat again at the Youghal courthouse. Hanlon's next of kin were represented by M.P. Mr T. Harrington, while

Thomas Rice was for the Crown. A large group of police were at the inquest, some were armed. Also present were County Inspector Brownrigg and District Inspector Sommerville. Thomas Rice stated immediately that he didn't really know what his role was there but had been requested to attend by the under Secretary and complied. He said his intention was not to interfere with the proceeding but to report to the government the findings.

THE COURT MESSENGER, PROTECTED BY THE POLICE, ENDEAVOURING TO SERVE AT MIDNIGHT THE SUMMONS OF THE BANKRUPTCY COURT ON A TENANT WHO HAD ADOPTED THE " PLAN OF CAMPAIGN," NEAR YOUGHAL

Notice being served on tenants of the estate

The proceedings opened more like a trial than an inquest when Harrington asked for the police report to be produced. Inspector Brownrigg immediately on the defensive said there was no report made and he refused to submit one. Harrington asked what was the Inspector's position on the case "would he state the truth or shield the police". It descended to exchanges of threats and insults between both sides until the coroner intervened and moved the proceedings on.

The remainder of the day was taken up with evidence of Head Constable Higgins who had been on the streets that night. He told how he didn't actually see what happened to Hanlon that night. When cross examined he admitted Sommerville could at anytime have retreated to the barracks before he charged the crowd.

The following day the inquest sat again but was moved to the town hall. There was some outbreak of fever at the courthouse. Sommerville was on the stand but said he didn't see what happen to Hanlon that night. During his cross examination by Mr Harrington the County Inspector sneered before the jury at the questions he was being asked. Harrington took great insult to this saying "your conduct is a scandal to your profession, bad as your profession is". This resulted in great cheering from the crowd in the room.

Acting Sergeant McKeague of Youghal told how he was on the streets at quarter past seven on the 8th March. He saw Sommerville and his men going towards the barracks, near the post office. Sommerville led with his sword drawn and all the others had their bayonets fixed on their rifles. The home rule band of Youghal was playing and the crowd including women and children were gathered all round the police. McKeague went back to the barracks to get his rifle and by the time he returned he had missed the charge on the crowd. The stone throwing continued and Sommerville ordered his men to retreat to the barracks as several had been injured.

On Monday the 14th the inquest was again to resume but there was great unrest in the town as a bankruptcy messenger had been spotted on the streets. Fr Keller was advised to lie low and keep out of sight but he refused to give in. He went to the inquest which was due to sit at the Mall house.

At the inquest that day District Inspector Sommerville was giving evidence when there was a sudden excitement in the room. The messenger arrived armed with six policemen in the middle of the proceeding to serve his summons on Fr Keller. He continued with his intentions despite objections from the Coroner and Mr Harrington. Both of whom said it was only being done to disrupt the proceedings of the inquest. After consulting with the County Inspector the messenger pushed his way through the crowd to get to the parish priest.

Parish priest Fr Keller

When he did Fr. Keller was served with a summons to appear at the Court of Bankruptcy in Dublin on the 16th. The summons requested him to act as witness in a bankruptcy case against a tenant. Quickly Harrington intervened and advised him not to accept it which he didn't. The envelope ended up on the floor and Harrington grabbed it and flung it out the window.

District inspector Sommerville resumed his evidence when the room settled down again but still refused to tell whether he had used his sword the night Hanlon was killed. He said a crowd followed his posse from the train station into the town on the 7th throwing stones at him and his men. He stated that the killing of Hanlon was in his opinion "justifiable homicide". Despite lengthy questioning from Mr Harrington he continually refused to answer whether he used his sword that night.

The Inspector did confirm that only three of his constables had been injured on the night. He also said the Chief Secretary Balfour's statement in the House of Commons that 21 of the constables were injured was not true.

Dr Charles Ronayne was questioned next, as the only justice of the peace in the town he said he felt it his duty to remain on the streets on the 7th. There was great excitement in the town that night due to the rumours but according to Ronayne very little damage was done. On the night of the 8th Dr Ronayne was called when Hanlon was stabbed. He found the victim dying due to the blood loss from his wound. The doctor examined the wound and found it was caused by a large double edged sword used with great force. As he could do nothing for poor Hanlon he went to the police barrack. When confronted Sommerville told him he knew nothing about a stabbing. The doctor examined all the constable's bayonets and found one to have blood on it. The stain was about eight inches from the point of the sword but Sommerville wasn't happy and asked him to stop interfering. The doctor caused a sensation in the room when he repeated what Sommerville told him in the barracks that night. Sommerville had said "I am sorry I did not fire on them"; Ronayne said he was shocked when he heard it.

The next day at the inquest Constables Irvine and Smith both refused to answer the question of had they seen Hanlon stabbed that night. Both refused on the grounds they may incriminate themselves. When a third Constable Balmer took the same line the coroner had enough. He issued a warrant for his arrest on contempt of court and handed it to district inspector Smith.

A woman and a labourer identified Constable Garrett Ward as the one who stabbed Hanlon. A Constable Moore also said he saw Ward stab Hanlon in the back as he ran away.

On Friday the Bankruptcy court messenger Malcolm Ellis was back in Youghal. This time he carried a warrant for the arrest of Fr Keller for contempt of court in failing to attend. Without any resistance Fr. Keller was arrested at the parochial house and taken by train to Dublin. He was held in Kilmainham gaol.

When the inquest sat on the 22nd of March it was its last day and a verdict would be reached. The Coroner asked the District Inspector why a warrant he issued for the arrest of Constable Balmer had not been executed. Previously Balmer had refused to be cross examined at the inquest. Coroner Rice said it was the first time in his long career he had to exercise this power. He said he only did so after convincing himself the constable had been told by his superiors not to answer questions. It was no surprise the warrant hadn't been executed but Smith made excuses as to why it wasn't. Eventually Balmer was produced before the jury but again refused to answer the questions. Much of the remainder of the day was taken up with recalling witnesses to answer particular questions the jury had.

The coroner asked was District Inspector Sommerville and Constable Ward present but received a reply that neither were. He said that it would be in their interest if both of them were present "well I think they ought to be here".

Mr Wynne addressed the jury saying how sure he was they would find Sommerville and his men had been attacked and were justified in their actions. The case for the prosecution Mr Harrington addressed the jury and explained the difference between murder, manslaughter and justifiable homicide. He said what took place that night was murder and nothing else. He asked why if a riot had taken place on the 8th of March that nobody had been arrested for being involved.

Finally the jury retired to consider their verdict and returned over an hour later having come to a conclusion. The foreman read the verdict, "we find Patrick Hanlon met his death in the North Main Street of Youghal on the night of March 8th by a stab with a sword bayonet, inflicted by constable Garret Ward and we say Constable Ward is guilty of wilful murder". Hearing this there was a loud applause in the room but the coroner intervened and calmed the crowd. The foreman read on "we also find the District Inspector Sommerville guilty of wilful murder for aiding and abetting him to commit the act".

The verdict was signed by thirteen of the jurors and Harrington immediately asked for a warrant for the arrest of those found guilty. Coroner Rice replied "of course I have no other option". Warrants were duly issued to arrest both men and place them in the county gaol. After some closing statements the jury were discharged of their duty.

The authorities were caught unawares by the coroner's actions and were unprepared for this eventuality. Amazingly the warrants were actually acted upon the day after the verdict and Sommerville was taken by train to the county gaol. Later Constable Ward was taken separately to the gaol. However any hopes the people of Youghal would get justice quickly faded. The Attorney General intervened in the case and accepted an application for bail for both the men after less than two weeks in custody.

Meanwhile back on the Ponsonby estate eight men were brought in to protect Park house from suspected outrages. The men were supplied by the Cork Defence Union, a landlords association set up to put down any boycotting. It was nearly the end of May when Fr Keller was released for Kilmainham gaol on the grounds of a technicality. He arrived back in Youghal triumphantly a few days later to a huge crowd.

In late July the Cork Assizes were in session, Mr Harrington applied to the judge about the Youghal case. He wasn't the judge to set a date for the trial of District Inspector Sommerville and Constable Ward on the charge of murder. However he was told the Attorney General had returned a *nolle prosequi* verdict and the case wouldn't be heard.

After all his work on the case Mr Harrington protested to the judge saying he wouldn't let it drop and would try elsewhere. Also in July the tenants tried to purchase the farms from the landlord, Ponsonby reckoned he was owed £19,600 in rent.

The stand off went on for a long time and evictions were carried out by force. In May 1889 a large force arrived on a train in Youghal catching everyone off guard.

The group consisted of 100 constables, 100 armed soldiers and 20 emergencymen. They also carried with them all the equipment such as a battering-ram which allows one to conjure the scene. The two tenants they came to evict had no option but to relent to such a force. Evictions went on throughout the year and into 1890. It was February of 1892 before some of the tenants finally agreed a settlement. Some of the tenants were able to purchase their holding they had fought over for years.

A shocking discovery
West beach, Cove 1848

1848 in the town centre of Cove (it would be another year before Queen Victoria visited and the town was renamed Queenstown in her honour), a young servant boy was up early one Sunday morning in May going about his normal duties when made a ghastly discovery. He noticed blood seeping from under a bedroom door upstairs.

He immediately raised the alarm in the house and a doctor was called for. It was almost seven in the morning when Dr Coppinger arrived; on his way there he presumed he was being called at such an early hour for William Grannell whose health had been poor for some time.

Entering the house the doctor was surprised when William's brother Richard informed him he had been called for Mary, William Grannell's wife. The doctor went upstairs and entered a small bedroom which faced out onto the harbour. There on the floor of the narrow room lay Mary Grannell in a pool of blood dressed in her night gown. It didn't take the doctor long to know there was nothing he could do. He found her throat had been cut several times so severely that the windpipe was exposed. It appeared that Mary Grannell had been dead for some time. There were also signs that a terrible struggle had taken place in the room judging by the marks on her arms and legs.

As the Grannell home was in the centre of town the police arrived quickly and began to make their inquiries. Everyone in the house was questioned but all claimed to have heard nothing during the night. Even Richard Grannell who slept in the room directly above where the murder had occurred said he never heard a thing. The police must have been suspicious as neighbours claimed to have heard a woman's screams during the night but didn't do anything about it. Young servant Patrick McCarthy was sure that nobody else was in the house during the night. The door was locked until he had opened it to let in another servant Mary Collins shortly after his discovery. It was clear no attempt had been made by the murderer to conceal the crime as the blood stained bread knife was found close to the body.

Grannell's drapery shop was at corner of West Beach
Image courtesy of the National Library of Ireland

The obvious suspect was the husband William but he didn't have any blood on his clothes that morning. Despite this the police arrested William for the murder of his wife but they had no evidence or witnesses.

The Grannell's were a most respectable family who ran a successful business in the centre of town for many years. William Grannell was a tailor and clothes dealer located at West Beach Cove. Much of his business was supplying the many ships that came to the busy port. When his health began to fail his younger brother returned from Liverpool to run the shop. It was rumoured that William was suffering from insanity for sometime.

The following day on 22nd of May 1848 the inquest was opened by coroner Mr S Foote and a jury of respectable men from the town were sworn in. The inquest was held in a room on the first floor in Grannell's, next to the room where the murder took place. The deceased woman Mary Grannell was still in her bedroom and the body would have been inspected by the jury. It began at six thirty in the morning almost exactly twenty four hours after the discovery was made.

The family's doctor John Cronin was called before the inquest to give evidence of Grannell's state of mind. He said William had been perfectly normal until November 1846 when he was struck with bouts of insanity. The doctor believed it had been caused by an inflammation of the brain and had been treating his patient by cooling his head as well as other treatments. The doctor went on to say William Grannell often needed to be restrained to prevent him doing harm. Cronin had previously recommended that William be sent to an asylum where he had the best chance of recovery.

Richard Grannell was next called; he recalled having a drink with his brother and his wife the Saturday night before the murder. He went to bed around eleven and didn't see anyone again until early the next morning when he learned Mary had been killed.

Doctor Cronin was recalled to give medical evidence as he had carried out a post mortem with Dr Coppinger. He described the wounds in detail saying he found one 3 inches long under her chin. Directly under the first wound was another four inches long, this severed the thyroid artery and the doctor said was the direct cause of death. A third wound was also found slightly lower on the neck. There were also several smaller wounds on the body, arms and knees which led the doctor to believe a great struggle had taken place. However he concluded the struggle must have occurred on the floor of the narrow room as the bed clothes were undisturbed. The bedclothes were carefully turned down to allow her get out of bed, so the doctor concluded she had not been dragged from her bed. Other than that there were no other signs of struggle or damage to anything in the small room. The doctor remarked that only for the marks on her body he would have thought she had cut her own throat. He also found that her legs were tied together with a handkerchief and assumed this was done by the murderer.

Young servant Patrick McCarthy was a key witness as he had discovered the crime. Patrick was up at about six that morning and met William about the house. He asked him for the keys but went himself to get them. It was then that he spotted the blood coming from under the door and entered the room to find Mrs Grannell dead. The boy said William looked pale and was not normally up so early. When asked about William's state at the time the servant said he "looked wild and frightened". Patrick McCarthy was sure nobody had got into the house during the night as all windows and doors were intact in the morning.

Dr Cronin again came forward and said since earlier giving evidence he had carried out an examination on William Grannell looking for signs of struggle. The constable had suggested it and the coroner agreed also. The doctor had found no marks indicating a struggle except a tiny scratch on his thumb and a little blood on the wrist. The doctor asked William where the blood had come from and wasn't expecting such a direct reply. William said "sure you know" and the doctor continued questioning. He next asked had he seen his wife lately but William said simply that he had. When asked did he know of his wife's death Grannell replied "it was I did it, I felt it was my duty and I did it". After this the doctor said William didn't go any further and refused to answer more questions.

Mary Collins was next called before the jury; she was the servant who knocked at the door just after Patrick had found Mrs Grannell dead. She informed the jury how she had seen the bloodstained knife on the wash stand in the room where the body lay. She recognised the knife which was normally in the kitchen.

After nearly six hours of hearing evidence, the jury left to deliberate at twelve o'clock. They returned after a short time and returned a verdict of wilful murder against William Grannell. They did however state they believed he was not of sound mind when he committed the horrendous crime.

Early in January of 1851 the entire premises that Grannell owned in the town was put up for sale. It was described as being the best location in the centre of town, complete with shop fixtures and house above. The building continued to be used as a drapers shop for many more years.

A feud gone too far
Creighmore, Gortaroo, Youghal August 1923

John Fennessy wanted to auction his farm in the townland of Creighmore; the auction was to take place on the 28th of October 1921. The farm had originally belonged to the O'Dea family. John Fennessy had married Hanna O'Dea about three years before. Fennessy now lived there with his elderly father-in-law Phillip and sister-in-law Ellen. It seems to be John having married the eldest daughter was now in charge. The farm consisted of 20 acres and included a good thatched farmhouse, stables and outhouses. It was situated less than half mile from Gortaroo and was about five miles from the town of Youghal.

On the day of the auction the highest bidder was a neighbouring farmer John Lee. He was a bachelor in his thirties who lived with his older sisters Ellen and Mary. It would seem a normal enough transaction, the farm was held in a fee simple which was a form of a freehold and was subject to an annuity of £11 14 s payable to the Land Commission.

However Fennessy refused to go ahead with the transaction and a dispute sparked off between the two men. It seems possible that Fennessy's in laws were trying to stop the sale but there is no evidence of this. Fennessy claimed that the price £393 was not a fair one and the sale was not conducted properly. Lee must have been frustrated wanting to pay and take possession of the farm. He was forced to take legal action and some time later it was called before a judge. In court it was decided that the contract agreed upon was not carried out. The sale price was to be lodged in court and Lee was allowed to deduct his legal costs from the sum.

Still Fennessy did not comply and refused to give up possession of the farm.

What now becomes a feud between neighbours drags on until the next year 1922. That year the civil war began and lasted 10 months but the trouble in Creighmore lasted longer.

The trouble continued well into August 1923, when there were shocking consequences that could not be foreseen. On Wednesday the first of August John Lee went to Youghal with a horse and cart. At about three in the afternoon as he returned home, turned into the boreen leading to his farm he found the lane blocked by a lorry. John Fennessy had sold hay from the land in question to a Mr Hennessy from Castlemartyr. The previous day Hennessy had removed a lorry load and now he was taking the remainder. The lorry was parked on the road while they drew the hay from the field with a horse and cart.

This didn't please Lee at all, he was instantly furious to find the road blocked especially as it involved the land he wished to purchase. He called Mr Hennessy a bum and a grabber saying he had no right to block the road. He turned on Fennessy shouting abuse at him, Fennessy told him there was room for him to get by. Eventually he did pass by the lorry with some difficulty and went to his own yard.

Lee took off his coat, walked back down the road to where the lorry was and continued the row where it had left off. Lee's claim was that the hay was on his land but Fennessy disagreed saying it was his. Lee was now joined by his sister Ellen who also began verbal abuse. Ellen shouted at Fennessy that it was the devil that had brought him and he might take him away again. Lee now pursued Fennessy and threw stones at him. Fennessy dodged around the lorry to get away and avoid being struck by a stone. One large stone was flung but Ellen Lee was caught between the men and received a blow on the side of her head. She fell to the ground, her face covered in blood. Their sister Mary arrived hurriedly on the scene and asked the workmen who had hit her sister. She must have been shocked to learn that it was her brother who had done it. Ellen was carried away home by her siblings but John Lee again returned to the scene to pursue Fennessy. He continued throwing stones but Fennessy fled to his own yard and avoided any harm. A doctor arrived on the scene, finding Ellen thrown on the settle unconscious. He treated her as best he could but knew there was little chance of a recovery.

Ellen Lee succumbed to her injuries and died the following morning. No time was wasted and an inquest was held in John Lee's house by the coroner Richard Rice that same morning. A jury was found from the locality with Patrick Smiddy a farmer from Ballymadog acting as foreman. The only witnesses giving evidence were John Fennessy and his wife, as well as Patrick Clarke from Castlemartyr and Patrick Twohig the workmen present.

Medical evidence was given by Dr Kennedy from Youghal who had attended Ellen the previous day. He had found the skull fractured and a puncture wound on the right side of the forehead. He told the inquest that he had done what he could for her but knew recovery was unlikely. The jury of the inquest reached a verdict that Ellen Lee died from a blow of a stone from her brother, but that her brother had no intention of hitting her.

Later that afternoon John Lee was arrested and taken into custody in Youghal. Within a matter of hours he appeared in court charged with the killing of his sister. State solicitor D Casey from Mitchelstown was in charge of the prosecution case, while Mr J.L Keane Youghal defended. Again the only witnesses were John Fennessy and some of the workmen who had been employed transporting the hay. In his evidence Patrick Twohig told of the threats spoken between the men before the stone was thrown. He heard Lee threaten to break every tooth in Fennessy's head for blocking the road. Fennessy replied that neither Lee nor any of his family would be fit to do it. It was at this he heard Lee tell his sister to clear out of his way so he could blow Fennessy's brains out. Patrick Twohig described the stone that he saw hit Ellen. He said it was round but cornered about the size of a half pint glass. He saw Ellen Lee stagger and fall after being hit by the stone. John Lee was heard saying to his sister that she was always in his way and that the stone was meant for Fennessy.

An Application was made to allow him bail so that he could attend the funeral. The judge however refused saying he could not grant it so Lee was remanded in custody to appear before the next district court.

A week later he was back in court again, this time the judge allowed bail for £500 and two sureties of £250 each. The case was sent to trial at the criminal court in Dublin.

It would be late the next year, 4th of December 1924 to be exact, before the case was heard again. In the criminal court house on Green Street in Dublin, with Justice O'Sullivan and a jury, John Lee now pleaded guilty to the charge of killing his sister almost 18 months previous.

Solicitor for the defence opened by saying how the case was one of the saddest that had ever come before the court. He described at length what occurred on that fateful day. He told how John Lee had supported his sister by hard work on his tiny farm.

The solicitor put the distance between Fennessy and Lee at 20 yards but Fennessy claimed it was only about ten. He reckoned that at 20 yards Lee had intended to hit his adversary but did not really expect to. The argument concluded saying there was no punishment which could be inflicted on Lee would ever be as bad as what had already occurred.

Criminal Court Green Street in Dublin where the case was heard

The local parish priest Fr Daniel Scanlan gave a character reference for the accused describing him as an honest, sober hardworking man. He went on to say it was obvious to those who knew him that he had a great affection for his sister. Finally the judge said he would consider the case and put off sentencing for another day.

The next day John Lee was again before the judge for sentencing with many others.

The judge agreed with the defence that John Lee had been punished already. He gave sentence of six months but suspended it binding him to keep the peace.

It would be almost another year before the dispute of the land sale was brought to a conclusion in court. By now Fennessy's elderly father-in-law Phillip O'Dea had died at the age of 82. On Tuesday the 17th of November 1925 the lawsuit was heard before a circuit court judge in Cork. This time John Lee was the plaintiff bringing the case against the defendants John Fennessy and his sister-in-law Ellen O'Dea. The lawsuit was for the non completion of the farm sale which was now four years later. After hearing how Fennessy wouldn't comply the judge said "these people need to be taught a lesson and made obey the law".

The defendants gave evidence but it didn't seem to change the judge's opinion of the case. Ellen O'Dea said she wouldn't like to be evicted but the judge quickly quipped "any trouble and worse than that will happen to you". The judge ordered that the sale money be again lodged in court and the lands to be transferred to the plaintiff. He again reminded the defendants that any trouble given to the sheriff and he would deal with them drastically. Warning them how they would have time to consider their position when in prison.

Glossary

Adze is a tool that dates back to the Stone Age, it is like an axe but the blade is turned at right angle to the handle. It is mostly used to shape wood and is often used in boat building.

Assizes periodic criminal courts held quarterly that heard the most serious cases before a jury.

Brigantine is a two masted sailing vessel with a square rig on the foremast.

Coroner is a person who conducts an inquest into the cause of death, is normally a magistrate or solicitor.

Emergencymen employed by the landlord to guard a property after an eviction.

Gibbets a gallows used to hang someone, gibbeting was the practice of hanging them in chains for display purposes.

Governor General or Seanascal this role was created with the formation of the Free State in 1922.The role was to be the official representative of the sovereign in Ireland. The role was a controversial one as the sovereign was still the king. The duties included giving royal assent to legislation and dissolving the Dáil.

Graffawn or graffaun hand tool like a pick axe but with a much wider blade used for digging or grubbing soil. Similar shaped to an adze but blade wouldn't be sharpened like an adze.

Grand Jury was normally made up of the largest local rate payers or put another way were the landlords. They acted as a form of local government as well as sitting as jury on more serious criminal cases. Members of a Grand Jury could also sit as magistrates judging lesser cases.

Gudgeon pin on a boat is the hinge like fitting where the rudder is attached.

Gunwale the upper edge or planking at the side of a boat.

Haggart is a small enclosed field or yard at the back of a farm cottage. Often used for storing winter supplies of hay, straw or fodder.

Inquest is a judicial inquiry held in public into the cause of death. A jury is required when the death is suspicious or a murder is suspected.

Nolle prosequi legal phrase used by the prosecutor to say the case is being dropped.

Martial Law usually a temporary measure where the military take over from the Government and impose law.

Paymaster non combatant army officer in charge of the regiment's pay and all financial aspects.

Pitch or tar was one time the primary waterproofing material especially on ships.

Riot Act a British law from 1714 which gave powers to local authorities. Any group of 12 persons or more could be declared unlawful and required to disperse. If the group did not go within an hour they were likely to face punishment.

Penal Servitude or hard labour was introduced in the 1770's and could also include transportation to a distant colony. By the 1850's transportation had been abolished but hard labour remained the norm. Not all labour was productive some prisons used punitive exercise such as a treadmill. As a form of punishment penal servitude was abolished in Britain in the 1950's but remained in Ireland until 1997 when the law was finally changed.

Petty Sessions local court of magistrates

Prima facie in simple terms legally means there is enough evidence for there to be a case to answer.

Provost Sergeant non commissioned officer who is responsible for the maintenance of order and discipline in the regiment.

Ticket of leave a system of parole where prisoners after good behaviour were given some freedoms and released from jail. The ticket was carried by the prisoner as identity to his status.

Under Secretary of Ireland up till 1922 was the head of the civil service.

Bibliography

Newspapers:

Belfast Newsletter 1738-1890

Cork Constitution

Cork Examiner 1841-

Dundalk Democrat

Evening Herald 1891-1949

Freeman's Journal 1763-1924

Irish Independent

Irish Press 1931-1995

Kerryman

Kerry Evening Post 1813-1917

Kerry Sentinel 1878-1916

Kerry Weekly Reporter 1883-1920

Leinster Express

Nation 1842-1897

Nenagh Guardian

Munster Express

Skibereen Eagle 1882-1922

Southern Star

Southern Reporter & Cork Commercial Courier

Tralee Chronicle and Killarney Echo

Tuam Herald 1837-

Websites:

www.dippam.ac.uk

www.historicgraves.com

www.findagrave.com

www.irishgenealogy.ie

http://www.nationalarchives.ie/

www.ancestry.co.uk

www.askaboutireland/Griffiths-valuation

www.landedestates.nuigalway.ie

Publications

Detective a life upholding the Law by Tom Connolly

The Leisure Hour 1866

The Journal of the Cork Historical and Archaeological Society 1975, The Gravestone Inscriptions of Co. Cork by R. Henchion.

The Journal of the Cork Historical and Archaeological Society 1964. The Letters and papers of James Cotter junior by Henry Blackall.

Hanging in Chains by Albert Hartshorne

A Global History of Execution and the Criminal Corpse by Richard Ward.

The Gentleman's Magazine

Curious Tales from North Cork by Edward Garner

Massacre at Rathcormac by Edward Garner

The Headstone Inscriptions of Gortroe Cemetery by John Arnold

Guys Almanac

Other Publications by the Author

Coming Soon in 2020...

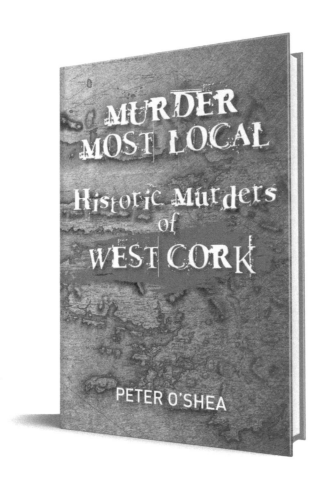

About the Author

Peter O'Shea is a native of Ballycotton. This is Peter's third book. His first book 'Well, Here I am in Ballycotton' combined his passion for postcards, his love of the sea and his appreciation for Ballycotton and its history. He wrote his second 'Murder Most Local, East Cork Historical Murders' following on from feedback he received about a local murder in his Ballycotton Book. Readers wanted to know more. Peter researched other local murders and wrote about 47 local East Cork murders. While researching the East Cork edition he found many other historical murders around Cork County.

Since January 2011 he has been Mechanic on the Ballycotton Lifeboat, he joined the Lifeboat as a volunteer many years before, when he was 18. During school and college Peter worked on local fishing boats and has always had a keen interest in all things maritime. Peter lives in Ballycotton with his partner Karen and their 3 sons James, Edward and Henry.

More information at www.facebook.com/ballycottonhistory